Dear Pam....
Teach ME Your Quick Quilting Techniques.

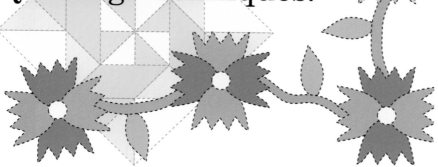

Pam Bono Designs, Inc.

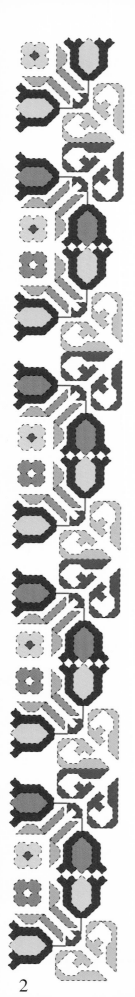

Dear Pam....
Teach ME Your Quick Quilting Techniques.

Published by

LEISURE ARTS

LEISURE ARTS
P. O. Box 55595
Little Rock, AR 72215
www.leisurearts.com

Produced by

Pam Bono Designs, Inc.

P.O. Box 659
Pagosa Springs, CO 81147
www.pambonodesigns.com

EDITORIAL STAFF

Editor-in-Chief:
Pam Bono
Editorial Assistants
Susan Clark and Nora Smith
Editors
Robert Bono, Susan Clark and Nora Smith
Art Director and Book Design
Pam Bono
Graphic Illustrations
Pam Bono
Photographer For Pam Bono Designs
Christopher Marona
Photographer For Zelda Wisdom
Shane Young
Photo Stylists for Pam Bono Designs
Christopher Marona, Pam and Robert Bono, Susan Clark and Nora Smith
Photo Stylists for Zelda Wisdom
Carol Gardner and Shane Young

Made in the United States of America.
Softcover ISBN 1-57486-348-7
10 9 8 7 6 5 4 3 2 1

Dedication:
To Ryan and Amy, and our beautiful new grandchild, Madeline Kinsey Bono. We hope someday to be able to teach our little "Maddy" all about the beauty of quilting, art, nature, and the gift of "Beautiful Music".

Credits

Designs by Pam and Robert Bono. "April Showers" design by Mindy Kettner. "Daily Bread" designed by Mindy Kettner, Pam and Robert Bono.

Quilting by Mary Nordeng and Faye Gooden.

Special Thanks To:

Sandra Case, Jeff Curtis, and everyone at Leisure Arts. It's great to have truly nice people like you to work with.

Mary Nordeng of Austin, Minnesota. I am always pleased when we find an extraordinary talent. I have never seen quilting on a long arm machine that compares to Mary's quilting, most of which is executed freehand. Thank you Mary for working us into your schedule and meeting torturing deadlines. Your beautiful work is greatly appreciated, and we are proud to present it in this book.

All of the ladies in Minnesota who pieced our quilts: Joan Holland, Bonnie Felt, Carolyn Matson, Carmen Christiansen, Joan Lewison, Margaret Ellsworth, Sue Sathre, Carol Jech, Sharon Morreim, Eunice Paaverud, And Kim Zenk. Our piecers in Pagosa Springs: Pam Thompson, Lorrie Andrews, Nora Smith and Susan Clark. Thanks for all of your hard work.

Special thanks to Susan and Nora for work above and beyond the call of duty. You are great to work with and terrific friends. Thanks to Chris for interrupting your busy schedule to drive to Pagosa to shoot in the flowers.

Joe and Carol Davis for allowing us to photograph in your exquisite home. We have never seen anything like it. You should be very proud.

Ray and Joan Laird for giving us a day to shoot in your beautiful log home. Thank you so much.

Alan and Kathy Fulmer for allowing us to photograph in your lovely home. Thank you.

Husqvarna Viking Sewing Machine Company for the loan of our Designer 1 machines.

RJR Fabrics for your supply of beautiful fabrics.

P & B Textiles for supplying us with your fabrics for projects in this book.

E. E. Schenck (Maywood Studio) for allowing us to create with your wonderful fabrics.

Carol Gardner, who made it possible for us, once again, to have the modeling sensation, Zelda (The Big "Z") in our book for everyone to enjoy. Put a smile on your face and look for more of Zelda on: www.zeldawisdom.com.

Dear Fellow Quilters,

We receive letters and emails on a daily basis from people around the globe who are becoming acquainted with our techniques. Quilt shops are teaching classes and introducing more and more quilters to those techniques.

It has been said many times, that once you learn the basics behind the different quick piecing "tricks" that we use, any of our patterns are possible to do.

Yes, in many of our designs there are small pieces, which are a breeze to do with the use of The Angler 2 and a little practice. If the quilt has many pieces that are alike, chain piecing makes it faster to accomplish.

We have also been told that our designs are very much like a jig saw puzzle. Units are assembled first; then the design begins to take form as units are joined. The results can be very rewarding. With these methods, you can achieve an appliqué look with quick piecing techniques. That is what this book is all about. Our basic techniques are introduced in the beginning of the book, and it is very helpful for you to read them, follow the many diagrams and practice before starting a project. You are also guided through the use of the techniques in each project.

All of our designs are organized in a logical step-by-step manner, so that the end result will be a quilt that you will be proud to display in your home, or enter in a quilt show.

The projects in the first part of the book are designed for those of you who are just beginning to piece, or quilters who wish to learn the way we put blocks and units together. You will find many graphics as an aid in assembling our designs, as I believe that most quilters are visual learners, including myself.

Yes, you can make the quilt on the cover! Yes, you can learn the "tricks" and piece any of the designs in this book. If you have just been introduced to piecing, take a class on how to use a rotary cutter and mat, and how the proper rulers and tools are used. At that time, begin learning the quick piecing techniques that we are sharing with you.

Always have a positive attitude about anything that you do, and don't be afraid to just "dive in!" You can do it!

Enjoy, and Happy Quilting!

Pam

Table of Contents

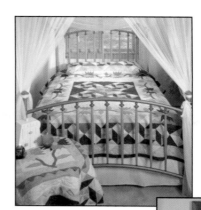

Cornflower
Pages 31-39

Learn as you piece!

Whirly Gig
Pages 13-15

On The Road Again.
Pages 40-46

Colorado Stars
Pages 16-22

Daily Bread
Tablecloth
Pages 47-51

Daily Bread
Place Mats
Pages 52-53

April Showers
Pages 23-25

Blooming
Desert
Pages 26-30

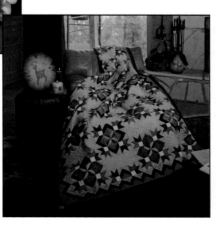

Rambling
Rose Quilt
Pages 54-60

5

Rambling
Rose
Tablecloth
Pages 61-64

Ring Around The Posie
Place Mats
Pages 89-90

String Of
Pearls
Pages 65-71

Butterflies Quilt
Pages 91-97

Pennsylvania Dutch
Table Runner
Pages 72-76

Grandmother's
Magnolias Quilt
Pages 98-104

Pennsylvania
Dutch Tablecloth
Pages 77-83

Dogwood Quilt
and Wall Quilt
Pages 105-116

Bottles Wall Quilt
Pages 117-123

Ring Around The
Posie Tablecloth
Pages 84-88

Into The Woods
Stockings
Pages 124-128

Learning Our Techniques

**The techniques that are shown on the following pages are used throughout projects in the book. Please refer to these techniques frequently, and practice them with scraps.

Strip piecing anti-directional sewing

 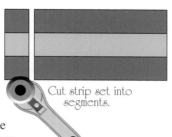

Cut strip set into segments.

For some projects, you'll join strips of different fabrics to make what is called a strip set. Project directions not only show illustrations of each strip set, but specify how many strip sets to make, how many segments are to be cut from each strip set, and the specific size of each strip and segment. To sew a strip set, match each pair of strips with right sides facing. Stitch through both layers along one long edge. When sewing multiple strips in a set, practice "anti-directional" stitching to keep strips straight. As you add strips, sew each new seam in the *opposite direction* from the last one. This distributes tension evenly in both directions, and keeps your strip set from getting warped and wobbly.

DIAGONAL CORNERS

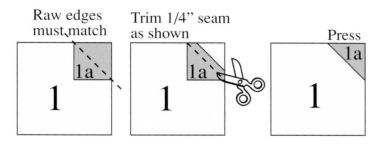

Raw edges must match   Trim 1/4" seam as shown   Press

This technique turns squares into sewn triangles. It is especially helpful if the corner triangle is very small, because it's easier to cut and handle a square than a small triangle. By sewing squares to squares, you don't have to guess where the seam allowance meets, which can be difficult with triangles. Project instructions give the size of the fabric pieces needed. These sizes given in the cutting instructions include seam allowance. The base triangle is either a square or rectangle, but the contrasting corner is <u>always</u> a square.

1. To make a diagonal corner, with right sides facing, match the small square to one corner of the base fabric. Trim the 1/4" seam on each diagonal corner as shown, trimming the center seam only. The back is left in tact for stability. The only exception to this rule is if the diagonal corner is very light in color. In this case, do not trim the center seam. If trimmed it will show through. For large diagonal or snowball corners, pin raw edges together so that they will remain even.

2. As a seam guide, you may wish to draw or press a diagonal line from corner to corner. For a quick solution to this time consuming technique, refer to our instructions on the following pages for The Angler 2.

3. Stitch the small square diagonally from corner to corner. Trim seam allowance as shown on the diagonal corner square only, leaving the base fabric untrimmed for stability and keeping the corner square. Press the diagonal corner square over as shown.

4. Many units in the projects have multiple diagonal corners or ends. When these are the same size, and cut from the same fabric, the identifying unit letter is the same. But, if the unit has multiple diagonal pieces that are different in size and/or color, the unit letters are different. These pieces are joined to the main unit in alphabetical order.

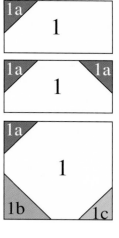

5. Many of our projects utilize diagonal corners on diagonal corners as shown below. In this case, diagonal corners are added in alphabetical order once again. First join diagonal corner, trim and press out; then add the second diagonal

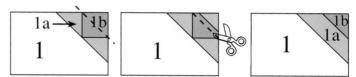

corner, trim and press out as shown.

6. Our designs also utilize diagonal corners on joined units such as strip sets. In this case, the joined units will have one unit number in the center of the unit as shown at right, with the diagonal corner having its own unit number.

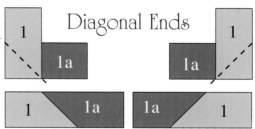

Diagonal Ends

Diagonal End - Left Slant   Diagonal End - Right Slant

1. This method joins two rectangles on the diagonal and eliminates the difficulty of measuring and cutting a trapezoid. It is similar to the diagonal corner technique, but here you work with two rectangles. Our project instructions specify the size of each rectangle.

2. To sew diagonal ends, place rectangles perpendicular to each other with right sides facing, matching corners to be sewn.

3. Before you sew, mark or press the diagonal stitching line, and check the right side to see if the line is angled in the desired direction.

4. Position the rectangles under the needle, leading with the top edge. Sew a diagonal seam to the opposite edge.

5. Check the right side to see that the seam is angled correctly. Then press the seam and trim excess fabric from the seam allowance.

6. As shown, the direction of the seam makes a difference. Make mirror-image units with this in mind, or you can put different ends on the same strip.

This technique is wonderful for making *continuous* binding strips. Please note on illustration below, diagonal ends are made first; then diagonal corners may be added in alphabetical order.

7. Refer to Step 6 in *diagonal corner section*. Diagonal ends may be added to joined units in the same manner as shown below.

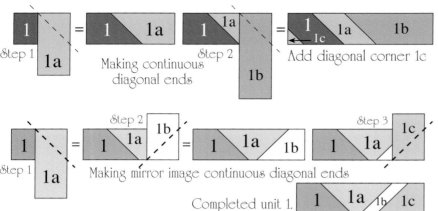

Making continuous diagonal ends

Add diagonal corner 1c

Making mirror image continuous diagonal ends

Completed unit 1.

Making mirror image combined unit diagonal ends.

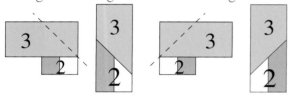

TRIANGLE SQUARES

1. Many patchwork designs are made by joining two contrasting triangles to make a square. Many people use the grid method when dozens of triangles are required in a design. However, for the designs in this book we use a simple way to make one or more half square triangles. To do so, draw or press a diagonal line from corner to corner on the back of the lightest colored square.

2. As an extra tip, we have found that spraying the fabric with spray starch before cutting the squares to be used keeps them from distorting. A bit more fabric may be used; however, it is a quick and easy technique. If you are chain piecing, and are using this technique, start your needle through a piece of stabilizer or a scrap so that the corner of the unit is not pulled down in the "hole".

3. Place squares right sides together and stitch on the line. Trim the seam as shown and press.

4. The illustration at right shows how triangle-square units are marked in the book. A diagonal line is always

 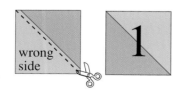

wrong side

shown, separating the two fabric colors. The unit number is always shown in the center of the square.

MACHINE PIECING

An accurate, consistent 1/4" seam allowance is essential for good piecing. If each seam varies by the tiniest bit, the difference multiplies greatly by the time the block is completed. Before you start a project, be sure your machine is in good working order and that you can sew a precise 1/4" seam allowance. Refer to instructions and illustrations for use of The Angler 2 in this section to aid with accurate seams.

1. Set your sewing machine to 12-14 stitches per inch. Use 100%-cotton or cotton/polyester sewing thread.

2. Match pieces to be sewn with right sides facing. Sew each seam from cut edge to cut edge of the fabric piece. It is not necessary to backstitch, because most seams will be crossed and held by another seam.

SEWING AN "X"

1. When triangles are pieced with other units, seams should cross in an "X" on the back. If the joining seam goes precisely through the center of the "X", the triangle will have a nice sharp point on the front.

PRESS AND PIN

1. To make neat corners and points, seams must meet precisely. Pressing and pinning can help achieve matched seams.

2. To press, set your iron on cotton. Use an up-and-down motion, lifting the iron from spot to spot. Sliding the iron back and forth can push seams out of shape. First press the seam flat on the wrong side; then open the piece and press the right side.

3. Press patchwork seam allowance to one side, not open as in dressmaking. If possible, press toward the darker fabric to avoid seam allowance showing through light fabric. Press seam allowances in opposite directions from row to row. By offsetting seam allowances at each intersection, you reduce the bulk under the patchwork. This is more important than pressing seam allowances toward dark fabric. Seams pressed in this manner are referred to as "locked" seams.

4. Use pins to match "locked" seam lines. With right sides facing, align opposing seams, nesting seam allowances. On the top piece, push a pin through the seam line 1/4" from the edge. Then push the pin through the bottom seam and set it. Pin all matching seams; then stitch the joining seams, removing pins as you sew.

EASING FULLNESS

1. Sometimes two units that should be the same size are slightly different. When joining such units, pin-match opposing seams. Sew the seam with the shorter piece on top. As you sew, the feed dogs ease the fullness on the bottom piece. This is called "sewing with a baggy bottom."

2. If units are too dissimilar to ease without puckering, check each one to see if the pieces were correctly cut and that the seams are 1/4" wide. Remake the unit that varies the most from the desired size.

CHAIN PIECING

1. Chain piecing is an efficient way to sew many units in one operation, saving time and thread. Line up several units to be sewn. Sew the first unit as usual, but at the end of the seam do not backstitch, clip the thread, or lift the presser foot. Instead, feed the next unit right on the heels of the first. There will be a little twist of thread between each unit. Sew as many seams as you like on a chain. Keep the chain intact to carry to the ironing board and clip the threads as you press.

 **The Angler 2**

Robert invented the first Angler between our first and second books for Oxmoor House/Leisure Arts. He watched me drawing diagonal line seam guides that took forever! He said: "There has got to be a quicker way!" He found a quicker way. This little tool is now used by millions of quilters all over the world with results that cut piecing time in half, after a bit of practice. It can be purchased where ever sewing notions are sold.

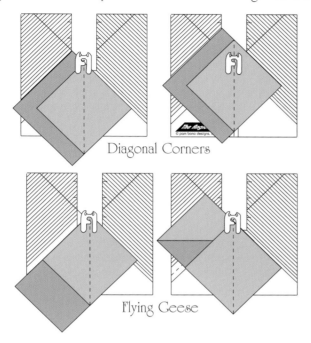

Diagonal Corners

Flying Geese

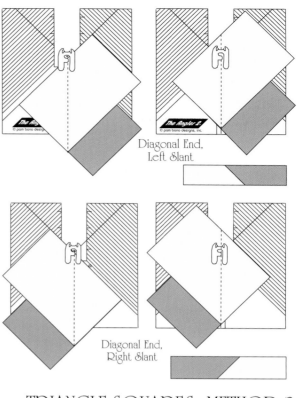

Diagonal End,
Left Slant

Diagonal End,
Right Slant

TRIANGLE-SQUARES, METHOD 2

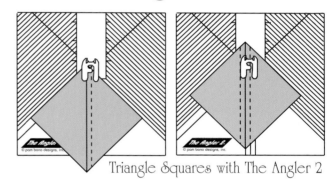

Triangle Squares with The Angler 2

DIAGONAL CORNERS & FLYING GEESE

1. Align diagonal corners with raw edges matching. Line fabric up so that right side of square is aligned with first 45° line on right as shown above, with the tip of the fabric under the needle. No seam guide lines will need to be drawn unless the square is larger than 7 3/4". As feed dogs pull the fabric through the machine, keep fabric aligned with the diagonal lines on the right until center line of The Angler 2 bottom is visible.
2. Keep the tip of the square on this line as the diagonal corner is fed through the machine. Trim seam as shown in our "quick piecing" technique section and press.
3. For Flying Geese, sew first diagonal corner. Trim seam and press; then join second diagonal corner. Trim seam and press. Overlap will give you an accurate 1/4" seam allowance.

DIAGONAL ENDS

1. For both slants, prepare rectangles with raw edges matching. For right slant, align top rectangle with the first 45° line on right side of The Angler 2.
2. Bottom rectangle should align on first 45° left line as shown. As feed dogs pull fabric through machine, keep fabric aligned with the diagonal lines on the right until center line on The Angler 2 bottom is visible. Keep the top of the rectangle on this line as it is fed through the machine. Trim seam and press.
3. For left slant, line top rectangle up with the first 45° line on left side of The Angler 2 as shown. As rectangles are fed through the machine, keep top rectangle aligned with left diagonal lines on The Angler 2. This technique is great for joining binding strips.

Prepare squares with right sides together and raw edges matching. Line up the right side of the squares on line 1 on the right side of The Angler 2 as shown. Left side of square needs to be aligned with dashed diagonal line on The Angler 2. As feed dogs pull square through machine, keep top part of square aligned with the diagonal lines on the Angler 2 until left seam line is visible as shown. Keep point on this line until seam is sewn. Turn square around and repeat for other seam. Seams will be 1/4" from center as shown. Cut triangle-squares apart on center line and trim off tips and press.
Although this method is not used in this book, when using the Angler 2 method, squares are always cut 7/8" larger than the finished size.

ACCURATE 1/4" SEAMS

Fabric is lined up on the computer generated 1/4" seam line on The Angler 2, and stitching is along center guide line. To take a full 1/4" seam, line fabric up on 1/4" seam line. If you want a "scant" 1/4" seam, line fabric up so that the seam guide line shows. We recommend a "scant" 1/4" seam as your seams end up being more accurate after they are pressed.

When using the Angler 2, watch the point of your fabric on the center line - NOT the needle.

9

ADDITIONAL QUICK PIECING TECHNIQUES.

Diagonal corners used as diagonal corners.

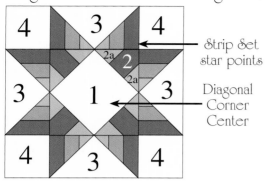

Strip Set star points

Diagonal Corner Center

Step 1. Begin with main diagonal corner Unit 2.

Step 2. Join diagonal corner 2a to main unit, stitching diagonally.

Step 3. Trim seam as shown and press.

Step 4. Join second diagonal corner 2a, and stitch diagonally.

Step 5. Trim seam as shown and press.

Step 6. Using the star center as an example, four of these units will need to be assembled.

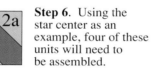

Star Center

Step 1. Place diagonal corners Unit 2 on Unit 1 as shown and stitch in place diagonally.

Step 2. Trim diagonal corner seams and press.

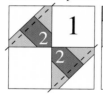

Step 3. Place remaining diagonal corners Unit 2 on Unit 1 as shown and stitch in place diagonally.

Step 4. Trim diagonal corner seams and press.

APPLIQUE TECHNIQUES

We have used Steam-A-Seam Lite and Steam-A-Seam 2 for appliqué projects in the book. Steam-A-Seam 2 was also used . We do not recommend it for large quilts, but it is an excellent product for smaller projects. Dashed lines within the designs show areas that fit behind another piece. If you have an appliqué pressing sheet, we highly suggest using it as you will not get unwanted

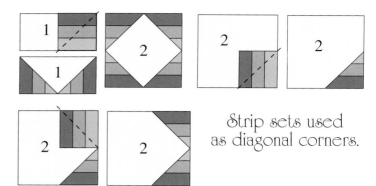

Strip sets used as diagonal corners.

Please note:

Stripes in the strip set are vertical in Flying Geese Unit 1. To end up with vertical stripes, they need to be placed on the main unit horizontally. For stripes to end up horizontally, place strip set vertically as shown. Strip set diagonal corners will overlap on the unit examples shown 1/4". This is your seam allowance.

- -

APPLIQUE TECHNIQUES CONTINUED

glue on your iron. We use an older steam iron when we do a lot of appliqué for this reason.

In the materials list, and the cutting list, specific sizes are given for the appliqué fabrics to be used. We have drawn the pattern pieces out and tested the sizes given so that there is plenty of fabric allowed. Follow manufacturers instructions for any fusible product.

Please note that specific instructions are given in each appliqué project.

Use a good press on, tear-a-way stabilizer behind your appliqués to keep them smooth.

LIST OF SUGGESTED SUPPLIES TO START

1. Rotary cutter: There are several different types of rotary cutters on the market. They are available in different shapes and sizes. Choose the one that is the most comfortable in your hand. Remember, the larger the blade, the longer it will last. Also purchase replacement blades.

2. Cutting mat: The size of the mat is based of course, on the size of your cutting area. We use the 23" x 35" June Tailor mat.

3. Sewing thread. Use a good quality cotton or cotton/poly thread.

4. Pins and pincushion. We especially like the long, thin, fine pins for quilting. Clover manufactures a great pin that we especially like. They are called"Patchwork Pins".

5. Seam ripper. We all use them frequently. We call them the "Un-sewers"!

6. Scissors. Here again, we use two or three different sizes to do different jobs.

7. Iron and ironing board. We use June Tailor's pressing mats next to our sewing machines for pressing smaller pieces.

8. Zip top bags, masking tape, and of course, The Angler 2 and Cut Right rulers!

9. Cut Right Acrylic rulers: Robert designed several sizes. They are: 8" x 24", 6 1/2" x 18", and the most used is the 3 1/2" x 12". Drawings on following page show how they work.

10. If you are going to do the blanket stitch appliqués by machine, you will need stabilizer and a supply of machine embroidery needles, as they should be changed every 8 hours of sewing.

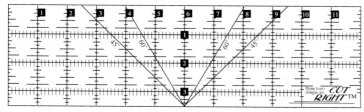

Your cutting time is cut in half with our practical rulers that minimize cutting errors.

Dear Quilting Friends,

Out of all of the different shapes and sizes of rulers that I have, I still make mistakes in my cutting, especially the 1/8" measurements; 1/8", 3/8", 5/8" and 7/8".

In talking to other quilters, it seems to be a common problem. Our new line of Pam Bono Designs rulers has helped me, and our quilting friends, especially with our changing eyesight.

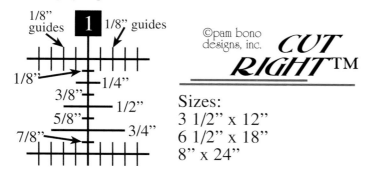

©pam bono designs, inc. **CUT RIGHT™**

Sizes:
3 1/2" x 12"
6 1/2" x 18"
8" x 24"

REVERSIBLE NAPKINS

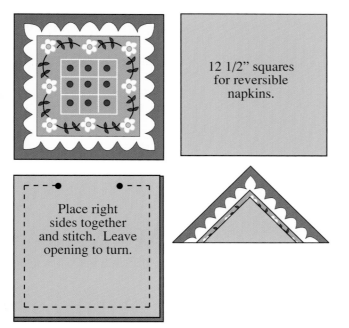

12 1/2" squares for reversible napkins.

Place right sides together and stitch. Leave opening to turn.

To finish, turn right side out and press. Place a small piece of Steam-A-Seam 2 (with paper removed from both sides) in the opening, close to the edge. We cut the piece the length of the opening and 1/4" wide. Press opening closed. This is a nice little trick that is quick and easy and eliminates hand stitching. It will stay together forever!!!

Using Our Instructions....

The following points explain how the instructions in our book are organized. You will find that all projects are made easier if you <u>read this section thoroughly</u> and follow each tip.

• Yardages are based on 44-45" wide fabric, allowing for up to 4% shrinkage. 100% cotton fabric is recommended for the quilt top and backing.

• At the beginning of each project, we tell you which techniques are used so you can practice them before beginning. Seam allowances *are included* in all stated measurements and cutting.

• The materials list provides you with yardage requirements for the project. We have included the exact number of inches needed to make the project, with yardages given to the nearest 1/8 yard. By doing this, we are giving you the option to purchase extra yardage if you feel you may need more.

• A color key accompanies each materials list, matching each fabric with the color-coded illustrations given with the project directions. We have made an effort to match the colors in the graphics to the actual fabric colors used in the project.

• Cutting instructions are given for each fabric, the first cut, indicated by a •, is usually a specific number of cross grain strips. The second cut, indicated by *, specifies how to cut those strips into smaller pieces, or "segments." The identification of each piece follows in parenthesis, consisting of the block letter and unit number that corresponds to the assembly diagram. For pieces used in more than one unit, several unit numbers are given.

• Organize all cut pieces in zip top bags, and label each bag with the appropriate unit numbers. We use masking tape on the bags to label them. This avoids confusion and keeps the pieces stored safely until they are needed. Arrange all fabric colors, in their individual bags with like fabrics together, making it easy to find a specific unit and fabric color.

We have carefully calculated the number of units that can be cut from specified strips, wasting as little fabric as possible.. "Stack this cut" will appear frequently in the cutting instructions. Refer

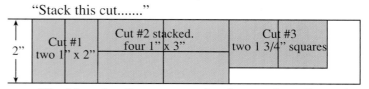

"Stack this cut......."

2" wide strip. Do not cut strips down unless directed.

to the diagram above. We utilize the width of the strip with the first units to be cut; then other units that can be stacked on top of each other to best utilize the strips are cut next. In doing this, units may be cut in two or three different places in the cutting instructions from a variety of strips. So that cut units may be organized efficiently, the units that appear in more than one strip are shown in red on the cutting list. These cuts are not only shown in red, but the words "add to" is shown within the parenthesis so that you know in advance that there will be more of the same size units.

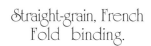
Straight-grain, French Fold binding.

Diagram 1
Joining binding strips.

Continuous Binding
Bias or straight-grain.

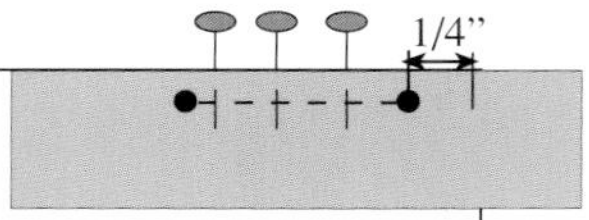

Diagram 2
Fold binding in half lengthwise and press. Matching right sides, and beginning at lower edge of project, pin raw edges of binding to project, (dot) leaving a 6" tail. Continue pinning to within 1/4" of corner. Mark this point on binding. Use a 1/4" seam allowance and stitch to your mark. Backstitch at beginning of stitching and again when you reach your mark. Lift needle out of fabric and clip thread.

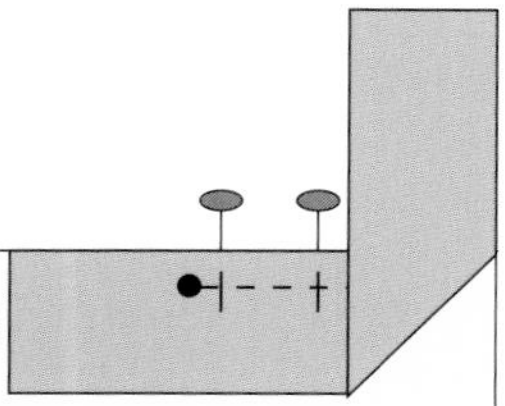

Diagram 3

Right side of project.

Fold binding as shown, matching raw edges.

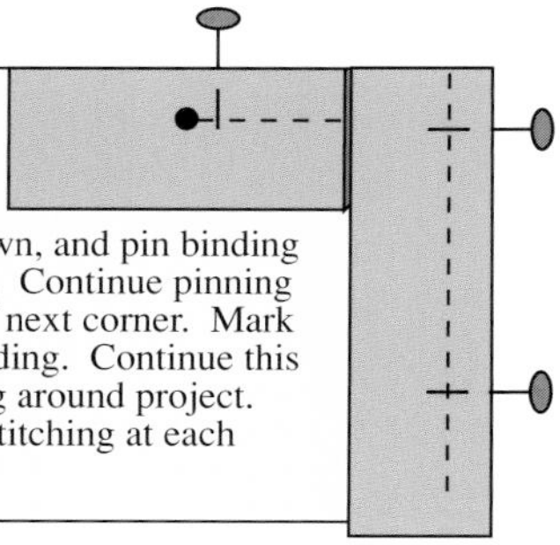

Diagram 4
Fold binding down, and pin binding to adjacent edge. Continue pinning to within 1/4" of next corner. Mark this point on binding. Continue this method, stitching around project. Reinforce your stitching at each marked point

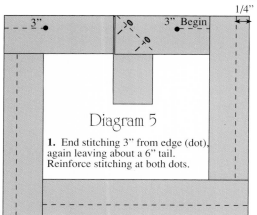
3"   3" Begin
Diagram 5

1. End stitching 3" from edge (dot), again leaving about a 6" tail. Reinforce stitching at both dots.

2. Fold left tail down at a 45° angle (perpendicular to top). Bring other tail straight across on top of folded bottom tail. Draw a 45° line from top left to bottom right where they meet, and pin in place as shown.
3. As there is plenty of room that is unsewn between the dots, pull the pinned binding out, and stitch the diagonal as shown on dashed 45° line. Trim seam 1/4" from stitching.
4. Complete sewing binding to project between dots, 1/4" from edge.
5. Trim batting and backing even with the seam allowance. Fold the binding over the seam allowance to the back. Blind stitch the folded edge to backing fabric. Fold and mitre into the binding at back corners.

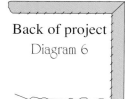
Back of project
Diagram 6

• Large pieces such as sashing and borders are generally cut first to assure you have enough fabric. To reduce further waste of fabric, you may be instructed to cut some pieces from a first-cut strip, and then cut that strip down to a narrower width to cut additional pieces.

• Cutting instructions are given for the entire project as shown. To make one block, see information below left on "How To Make One Block".

• Cutting and piecing instructions are given in a logical step-by-step progression. Follow this order always to avoid having to rip out in some cases. Although there are many assembly graphics, we strongly suggest reading the written instructions along with looking at the graphics.

• Every project has one or more block designs. Instructions include block illustrations that show the fabric color, and the numbered units.

• Individual units are assembled first. Use one or more of the "quick piecing" techniques described on pages 7 and 8.

• Strip set illustrations show the size of the segments to be cut from that strip set. The illustration also designates how many strip sets are to be made, and the size of the strips. Keep strip set segments in their own labeled zip top bag.

• Each unit in the assembly diagram is numbered. The main part of the unit is indicated with a number only. A diagonal line represents a seam where a diagonal corner or end is attached. Each diagonal piece is numbered with the main unit number plus a letter (example: 1a).

• Many extra illustrations are given throughout the projects for assembly of unusual or multiple units for more clarity.

• Piecing instructions are given for making one block. Make the number of blocks stated in the project illustrations to complete the project as shown.

• We have developed many other quick piecing techniques to assemble units and combined units quickly. These methods are shown in projects where they are applicable.

All "Q" units in cutting instructions stand for quilt top. These are units that are not incorporated into the specific blocks, but are on the quilt top.

HOW TO MAKE ONE BLOCK

Cutting instructions are given for making the project as shown. There may be times that you want to make just one block for a project of your own design. All you have to do is count, or divide if preferred.

With each cutting list there is an illustration for the blocks (s). Unit numbers in the cutting list correspond with the units in the illustration. Count how many of each unit are in the block illustration. Instead of cutting the number shown on the cutting list, cut the number you need for one block. Should you wish to make two or more blocks, multiply the number of units X the number of blocks you wish to make.

Whirly Gig

Patriotism is foremost in our minds in these times, and there are so many ways to express our love of country. This cheerful beginner design can be used for many festive occasions. Chris captured it best on film with a flag flying above the beauty of new growth.

Materials

☐ Fabric I (white on white print)   Need 46 1/2"   1 3/8 yards

◻ Fabric II (med. blue print)   Need 49"   1 1/2 yards

■ Fabric III (navy print)   Need 17 1/2"   5/8 yard

■ Fabric IV (red print)   Need 34 1/2"   1 1/8 yards
   Backing   3 1/4 yards

Finishes to: 52" square.
Techniques used:
Strip sets as diagonal corners and triangle-squares.

13

Cutting

 From Fabric I, cut: (white on white print)
- One 9 1/2" wide strip. From this, cut:
  * Four 9 1/2" squares (Q7)
- Three 6 1/2" wide strips. From these, cut:
  * Nine - 6 1/2" squares (Q1, Q7a, B1)
  * Sixteen - 3 1/2" x 6 1/2" (Q2, A3)
- Five 3 1/2" wide strips. From these, cut:
  * Four - 3 1/2" x 30 1/2" (Q5)
  * Four - 3 1/2" x 9 1/2" (Q3)
  * Eight - 3 1/2" squares (A4, B3)

From Fabric II, cut: (medium blue print)
- Three 3 1/2" wide strips. From these, cut:
  * Twenty-eight - 3 1/2" squares (A1, A3a, B3, B4)
- Fourteen 2 1/2" wide strips. Six for straight-grain binding. From remainder, cut:
  * Four - 2 1/2" x 26 1/2" (Q9) Join two together to = two 52 1/2" lengths.
  * Four - 2 1/2" x 24 1/2" (Q8) Join two together to = two 48 1/2" lengths.
- Two 1 3/4" wide strips for Strip Set 1

From Fabric III, cut: (navy print)
- Five 3 1/2" wide strips. From these, cut:
  * Four - 3 1/2" x 30 1/2" (Q4)
  * Twenty - 3 1/2" squares (Q7b, A2, B2)

From Fabric IV, cut: (red print)
- One 9 1/2" wide strip. From this, cut:
  * Four - 9 1/2" squares (Q7)
- One 6 1/2" wide strip. From this, cut:
  * Four - 6 1/2" squares (Q1)
- Four 3 1/2" wide strips. From these, cut:
  * Four - 3 1/2" x 30 1/2" (Q6)
- Two 2 1/4" wide strips for Strip Set 1.

Strip Set Assembly

Strip Set 1. Make 2. Cut into sixteen 3 1/2" segments

1. As strip sets are used in this design as diagonal corners, it is important that they are as accurate as possible so that the square to be used is a true 3 1/2" square. Refer to page 7 for strip set assembly instructions. This design will help you to learn how accuracy effects the completed design.
2. When sewing your strips together, measure your 1/4" seam, making sure that it is correct. A "scant" 1/4" seam is the most desirable as it will end up to be a true 1/4" after it is pressed. The joined strips should measure 3 1/2" wide.

Triangle-Squares For This Project.

Use this assembly for Block B, Unit 3.

Place 3 1/2" squares of fabrics I and II right sides together, matching raw edges, and stitch a diagonal line from corner to corner as shown. Press open and trim center seam, leaving the top and base fabric.

Unit 3 for Block B assembly. Make 4.

Making Unit 4 for Block A, and Unit Q1. Make 4 of each.

Use this assembly for Block A, Unit 4.

Place a 3 1/2" square of fabrics I and Strip Set 1 segment right sides together, matching raw edges, and stitch a diagonal line from corner to corner as shown. Trim 4a seam, leaving the top and base fabric. Press 4a as shown.

Use this assembly for Unit Q1. Place 6 1/2" squares of fabrics I and IV right sides together, pinning raw edges, and stitch diagonal as shown.

Block A Assembly

Step 1. Place Strip Set 1 segment on Unit 3 as shown. Stitch diagonally.

Step 2. Trim diagonal corner 3b seam.

Step 3. Press diagonal corner 3b seam.

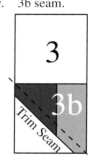

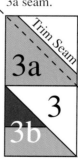

Step 4. Join diagonal corner 3a, stitching a diagonal as shown.

Step 5. Trim 3a seam.

Step 6. Press 3a corner.

Making Unit 3 for Block A. Make 12.

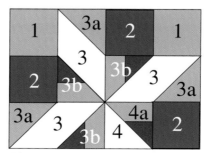

Block A. Make 4. When completed block should measure 9 1/2" x 12 1/2"

1. Now that all units for Block A have been prepared, the block can be assembled. I always work from left to right if possible. Begin by joining units 1 and 2; then add Unit 3 to right side of combined 1/2 units. Turn Unit 3 and join to bottom of combined units.

2. For right hand section, join units 2 and 1; the add another Unit 3 Join units 4 and 2 as shown. Add these to bottom of 1-3 combined units.

3. Join the two combined unit sections to complete Block A. Make 4.

Block B Assembly

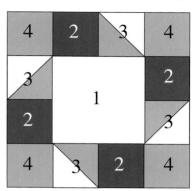

Block B. Make 1. When completed, block should measure 12 1/2" square.

1. Refer to page 14 for making triangle-square Unit 3.

2. To assemble Block B, join units 2 and 3 as shown. Make four, referring to Block B diagram frequently for correct placement of Unit 3. Join two of the combined 2/3 units to opposite sides of Unit 1.

3. Join Unit 4 to opposite sides of remaining 2/3 combined units as shown. Join these rows to top and bottom of center section to complete Block B. Make 1.

Step 1. Place Unit Q7a square on top of Fabric IV, Unit Q7, with raw edges matching. Stitch in place diagonally

Step 2. Do not trim seam as Q7a is a white diagonal corner on a dark fabric. If seam is trimmed, the darker fabric will show through on the corner.

Step 3. Place Unit Q7b on top of Q7a corner.Stitch a diagonal as shown.

Step 4. Trim Unit Q7b seam and press.

*Making Unit Q7.
Diagonal corners
on diagonal
corners*

Step 5. Place Unit Q7 from Fabric I on top of combined Q7 units with raw edges matching and stitch diagonally.

Step 6. Do not trim seam of Fabric I, Unit Q7 as it is a white fabric on top of a darker fabric. Press it as shown.

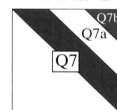

Quilt Top Assembly

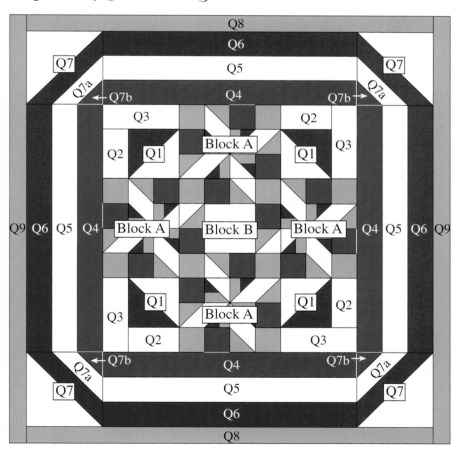

3. Again referring to Quilt Top diagram for correct placement of units, join the Q1-Q3 combined units to opposite sides of one Block A. Make two of these rows. Join two of Block A to opposite sides of Block B, matching seams to complete center row. Join the three rows together as shown.

4. Join units Q4, Q5, and Q6 as shown. Join two of these rows to top and bottom of quilt center. Join completed Unit Q7 to opposite sides of remaining Q4-Q6 rows. Join these to two rows to opposite sides of the quilt top, carefully matching seams to complete the outer stripes.

5. Join Unit Q8 to top and bottom of quilt; then add Unit Q9 to sides to complete the quilt top.

6. Mary used a swirled fill on larger open white spaces with medium blue thread, and "ditched" the patchwork.

7. Refer to page 12 for instructions on how to make straight-grain, French Fold binding. Use the six 2 1/2" wide strips of Fabric II, and bind your quilt.

1 Before quilt top assembly begins, refer to diagrams and instructions at top right and make four of Unit Q7.

2. To assemble the quilt top, refer frequently to diagram above for correct placement of units. Begin by joining units Q1 and Q2; then add Unit Q3 to side of combined units as shown.

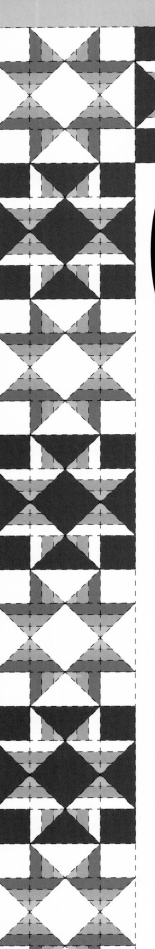

Colorado Stars

Robert and I gave a demonstration and a lecture about two years ago showing all of the wonderful things that can be done with quick piecing techniques. A part of this design was the central theme as the Ohio Star is a very traditional block.

Through the years I have learned how to change the look of a design by using different techniques and color combinations. The entire look of the block can be changed just by moving the colors in the design to different positions. We wanted to show how many things could be done to change the appearance of the Ohio Star.

Everyone at the demonstration said "You need to put this in a book!" So here it is............

Quilt finished size: 92" x 104"
Table topper finished size: 38" square.
Techniques used: Strip sets and diagonal corners used as diagonal corners.

Materials

	Fabric	Need
	Fabric I (light tan print) 4 3/4 yards	Need 164 1/2"
	Fabric II (honey tan print) 3 1/8 yards	Need 106"
	Fabric III (dark brown print) 2 7/8 yards	Need 96"
	Fabric IV (dark blue print) 2 1/8 yards	Need 72"
	Fabric V (medium blue print) 1 7/8 yards	Need 61 1/2"
	Backing	8 1/4 yards

Cutting

From Fabric I, cut: (light tan print)
- One 10 1/2" wide strip. From this, cut:
  - * Four - 10 1/2" squares (Q12)
- Twelve 6 1/2" wide strips. From these, cut:
  - * Ten - 6 1/2" squares (B2, C1)
  - * 116 - 3 1/2" x 6 1/2" (A1, B1, F1)
  - * Four - 1 1/2" x 26 3/4" (Q18) Stack this cut.
- Eleven 3 1/2" wide strips. From these, cut:
  - * Four - 3 1/2" x 15 1/2" (Q9)
  - * Six - 3 1/2" x 12 1/2" (Q4, Q8)
  - * Eighty-eight - 3 1/2" squares (A2, B3)
- Four 1 1/2" x 42 1/2" strips for (Q19) Piece two together to = two 84 1/2" lengths.
- Twenty-one 1 1/2" strips. Thirteen for Strip Sets 2 and 4. From remainder, cut:
  - * Two - 1 1/2" x 42" (Q18). Piece together with two 1 1/2" x 26 3/4" (above) joined to opposite ends to = two 94 1/2" lengths.
  - * Two - 1 1/2" x 36 1/2" (Q13)
  - * Four - 1 1/2" x 33 1/2" (Q10) Piece two together to = two 66 1/2" lengths.
  - * Four - 1 1/2" x 9 1/2" (Q11)

From Fabric II, cut: (honey tan print)
- Three 12 1/2" wide strips. From these, cut:
  - * One - 12 1/2" x 18 1/2" (Q1)
  - * Six - 9 1/2" x 12 1/2" (Q2)
  - * Six - 6 1/2" x 12 1/2" (Q3, Q6)
  - * Twenty-two - 1 1/2" x 2 1/2" (A6)
- Five 6 1/2" wide strips. From these, cut:
  - * Sixty - 3 1/2" x 6 1/2" (G1)
- Twenty-four 1 1/2" wide strips. Twenty-one for Strip Sets 1, 3 and 4. From remainder, cut:
  - * Forty-four - 1 1/2" x 2 1/2" (add to A6)

From Fabric III, cut: (dark brown print)
- Thirteen 3 1/2" wide strips. From these, cut:
  - * Four - 3 1/2" x 34 1/2" (Q14) Piece two together to = 68 1/2" lengths.
  - * Four - 3 1/2" x 28 1/2" (Q15) Piece two together to = 56 1/2" lengths.
  - * Sixteen - 3 1/2" x 6 1/2" (C2, D1, E1)
  - * Twenty-four - 3 1/2" squares (Q7, Q20, C3, D2, E2)
  - * Sixty-four - 1 1/2" x 3 1/2" (A7)
- Ten 2 1/2" wide strips for straight-grain binding.
- Seventeen 1 1/2" wide strips. Six for Strip Set 5. From remainder, cut:
  - * Four - 1 1/2" x 42" (Q21, Q22)
  - * Four - 1 1/2" x 30 3/4" (Q21) Piece two to opposite sides of two 42" strips to = two 102 1/2 lengths.
  - * Four - 1 1/2" x 25 3/4" (Q22) Piece two to opposite sides of two 42" strips to = two 92 1/2 lengths.

From Fabric IV, cut: (dark blue print)
- Forty-eight 1 1/2" wide strips. Thirty-seven for Strips Sets 1, 2, 3, 4, and 5. From remainder, cut:
  - * Two - 1 1/2" x 42" (Q16)
  - * Four - 1 1/2" x 41 1/2" (Q17) Piece two together to = two 82 1/2" lengths.
  - * Four - 1 1/2" x 25 3/4" (Q16) Piece two to opposite sides of 42" strips to = two 92 1/2" lengths.
  - * Sixty-four - 1 1/2" squares (A3)

From Fabric V, cut: (medium blue print)
- Forty-one 1 1/2" wide strips. Thirty-four for Strips Sets 1, 2, 3, and 5. From remainder, cut:
  - * Sixty-four - 1 1/2" x 2 1/2" (A5)
  - * Sixty-four - 1 1/2" squares (A4)

Strip Sets

Strip Set 1. Make 13. Cut into 152 - 3 1/2" segments

Strip Set 2. Make 10. Cut into 120 - 3 1/2" segments

Strip Set 3. Make 5. Cut into 56 - 3 1/2" segments

Strip Set 4. Make 3. Cut into 32 - 3 1/2" segments

Strip Set 5. Make 6. Cut into 64 - 3 1/2" segments

1. Refer to page 7 for strip piecing instructions. Make the strip sets above as shown and cut them into the number of segments as instructed.

2. As strip sets are used in this design as diagonal corners, it is important that they are as accurate as possible so that the square to be used is a true 3 1/2" square. This design will help you to learn how accuracy effects the completed design.

3. When sewing your strips together, measure your 1/4" seam, making sure that it is correct. A "scant" 1/4" seam is the most desirable as it will end up to be a true 1/4" after it is pressed. The joined strips should measure 3 1/2" wide.

Block A Assembly

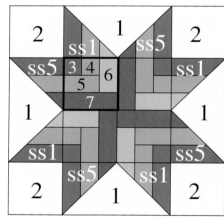

Block A. Make 16. When block is complete, it should measure 12 1/2"

1. Refer to diagram at the bottom of the page for making the center section of Block A. This is a small Log Cabin block that comprises the center of the star when four are sewn together. Follow the instructions and diagrams below and make a total of 64 Log Cabin blocks, four for each star. Join them together as directed.

2. The diagram at the top of page 19 shows you how to place

A Small Log Cabin Center

Join units in numerical order.

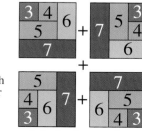

Make 64. Four for each Block A star center.

Join the four sections together as shown, with Unit A3 facing outward.

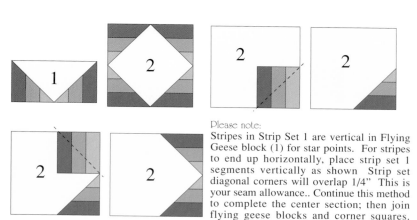

Please note:
Stripes in Strip Set 1 are vertical in Flying Geese block (1) for star points. For stripes to end up horizontally, place strip set 1 segments vertically as shown. Strip set diagonal corners will overlap 1/4" This is your seam allowance.. Continue this method to complete the center section; then join flying geese blocks and corner squares.

Block C Assembly

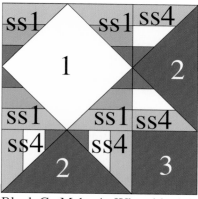

Block C. Make 4. When block is complete, it should measure 9 1/2" square

1. Block C is assembled in the same manner as Blocks A and B, however one of the strip sets and colors are different, and the block is incomplete compared to the other blocks. This is because in order to assemble the quilt top correctly, this star must be broken up.
2. Refer to diagrams for Blocks A and B for correct placement of strip sets. Make four of Block C.

your strip set segment to achieve the desired effect. Refer to the illustration above, and read the instructions, as this technique can be used in many places.

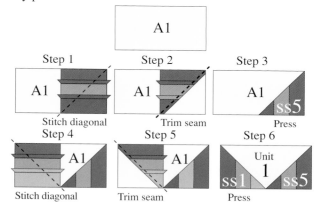

Step 1 · **Step 2** · **Step 3**
Stitch diagonal · Trim seam · Press
Step 4 · **Step 5** · **Step 6**
Stitch diagonal · Trim seam · Press

3. For Block A star points, refer to the illustration above and place the strip sets as shown. The strip sets must be a 3 1/2" square if you are to achieve an accurate corner. Trim them if necessary, and pin corners to keep them from shifting if you need to. Join the strip sets as instructed. You will need to make four of Unit 1 for each block.
4. Join Unit 1 to top and bottom of center section, matching the stripe seams. Join Unit 2 to opposite short ends of the two remaining Unit 1's and press. Join these combined units to opposite sides of the center to complete the star. Make 16.

Block D Assembly

Block D. Make 4 mirror image. When block is complete, it should measure 3 1/2" x 9 1/2".

1. Block D is part of the Block C star and is made in the same manner as the other star blocks. Refer to illustration of Unit A1 to join Strip Set 4 segments correctly. You will make four of this block, two will have Unit 2 joined on the right side, and two will have it joined on the left side.

Block E, F, and G Assembly

Block E. Make 4. When completed, block should measure 3 1/2" x 12 1/2"

1. All three of these blocks are assembled as the other star point blocks. Block E is part of the Block C star and Unit 2 is joined to opposite short ends when Flying Geese star points are completed. Make 4 of this block.
2. Refer to the illustrations at left for blocks F and G. Make the required number of these blocks as shown.

Block F. Make 28. When completed, block should measure 3 1/2" x 6 1/2"

Border Block G. Make 60. When completed, block should measure 3 1/2" x 6 1/2"

Block B Assembly

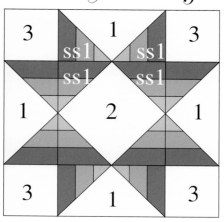

Block B. Make 6. When block is complete, it should measure 12 1/2"

1. Block B is constructed in much the same manner as Block A, with the exception of the center, Unit 2. Refer to the diagram at the top of this page for correct placement of Strip Set 1 segments.
2. Complete the center section; then complete the star points using the Strip Set 1 segments as shown. Join the block together as in Step 4 for Block A. Make six of Block B.

19

Quilt Top Assembly

1. Side sections of the quilt top are assembled first, beginning with the Block C star corners. Refer to the diagram above frequently for correct placement of all blocks and "Q" units, as the sides are mirror images. Beginning with the corners, join Block C and Unit Q11 together; then add Unit Q12 as shown. Make four of these corners, checking diagram for mirror image unit placement. Set aside.

2. Beginning at the top of the quilt top, directly below the corners, join two of Block F together as shown. Make twenty of these pairs. Ten are for the right side of the quilt top and ten are for the left side. Referring to illustration above, join a pair of Block F to the top of Block A. Join a Q7 corner to one short end of another Block F pair and join Unit Q9 to these combined blocks. Join to side of Block A combination. Make two of these, referring to diagram as the placement of the Q9 unit will be different at the bottom. Join Block A and Unit Q6. Make two. Join Unit Q8, a pair of the F blocks and Block A in a row.

3. To complete the side rows, join the Block A/Q6 rows to top and bottom of the Q8 row; then join the top and bottom Q9 combination to opposite short ends of the combined star rows. Join pieced Unit Q10 to side of these rows as shown. Referring to illustration for correct placement, join the Block C corners to opposite short ends of the side rows.

4. For the center section of the quilt, join Unit Q4, a pair of F blocks, Block A, Unit Q2, Block B, Unit Q3, Block B, Unit Q2, Block A, a pair of F blocks, and Unit Q4 in a vertical row. Make two. For the center row, join Block A, Unit Q2, Block B, Unit Q1, Block B, Unit Q2, and Block A. Join the three rows together; then add Unit Q13 to top and bottom of the center section. Join the previously completed side sections to the center section as shown.

5. For top and bottom row of quilt top, join Block D to opposite short ends of Unit Q15 as shown, checking for correct placement of mirror image Block D. Make two and join to top and bottom of quilt top, matching Block D seams. For sides, join Block E to opposite short ends of pieced Unit Q14 as shown. Make two and join to opposite sides of quilt top, matching the star points to complete the corner star.

6. Join pieced Unit Q16 to opposite sides of quilt top; then add pieced Unit Q17 to top and bottom. Join pieced sashing Unit Q18 to opposite sides of quilt; then join pieced Unit Q19 to top and bottom.

7. For the border, refer to diagram and join sixteen of Block G together as shown, with Unit 1 of Block G facing in opposite directions. Please note that two of the Block G units will face in the same direction in th center of the border. Make 2 and join them to opposite sides of quilt top. Join fourteen of border Block G together as you did for the sides, again taking note that two of the blocks face in the same direction in the center of the border. Join Unit Q20 to opposite short ends, and join to top and bottom of quilt top matching Unit Q20 seams to corner. Join pieced border Q21 to opposite sides of quilt. Join pieced border Unit Q22 to top and bottom to complete the quilt top.

8. Faye quilted some spectacular circular motifs in the Block B centers and Q12 blocks using dark brown thread. A lovely feather design is quilted in the honey tan sections with dark brown thread. The patchwork was "ditched".

9. Refer to page 12 for making straight-grain binding, and using the 2 1/2" wide strips of Fabric III, make the binding. Bind your quilt as directed on Page 12.

Designing Your Own Block

3 1/2" x 6 1/2"

When working on a design such as this, you will note that it is divided into four sections. The size of the block *finished* is a 12" square. This measurement divided by four is 3". The center square is 6" finished. It is the total finished size of the flying geese blocks.

To calculate what sizes must be cut, seam allowance is added to all of the units. To do this, keep in mind that seam allowance all the way around the unit is 1/4", meaning that you will add 1/2" to *all finished* sizes.
This means that the center square will be a 6 1/2" square when cut. Cut sizes are shown on the illustration at left.

The star point sections will be 3 1/2" when cut. To calculate the size of the diagonal corner square in the center, you will need to divide the center square *finished* size in half. This measurement is 3". Adding seam allowance, it becomes 3 1/2". This measurement is consistant with the 3 1/2" width of the star points.

We calculated the center diagonal corner on diagonal corner square so that the navy would be a 1" width between the gold diagonal corners when *finished*, thus making the gold corners 2 1/2" squares.. The navy center (finished) is the exact width of the strip set points, which is 1".

To calculate your strip size, take the *finished* measurement, which is 3" and divide it by three, giving you three 1" wide strips when *finished*. Add 1/2" for seam allowance to the strips, making them 1 1/2" wide strips.

A good example of this would be if you wanted only two stripes on your star points. Divide the *finished* size, which is 3" by two, giving you 1 1/2" *finished*. Adding 1/2" seam allowance, the strips would be cut 2" wide.

Another approach

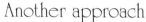

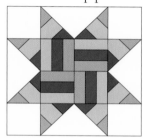

A Rail Fence strip set center with diagonal corners used as diagonal corners for the star points.

Your center section diagonal corner navy square is once again a 3" square *finished*. To determine the size of the small diagonal corners, remember that the navy should end up to be the width (finished) of the star point strips, which is 1 1/2". Divide the *finished* size of the center square in half, giving you 1 1/2". Add seam allowance to the gold square to give you a square that is to be cut 2". Always remember to work with the *finished* size and add 1/2" seam allowance.

Additional Borders

Use your own color scheme.

21

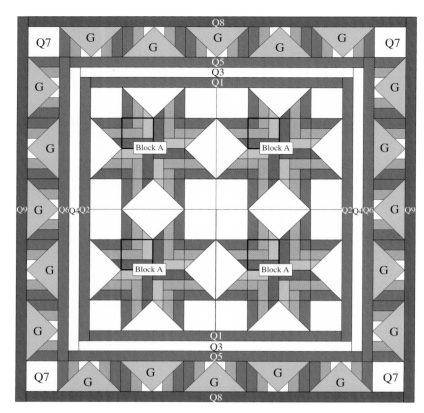

Table Topper Materials

	Fabric I (light tan print) 7/8 yard	Need 26 1/2"
	Fabric II (honey tan print) 5/8 yard	Need 17"
	Fabric III (dark brown print) 5/8 yard	Need 20 1/2"
	Fabric IV (dark blue print) 3/4 yard	Need 24"
	Fabric V (medium blue print) 1/2 yard	Need 15"
	Backing	1 3/8 yards

Table Topper Assembly

Border Block G. Make 20

Strip Set 1. Make 2. Cut into 16 - 3 1/2" segments

Strip Set 2. Make 4. Cut into 40 - 3 1/2" segments

Strip Set 5. Make 2. Cut into 16 - 3 1/2" segments

1. Refer to strips set assembly, and Block A assembly for quilt on pages 18 and 19. Sew and cut the strip set segments as directed on the left.

2. Assemble Block A as instructed for quilt. Make 4 of Block A and join them together as shown in table topper diagram.

3. Refer to page 19 for Block G assembly, and make 20 of Block G. For the border, refer to diagram and join five of Block G together as shown, with Unit 1 of Block G facing in opposite directions. Make four sets for border.

4. Join Unit Q1 to top and bottom of combined Block A center; then add Unit Q2 to opposite sides. Join Unit Q3 to top and bottom of table topper; then join Unit Q4 to sides. Join Unit Q5 to bottom of table topper; then join Unit Q6 to opposite sides.

5. Refer to illustration of table topper for correct placement of Block G borders. Join a set to top and bottom of table topper. Join Unit Q7 to opposite short ends of the two remaining joined borders. Join these two rows to opposite sides of table topper. Join Unit Q8 to top and bottom of table topper; then add Unit Q9 to opposite sides to complete the pieced top.

6. Faye ditched the patchwork. Join the five 2 1/2" wide strips of Fabric III together for straight-grain binding as shown on page 12. Bind the table topper.

Table Topper Cutting

From Fabric I, cut: (light tan print)
- Five 3 1/2" wide strips. From these, cut:
  * Sixteen - 3 1/2" x 6 1/2" (A1)
  * Twenty - 3 1/2" squares (Q7, A2)
  * Two - 1 1/2" x 26 1/2" (Q3)
- Six 1 1/2" wide strips. Four for Strip Set 2. From remainder, cut:
  * Two - 1 1/2" x 28 1/2" (Q4)

From Fabric II, cut: (honey tan print)
- Four 3 1/2" wide strips. From these, cut:
  * Twenty - 3 1/2" x 6 1/2" (G1)
  * Sixteen - 1 1/2" x 2 1/2" (A6)
- Two 1 1/2" wide strips for Strip Set 1.

From Fabric III, cut: (dark brown print)
- Four 2 1/2" wide strips for straight-grain binding
- Seven 1 1/2" wide strips. Two for Strip Set 5. From remainder, cut:
  * Two - 1 1/2" x 38 1/2" (Q9)
  * Two - 1 1/2" x 36 1/2" (Q8)
  * Sixteen - 1 1/2" x 3 1/2" (A7)

From Fabric IV, cut: (dark blue print)
- Sixteen 1 1/2" wide strips. Eight for Strip Sets 1, 2, and 5. From remainder, cut:
  * Two - 1 1/2" x 30 1/2" (Q6)
  * Two - 1 1/2" x 28 1/2" (Q5)
  * Two - 1 1/2" x 26 1/2" (Q2)
  * Two - 1 1/2" x 24 1/2" (Q1)
  * Sixteen - 1 1/2" squares (A3)

From Fabric V, cut: (medium blue print)
- Ten 1 1/2" wide strips. Eight for Strip Sets 1, 2, and 5. From remainder, cut:
  * Sixteen - 1 1/2" x 2 1/2" (A5)
  * Sixteen - 1 1/2" squares (A4)

When ripping (unsewing) a seam, clip every 3rd to 5th thread on one side of the fabric; then pull the back thread out. Scotch tape is good to pick out the smaller threads.

APRIL SHOWERS

This adorable beginner baby quilt finishes to: 47" square.
Techniques used: diagonal corners.

Materials

Fabric I (medium blue 30's print) 1 1/8 yards	Need 33"	
Fabric II (light blue dot print) 5/8 yard	Need 17 1/2"	
Fabric III (light yellow print) 1/2 yard	Need 11"	
Fabric IV (medium pink 30's print) 1/2 yard	Need 10 1/2"	
Fabric V (dark green print) 1/4 yard	Need 7 1/2"	
Fabric VI (medium green 30's print) 1/4 yard	Need 5"	
Fabric VII (solid orange) 1/8 yard	Need 3"	
Fabric VIII (white on white print) 7/8 yard	Need 26"	
Backing	3 yards	

Cutting

From Fabric I, cut: (medium blue 30's print)
- One 5 1/2" wide strip. From this, cut:
  * One - 5 1/2" x 11 1/2" (A1)
  * Two - 2 1/2" x 24 " (Q6) Join two together to = two 47 1/2" lengths.
  * Four - 1 1/2" squares (Q2)
- Eleven 2 1/2" wide strips. Five for straight-grain binding. From remainder, cut:
  * Two - 2 1/2" x 24 " (add to Q6)
  * Four - 2 1/2" x 22" (Q5) Join two together to = two 43 1/2" lengths.

From Fabric II, cut: (light blue dot print)
- One 5 1/2" wide strip. From this, cut:
  * Four - 5" x 5 1/2" (B3)
  * Four - 3 1/2" x 5 1/2" (B10)
  * Four - 1 1/2" x 5 1/2" (B9)
- One 4 1/2" wide strip. From this, cut:
  * Four - 4 1/2" squares (B20)
  * Four - 2 1/2" x 4 1/2" (B17)
  * Four - 1 1/2" x 4" (B2)
  * Eight - 1 1/2" x 2 1/2" (B6, B15)
- One 3 1/2" wide strip. From this, cut:
  * Four - 3 1/2" x 9 1/2" (B16)
  * Four - 1 3/4" squares (B1a)
- One 2 1/2" wide strip. From this, cut:
  * Eight - 2 1/2" squares (B4a, B8)
  * Four - 2 1/2" x 3" (B11)
- One 1 1/2" wide strip. From this and scrap, cut:
  * Four - 1 1/2" x 6 1/2" (B18)
  * Twelve - 1 1/2" squares (B1b, B13, B19a)

From Fabric III, cut: (light yellow print)
- Two 5 1/2" wide strips. From these, cut:
  * Four - 5 1/2" x 8 1/2" (B4)
  * Four - 3" x 5 12" (C1)
  * Four - 4" x 4 1/2" (B1)
  Stack these cuts:
  * Four - 1 1/2" x 6 1/2" (B19)
  * Twelve - 1 1/2" squares (Q4)

From Fabric IV, cut: (medium pink 30's print)
- Two 3" wide strips. From these, cut:
  * Four - 3" x 5 1/2" (C2)
  * Eight - 3" squares (C1b)
  * Four - 1 1/2" x 13 1/2" (Q1)
- Three 1 1/2" wide strips. From these, cut:
  * Eight - 1 1/2" x 13 1/2" (add to Q1)

From Fabric V, cut: (dark green print)
- Five 1 1/2" wide strips. From these, cut:
  * Twelve - 1 1/2" x 13 1/2" (Q3)
  * Four - 1 1/2" x 6 1/2" (C5)

From Fabric VI, cut: (medium green print)
- Two 2 1/2" wide strips. From these, cut:
  * Eight - 2 1/2" x 5 1/2" (C7)

From Fabric VII, cut: (solid orange)
- Two 1 1/2" wide strips. From these, cut:
  * One - 1 1/2" x 6 1/2" (A9)
  * Thirteen - 1 1/2" x 2 1/2" (A6, B5, B7, B14)
  * Five - 1 1/2" squares (A5, B12)

From Fabric VIII, cut: (white on white print)
- Two 5 1/2" wide strips. From these, cut:
  * One - 5 1/2" x 7 1/2" (A10)
  * One - 4 1/2" x 5 1/2" (A3)
  * Eight - 3 1/2" x 5 1/2" (C3)
  * Sixteen - 2 1/2" x 5 1/2" (C6, C8)
- One 3 1/2" wide strip. From this, cut:
  * Two - 3 1/2" squares (A1a)
  * One - 2 1/2" x 3 1/2" (A7)
  * Eight - 2 1/4" squares (C1a)
  * Nine - 1 1/2" squares (A4, C2a)
- One 2 1/2" wide strip. From this, cut:
  * Sixteen - 2 1/2" squares (C7a)
- Six 1 1/2" wide strips. From these, cut:
  * Ten - 1 1/2" x 13 1/2" (A11, C10)
  * Nine - 1 1/2" x 11 1/2" (A2, C4, C9)
  * One - 1 1/2" x 6 1/2" (A8)

Block A Assembly

1. Use diagonal corner technique to make one of Unit 1. Do NOT trim center seam on diagonal corner as the corner is a white fabric over a darker fabric, and the dark will show through. Press the corners.

2. To assemble Block A, begin by joining units 1 and 2. Join units 4 and 5. Join units 6 and 7. Join the 4/5 units and the 6/7 units as shown in Block A diagram, then add Unit 3 to top of combined units, and Unit 9 to right side. Join Unit 8 to bottom of combined units; then add Unit 10 to right side. Join the umbrella top to the umbrella bottom. Join Unit 11 to opposite sides of umbrella to complete the block. Make 1

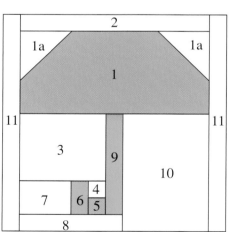

Block A, Make 1. When block is completed it should measure 13 1/2" square.

Block B Assembly

.1. To assemble the duck, use diagonal corner technique to make one each of units 1, 4 and 19.

2. Join units 1 and 2; then add Unit 3 to left side of combined units. Join Unit 4 to bottom.

3. Although you can't see it, Unit 18 is a solid light blue strip, and Unit 19 is a solid yellow strip with diagonal corner 19a on its corner. Join these two units together; then add Unit 17 to top of these combined units. Join these combined units to duck combined units, referring to diagram for correct placement of units.

4. Join diagonal corner, Unit 20 to bottom left corner of combined units. Stitch the diagonal, trim seam and press. We use this little

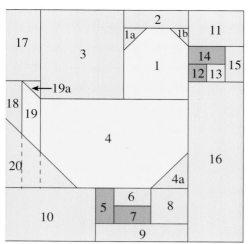

Block B, Make 4. When block is completed it should measure 13 1/2" square.

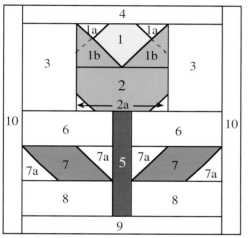

Block C , Make 4. When block is completed it should measure 13 1/2" square.

Block B. Join sashing Unit 3 to left side on one Block C, and right side of the other. Join Block C to opposite sides of Block B as shown. Make two of these rows. One for the first row, and one for the third row.

2. For center row, join sashing Unit 1 to opposite sides of Block A. Join sashing Unit 3 to right side of one Block B and the other side of remaining Block B as shown.

3. For center sashing rows, join Unit 4, Unit 1, Unit 2, Unit 1, Unit 2, Unit 1, and Unit 4, in a long horizontal row. Make two of these rows. Join them to top and bottom of center row, matching sashing square seams. Join top and bottom row to opposite sides of center sashing row.

4. For top and bottom sashing rows, join Unit 4, Unit 3, Unit 4, Unit 3, Unit 4, Unit 3 and Unit 4 in a long horizontal row as shown. Join to top and bottom of quilt, again matching sashing square seams.

5. Join pieced Unit 5 to opposite sides of quilt top; then add pieced Unit 6 to top and bottom to complete the quilt top.

6. Faye "ditched" all of the patchwork and quilted small rain drops under the umbrella.

7. Use the five 2 1/2" wide strips of Fabric I and make straight-grain binding. Bind your quilt as illustrated on page 12.

trick when ever we can so that seams do not have to be matched.

5. For duck feet, join units 6 and 7; then add Unit 5 to left side of combined units, and Unit 8 to right side. Join Unit 9 to bottom of combined units; then add Unit 10 to left side as shown. Add these units to bottom of duck.

6. For beak assembly, join units 12 and 13; then add Unit 14 to top of 12/13 combined units. Join Unit 15 to right side; then add Unit 11 to top of combined units, and Unit 16 to bottom. Join the beak section to duck, matching seams. This completes the block. Make 4.

Block C Assembly

1. To assemble Block C units, use diagonal corner technique to make one each of Unit 1 (illustrated above), and 2. Make two of mirror image Unit 7. To assemble Unit 1, all diagonal corners are joined in alphabetical order as shown. Join Unit 1a. Do NOT trim center seam as the white is on a darker fabric and will show through if seam is trimmed. Press towards corner. Join diagonal corner Unit 1b as shown. Trim seams and press.

2. To assemble the block, join units 1 and 2; then add Unit 3 to opposite sides of combined 1/2 units. Join Unit 4 to top of combined units. Join units 6, 7, and 8 in a vertical row, checking Block C diagram for correct placement of mirror image Unit 7. Make two row.s. Join to opposite sides of Unit 5. Join Unit 9 to bottom of these combined units.

3. Join flower top section to the flower leaf section; then add Unit 10 to opposite sides of the flower to complete the block. Make four.

Quilt Assembly

1. To assemble the quilt top, begin by joining top row. To do so, join sashing Unit 1 to opposite sides of

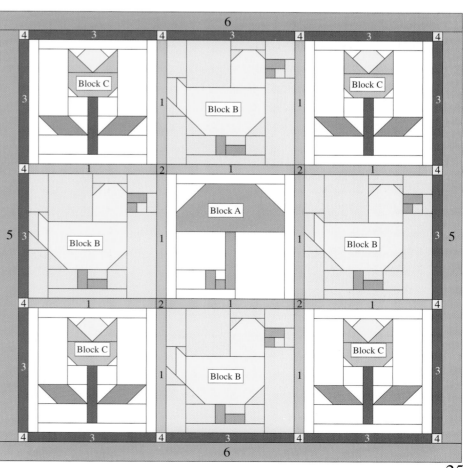

Quilt finishes to: 71" x 103".
Techniques used: Diagonal corners, diagonal ends, and triangle-squares.

Materials

	Fabric I (sand)	Need 97 1/2"	3 yards
	Fabric II (light aqua print)	Need 67 1/2"	2 yards
	Fabric III (burgundy print)	Need 60"	1 3/4 yards
	Fabric IV (light rose print)	Need 68 5/8"	2 1/8 yards
	Fabric V (dark rose print)	Need 21 1/2"	3/4 yard
	Fabric VI (dark olive print)	Need 43 1/2"	1 3/8 yards
	Fabric VII (light olive print)	Need 7 1/2"	1/4 yard
	Fabric VIII (dark turquoise print)	Need 68 1/2"	2 1/4 yards
	Fabric IX (bright turquoise print)	Need 44 3/8"	1 1/2 yards
	Fabric X (light yellow print)	Need 12"	1/2 yard

Cutting

From Fabric I, cut: (sand)
- Three 12 1/2" wide strips. From these, cut:
  * Twenty-seven - 4 1/2" x 12 1/2" (Q1)
- Five 2 1/2" wide strips. From these, cut:
  * Seventy-two - 2 1/2" squares (A14)
- Fifteen 2" wide strips. From these, cut:
  * 120 - 2" x 3" (A2, A9, B2, B9, C2, C9)
  * 124 - 2" squares (A1, A8, B1, B8, C1, C8, Q4)
- Ten 1 3/4" wide strips. From these, cut:
  * 240 - 1 3/4" squares (A3a, A4a, A10a, A11a, B3a, B4a, B10a, B11a, C3a, C4a, C10a, C11a)

From Fabric II, cut: (lt. aqua print)
- Twenty-seven 2 1/2" wide strips. From these, cut:
  * 232 - 2 1/2" x 3" (A7a, B7a, C7a)
  * 152 - 2 1/2" squares (D1b)

From Fabric III, cut: (burgundy print)
- Fifteen 4" wide strips. From these, cut:
  * 240 - 2 1/2" x 4" (B7, C7, D1)
  * Four - 2" squares (E1a)

From Fabric IV, cut: (light rose print)
- One 4 1/2" wide strip. From this, cut:
  * Four - 4 1/2" squares (E1a)
  * Thirty-six - 1 1/2" squares (A10b)
- Thirteen 3" wide strips. From these, cut:
  * 152 - 2 1/2" x 3" (D1a)
  * Seventy-two - 1 3/4" x 3" (A3, A4)
  * Thirty-six - 1 1/2" x 2" (A12)
- Six 2 1/2" wide strips. From these, cut:
  * Eighty-eight - 2 1/2" squares (B7b, C7b)
  * Eleven - 2" squares (A9a)
- Three 2" wide strips. From these, cut:
  * Sixty-one - 2" squares (add to A9a)
- Three 1 3/8" wide strips. From these, cut:
  * Eighty - 1 3/8" squares (B14a)

From Fabric V, cut: (dark rose print)
- Three 3" wide strips. From these, cut:
  * Seventy-two - 1 3/4" x 3" (A10, A11)
- Four 2" wide strips. From these, cut:
  * Seventy-two - 2" squares (A2a)
  * Sixteen - 1 1/2" x 2" (A5)
- Three 1 1/2" wide strips. From these, cut:
  * Twenty - 1 1/2" x 2" (add to A5)
  * Thirty-six - 1 1/2" squares (A3b)

Blooming Desert

From Fabric VI, cut: (dark olive print)
- Nine 4" wide strips. From these, cut:
  * 144 - 2 1/2" x 4" (A7)
- Three 2 1/2" wide strips. From these, cut:
  * Forty - 2 1/2" squares (B14)

From Fabric VII, cut: (light olive print)
- Three 2 1/2" wide strips. From these, cut:
  * Forty - 2 1/2" squares (B14)

From Fabric VIII, cut: (dark turquoise print)
- Two 3" wide strips. From these, cut:
  * Forty-eight - 1 3/4" x 3" (B10, B11, C10, C11)
- Fourteen 2 1/2" wide strips. Nine for straight-grain binding. From remainder, cut:
  * Seventy-two - 2 1/2" squares (A14)
  * Eleven - 2" squares (B2a, C2a)
- Thirteen 2" wide strips. From these, cut:
  * Two - 2" x 41 1/2" (Q3)
  * Four - 2" x 30" (Q3) Piece on opposite ends of 2" x 41 1/2" strips to = two 100 1/2" long strips.
  * Four - 2" x 34 1/2" (Q2) Piece two together to = two 68 1/2" strips.
  * Thirty-seven - 2" squares (add to B2a, C2a)
  * Twenty-four - 1 1/2" x 2" (B5, C5)
- One 1 1/2" wide strip. From this, cut:
  * Twenty-four - 1 1/2" squares (B3b, C3b)

From Fabric IX, cut: (bright turquoise print)
- Two 3" wide strips. From these, cut:
  * Forty-eight - 1 3/4" x 3" (B3, B4, C3, C4)
- Nine 2 1/2" wide strips. From these, cut:
  * 144 - 2 1/2" squares (A7b)
- Three 2" wide strips. From these, cut:
  * Forty-eight - 2" squares (B9a, C9a)
  * Twenty - 1 1/2" x 2" (B12, C12)
- Two 1 1/2" wide strips. From these, cut:
  * Four - 1 1/2" x 2" (add to B12, C12)
  * Twenty-four - 1 1/2" squares (B10b, C10b)
- Five 1 3/8" wide strips. From these, cut:
  * 144 - 1 3/8" squares (A14a)

From Fabric X, cut: (light yellow print)
- Six 2" wide strips. From these, cut:
  * 120 - 2" squares (A6, A13, B6, B13, C6, C13)

Block A Assembly

1. Use diagonal corner technique to make two each of units 2, 3, 4, 9, 10, and 11. Use diagonal end technique to make four of Unit 7. For Unit 7 assembly, see diagram above right, keeping in mind that Unit 7 is a mirror image, which is shown. Make diagonal end first; then join diagonal corner 7b. Refer to block diagrams for color changes within the blocks, and make units 2 and 9 according to the instructions above.

2. Unit 14 has another interesting quick piecing technique. Make the triangle-squares shown on page 29 according to the instructions in the gold box; then add diagonal corners to form the leaves for the center of the blocks.

3. After all units are constructed, assemble Block A. Begin by joining the four Unit 14's in the center as shown. Check illustration for correct placement.

4. Join four pairs of Unit 7 as shown. Add two to top and bottom of center section.

5. For side sections of the block, join units 1 and 2. Join units 3 and 4. Join units 5 and 6. Again referring to the illustration, join the combined 3/4 units and the combined 5/6 units together; then add combined units 1/2 to the top. Join another pair of

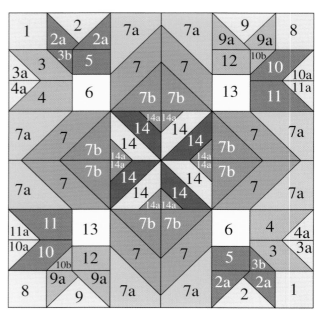

Block A. Make 18. When completed, block should measure 12 1/2" square.

Making Unit 7 for Blocks A, B, and C. Make 4 of each for Blocks A & B. Make one for Block C. Refer to block diagrams for color changes.

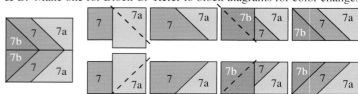

Making Units 2 and 9 for Blocks A and B. Make 2 for each block. For Block C, make one of each. Refer to block diagrams for color changes. Diagonal corners will overlap.

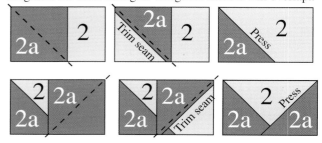

Unit 7's to other combined units. For the remaining flower, join units 10 and 11. Join units 12 and 13, and join units 8 and 9. Assemble the flower by joining units 10 and 11; add combined units 12 and 13 to right side of the 10/11 combined units. Join combined units 8/9 to bottom to complete the flower. Join the flower to other combined units. Make two of these rows. Refer to illustration for correct placement as the remaining side row will be turned around. Join the flower rows to the center row to complete Block A. Make 18.

Block B Assembly

1. Block B is exactly the same as Block A. The only difference is the col.or change. Follow all instructions for Block A assembly, changing the colors that you have cut.

Block C Assembly

1. As you can see, Block C is 1/3 of Block B. Follow the instructions for Block A, and refer to Block B diagram frequently for color changes.

Block A

Block B

Use this assembly for Blocks A and B, Unit 14.

For Block A, place 2 1/2" squares of fabrics I and VIII right sides together, matching raw edges, and stitch a diagonal line down the center as shown. Press open and trim center seam, leaving the top and base fabric.

Join 1 3/8" squares of Fabric IX for diagonal corners. Stitch seams, trim and press.

For Block B, place 2 1/2" squares of Fabrics VI and VII right sides together, matching raw edges, and stitch a diagonal line down the center as shown. Press open and trim center seam, leaving the top and base fabric.

Join 1 3/8" squares of Fabric IV for diagonal corners. Stitch seams, trim and press.

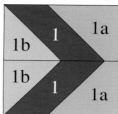

Each section when completed should measure 2 1/2" x 4 1/2"

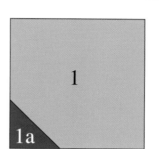

Mirror image Block D. Make 76. Completed block should measure 4 1/2" square

Quilt Assembly

1. To assemble the quilt, we will work from left to right, beginning with the left vertical row. Beginning with Block A, join six of Block A with Unit Q1 between them. These are the "Block A" rows. Make three.

2. For the Block B rows, begin by joining Block C, and Unit Q1. Join five of Block B with Unit Q1 between them. For bottom of the row, join another Unit Q1 with Block C as shown. Add these combined units to bottom of Block B row; the add the remaining Block C/Unit Q1 to top of Block B row. Make two of these rows.

3. Refer to quilt diagram and join the rows together, beginning with left side of quilt and Block A row. Match flower seams as shown.

4. For the border, if you haven't already done so, join mirror image Block D's together in pairs as shown above. Join fifteen pairs in a long horizontal row as shown. Make two of these rows. Join to top and bottom of quilt.

5. Corner Block E is a square with a diagonal corner. Complete adding the diagonal corner to all four of the squares.

6. Join twenty-three pairs of Block D together in a long row as shown. Make two of these rows. When the rows are completed, add Block E to opposite short ends of the rows, checking illustration for correct placement of Block E. Join these rows to opposite sides of the quilt, matching corner seams.

7. Join pieced Unit Q2 to top and bottom of quilt top. Join corner Unit Q4 to opposite short ends of pieced Unit Q3 and join this border to opposite sides of quilt, matching Q4 corners.

8. Mary "ditched" the patchwork and quilted leaves in the open Q1 spaces.

9. Join the nine 2 1/2" strips of Fabric VIII together to make straight-grain binding. Refer to instructions and illustrations on Page 12 and bind your quilt.

Block E. Make 4 When completed it should measure a 4 1/2" square.

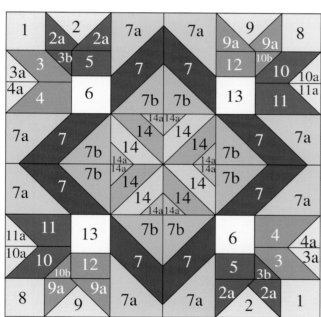

Block B. Make 10. When completed, block should measure 12 1/2" square

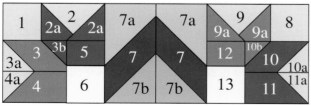

Block C. Make 4. When finished, block should measure 4 1/2" x 12 1/2"

Border Block D

1. Border Block D is the same as Unit 7 for blocks A, B, and C. Only the colors are different. Use chain piecing and make 76 of this block.

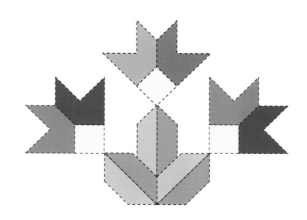

29

Cornflower

Having lived with quilting for such a long time, I truly believe that there are some quilts that make us very aware of our surroundings and have a little story of their own to tell. There are two such quilts in this book, beginning with this one.

In March, we bought a new home, and moved to Pagosa Springs, Colorado, which is absolutely gorgeous. I am fortunate enough to be able to see the mountains and beautiful Ponderosa pines from my office window. I never take it for granted!

There is a plant here that the local people refer to as a "weed", however in my case it proved to be much more than a weed. It is called "Mules Ears". It has long, broad leaves and produces a yellow daisy type of flower. The first part of June we noticed a few of them scattered on our land, but didn't pay much attention to them as there were other wildflowers mixed in.

Chris, our photographer, was busy shooting a catalog, and I knew that he would not be available for several weeks. Robert and I had been hard at work on several projects that had to be finished in a short period of time. This, along with our move, and hiring new people gave us little time to notice much of anything.

It is important for you to know that the middle of July, in our part of Southwest Colorado is the peak of the wildflower season, so we generally do not look for flowers until that time. In order to get the perfect shot of a quilt in the wildflowers, one must take at least two days off and drive around in search of the appropriate spot. Although it is pleasant, it is also very time consuming. Great shots do not just happen. They are generally planned very carefully.

There is a 3 acre lot next to us that meets national forest land, with "Eagle Peak", one of the highest in Pagosa, proudly standing in the background. One afternoon I decided to take the Bulldogs for a little walk on that lot, and as I started in that direction, and looked up, I stopped dead in my tracks! The entire lot, along with the national forest land was a sea of yellow daisies. I have never seen anything like it in my 18 years of pursuing wildflowers in Colorado.

I ran inside and called the lady who was piecing the quilt. She was not finished with it to my dismay. I then called Chris and said "Chris, tell me that there is no way you can drive the 50 miles to Pagosa to get a great shot.....It will make me feel much better!" He asked what it was, and I elaborated. His response was: "Well, I could throw my camera in the car at 5:00. How long do the flowers last?" I had no idea, but I knew that our time was limited. This was "heaven" right next to me in the form of hundreds of Mules Ears!!!

Robert and I drove to Durango, picked up the quilt, and spent two nights in a row until 3:00 a.m. finishing it. We then sent it overnight to our quilter in Minnesota. Mary finished it in a day and a half and sent it back overnight. Chris did jump in his car at 5:00 p.m. and made it here in time. The flowers were still at their peak. My new friend Susan, who is our best piecer loaned us her log headboard and we ran extension cords out into the field so that Chris could set up his lights. The extension cords didn't work properly and it was closing in on dusk. Everyone looked very disappointed except for Chris. Never give up hope my fellow quilters.

The photo on page 1 of this book is the result of the efforts of some very good friends, a talented, dedicated photographer, a great quilter, and persistence.

Enjoy!

P.S. Mary deserved flowers, so we sent them, but we couldn't find a florist who had Mules Ears!

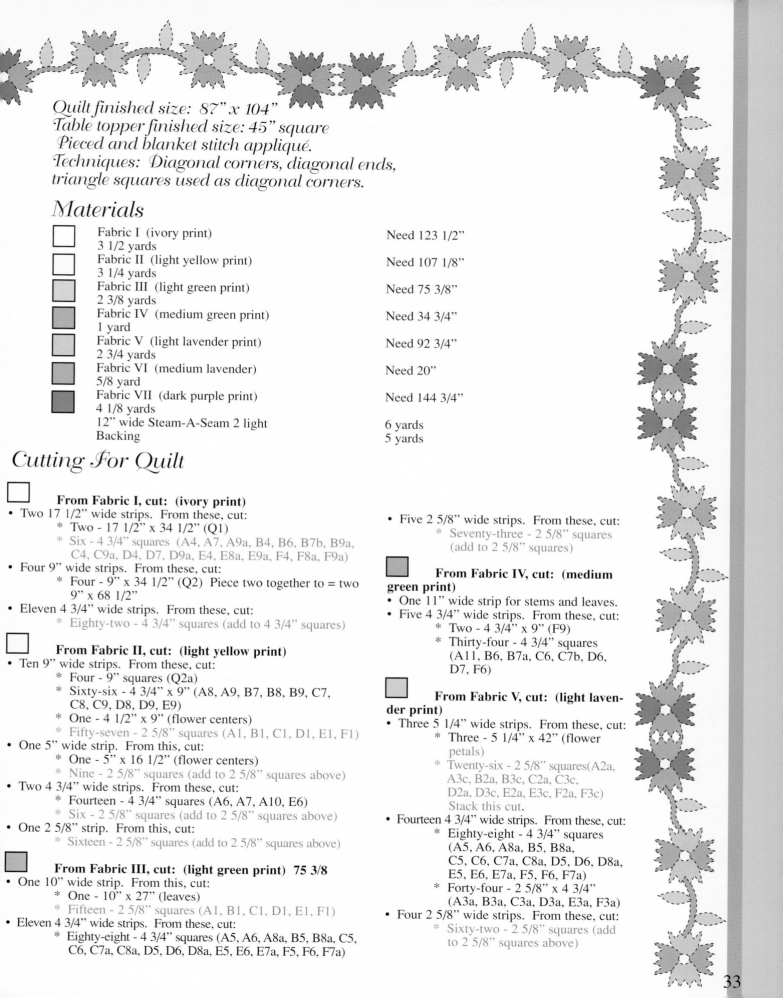

Quilt finished size: 87" x 104"
Table topper finished size: 45" square
Pieced and blanket stitch appliqué.
Techniques: Diagonal corners, diagonal ends,
triangle squares used as diagonal corners.

Materials

☐	Fabric I (ivory print) 3 1/2 yards	Need 123 1/2"
☐	Fabric II (light yellow print) 3 1/4 yards	Need 107 1/8"
☐	Fabric III (light green print) 2 3/8 yards	Need 75 3/8"
☐	Fabric IV (medium green print) 1 yard	Need 34 3/4"
☐	Fabric V (light lavender print) 2 3/4 yards	Need 92 3/4"
☐	Fabric VI (medium lavender) 5/8 yard	Need 20"
☐	Fabric VII (dark purple print) 4 1/8 yards	Need 144 3/4"
	12" wide Steam-A-Seam 2 light	6 yards
	Backing	5 yards

Cutting For Quilt

☐ From Fabric I, cut: (ivory print)
• Two 17 1/2" wide strips. From these, cut:
   * Two - 17 1/2" x 34 1/2" (Q1)
   * Six - 4 3/4" squares (A4, A7, A9a, B4, B6, B7b, B9a, C4, C9a, D4, D7, D9a, E4, E8a, E9a, F4, F8a, F9a)
• Four 9" wide strips. From these, cut:
   * Four - 9" x 34 1/2" (Q2) Piece two together to = two 9" x 68 1/2"
• Eleven 4 3/4" wide strips. From these, cut:
   * Eighty-two - 4 3/4" squares (add to 4 3/4" squares)

☐ From Fabric II, cut: (light yellow print)
• Ten 9" wide strips. From these, cut:
   * Four - 9" squares (Q2a)
   * Sixty-six - 4 3/4" x 9" (A8, A9, B7, B8, B9, C7, C8, C9, D8, D9, E9)
   * One - 4 1/2" x 9" (flower centers)
   * Fifty-seven - 2 5/8" squares (A1, B1, C1, D1, E1, F1)
• One 5" wide strip. From this, cut:
   * One - 5" x 16 1/2" (flower centers)
   * Nine - 2 5/8" squares (add to 2 5/8" squares above)
• Two 4 3/4" wide strips. From these, cut:
   * Fourteen - 4 3/4" squares (A6, A7, A10, E6)
   * Six - 2 5/8" squares (add to 2 5/8" squares above)
• One 2 5/8" strip. From this, cut:
   * Sixteen - 2 5/8" squares (add to 2 5/8" squares above)

☐ From Fabric III, cut: (light green print) 75 3/8
• One 10" wide strip. From this, cut:
   * One - 10" x 27" (leaves)
   * Fifteen - 2 5/8" squares (A1, B1, C1, D1, E1, F1)
• Eleven 4 3/4" wide strips. From these, cut:
   * Eighty-eight - 4 3/4" squares (A5, A6, A8a, B5, B8a, C5, C6, C7a, C8a, D5, D6, D8a, E5, E6, E7a, F5, F6, F7a)

• Five 2 5/8" wide strips. From these, cut:
   * Seventy-three - 2 5/8" squares (add to 2 5/8" squares)

☐ From Fabric IV, cut: (medium green print)
• One 11" wide strip for stems and leaves.
• Five 4 3/4" wide strips. From these, cut:
   * Two - 4 3/4" x 9" (F9)
   * Thirty-four - 4 3/4" squares (A11, B6, B7a, C6, C7b, D6, D7, F6)

☐ From Fabric V, cut: (light lavender print)
• Three 5 1/4" wide strips. From these, cut:
   * Three - 5 1/4" x 42" (flower petals)
   * Twenty-six - 2 5/8" squares (A2a, A3c, B2a, B3c, C2a, C3c, D2a, D3c, E2a, E3c, F2a, F3c) Stack this cut.
• Fourteen 4 3/4" wide strips. From these, cut:
   * Eighty-eight - 4 3/4" squares (A5, A6, A8a, B5, B8a, C5, C6, C7a, C8a, D5, D6, D8a, E5, E6, E7a, F5, F6, F7a)
   * Forty-four - 2 5/8" x 4 3/4" (A3a, B3a, C3a, D3a, E3a, F3a)
• Four 2 5/8" wide strips. From these, cut:
   * Sixty-two - 2 5/8" squares (add to 2 5/8" squares above)

33

From Fabric VI, cut: (medium lavender print)
- Four 5" wide strips for flower petals.

From Fabric VII, cut: (dark purple print)
- One 10 1/2" wide strip. From this, cut:
  * One - 10 1/2" x 30" (flower petals)
- Three 6 7/8" wide strips. From these, cut:
  * Forty-four - 2 5/8" x 6 7/8" (A3, B3 ,C3, D3, E3, F3)
- Seven 2 5/8" wide strips. From these, cut:
  * Forty-four - 2 5/8" x 4 3/4" (A2, B2, C2, D2, E2, F2)
  * Forty-four - 2 5/8" squares (A3b, B3b, C3b, D3b, E3b, F3b)
- Ten 2 1/2" wide strips for straight-grain binding.
- Eleven 4 3/4" wide strips. From these, cut:
  * Twelve - 4 3/4" x 9" (E7, E8, F7, F8)
  * Sixty-four - 4 3/4" squares (A4, A5, B4, B5, C4, C5, D4, D5, E4, E5, F4, F5)
- Twelve 1 1/2" wide strips. From these, cut:
  * Four - 1 1/2" x 42" (Q3, Q4)
  * Four - 1 1/2" x 30 3/4" (Q3) Join to opposite ends of (Q3) above to = two 102 1/2" lengths.
  * Four - 1 1/2" x 23 1/4" (Q4) Join to opposite ends of (Q4) above to = two 87 1/2" lengths.

Block A

Use this assembly for Blocks A-F.

For Block A, Unit 4, place 4 3/4"" squares of fabrics I and VII right sides together, matching raw edges, and stitch a diagonal line down the center as shown. Press open and trim center seam, leaving the top and base fabric. Use this technique for all blocks, Unit 1.

For Unit 5, place 4 3/4" squares of fabrics III and V right sides together and stitch a diagonal as shown. Trim seam and press open. Place this triangle-square right sides together on 4 3/4" square of Fabric VII as shown. Stitch diagonal, trim seam and press as shown.

Use this technique for units 5 and 6 in blocks E and F.

Use this technique on all triangle-squares.

Block A Assembly

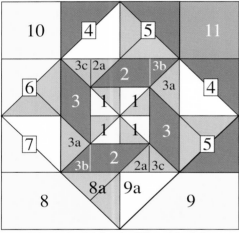

Block A. Make 4. When block is completed, it should measure 17 1/2" square

1. Use diagonal corner technique to make two of Unit 2 and one of Unit 9. Refer to illustrations of triangle squares and read the instructions in the gold box. Refer to drawing of Unit 8. This shows a triangle-square used as a diagonal corner. Refer to this diagram frequently as this technique is used throughout this project.

2. Use diagonal end technique to make two of Unit 3. Refer to the drawing at left showing how to make Unit 3.

Making Unit 3 for all blocks.

3. Assemble the center section first. Begin by joining triangle-square Units 1 together as shown. Join Unit 2 to top and bottom of combined Units 1; then add Unit 3 to opposite sides.

4. Refer to Block A diagram for correct placement, and join units 4 and 5. Make two, making sure the second pair is joined according to drawing. Join units 6 and 7. Join the 6/7 combined units to left side of center section and combined units 4/5 to right side, checking illustration for correct placement of the 4/5 units. Join Unit 10 to left side of remaining 4/5 combined units, and Unit 11 to right side. Join these combined units to top of center section. Join units 8 and 9 and add them to bottom of center section to complete the block. Make 4.

Block B Assembly

1. Use diagonal corner technique to make two of units 2 and 8, and one each of units 7 and 9. Refer to Block A, steps 2 and 3 for assembling the center section of the block. Use triangle-square technique shown above to make any triangle-squares.

2. Join units 4 and 5 as shown in Block B diagram . Join units 5 and 6 as shown. To assemble the block, join combined 4/5 units to left side of center section, and combined units 5/6 to right side. Join units 7 and 8 and add them to the top of the center section; then join units 8 and 9 and join them to bottom of center section to complete the block. Make 4.

Block B. Make 4. When block is completed, it should measure 17 1/2" square

Making Unit 8 for blocks A, B, C, and D. Triangle-Squares used as diagonal corners. Use this technique for blocks E and F, Unit 7.

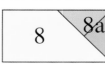

Join Fabric III and Fabric V together for triangle-square.

Use triangle-square as a diagonal corner. Stitch.

Press 8a corner.

Block C Assembly

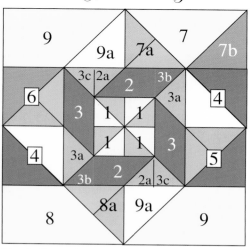

Block C. Make 4. When block is completed, it should measure 17 1/2" square

1. Use diagonal corner technique to make two of units 2 and 9, and one each of units 7 and 8. Refer to Block A, steps 2 and 3 for assembling the center section of the block. Use triangle-square technique shown on page 34 to make any triangle-squares. 2. Join units 4 and 6. Join units 4 and 5 as shown. Join the combined units 4/6 to left side of center section; then join combined units 4/5 to right side. 3. Join units 9 and 7 as shown. Join units 8 and 9. Join the 9/7 combined units to top of center section, and combined units 8/9 to the bottom to complete the block. Make 4.

Block D Assembly

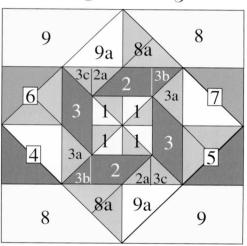

Block D. Make 6. When block is completed, it should measure 17 1/2" square

1. Use diagonal corner technique to make two of units 2, 8, and 9. Refer to Block A, steps 2 and 3 for assembling the center section of the block. Use triangle-square technique shown on page 34 to make any triangle-squares. 2. Join units 4 and 6. Join units 7 and 5 as shown. Join the combined units 4/6 to left side of center section; then join combined units 7/5 to right side. Join mirror image units 8 and 9 as shown . Join the 9/8 combined units to top of center section, and combined units 8/9 to the bottom to complete the block. Make 6.

Block E Assembly

1. Use diagonal corner technique to make two of units 2, and 7, and one each of units 8 and 9.. Refer to Block A, steps 2 and 3 for assembling the center section of the block. Use triangle-square technique shown on page 34 to make any triangle-squares.
2. Join units 5 and 4. Join units 4 and 6 as shown. Join the combined units 5/4 to left side of center section; then join combined units 4/6 to right side.
3. Join units 8 and 7 as shown.. Join units 7 and 9. Join the8/7 combined units to top of center section, and combined units 7/9 to the bottom to complete the block. Make 2.

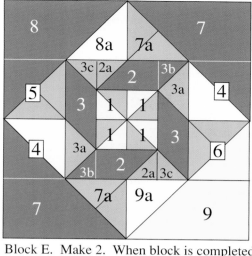

Block E. Make 2. When block is completed, it should measure 17 1/2" square

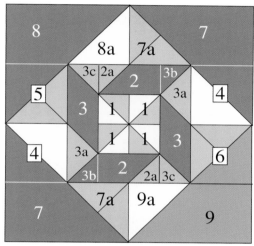

Block F. Make 2. When block is completed, it should measure 17 1/2" square

Block F Assembly

1. Use diagonal corner technique to make two of units 2, and 7. Refer to Block A, steps 2 and 3 for assembling the center section of the block. Use triangle-square technique shown on page 34 to make any triangle-squares.
2. Join units 5 and 4. Join units 4 and 6 as shown. Join the combined units 5/4 to left side of center section; then join combined units 4/6 to right side.
3. Join units 8 and 7 as shown. Join units 7 and 9. Join the 8/7 combined units to top of center section, and combined units 7/9 to the bottom to complete the block. Make 2.

Quilt Assembly

1. To assemble the quilt top, refer to the quilt diagram on page 36 and begin in the center with blocks E and F. Turn them so that the center yellow and green form the quarter triangle-square as shown. Join Unit Q1 to top and bottom of joined blocks. Use diagonal corner technique to make two of Unit Q2 and join to opposite sides of center section.
2. Beginning at the top, join blocks C, D, and B in a row. Join this row to the top of the center section. Join blocks B, D, and C. Join to the bottom of the center section.
3. Join the following blocks in a vertical row as shown: A, B, D, D, C, and A. Join this block row to the left side of the quilt. Join

blocks A, C, D, D, B, and A in a vertical row and join them to the bottom of the quilt. Join pieced Unit Q3 to opposite sides of quilt top; then add pieced Unit Q4 to top and bottom to complete the pieced part of the quilt.top; then add pieced Unit Q4 to top and bottom to complete the pieced part of the quilt.

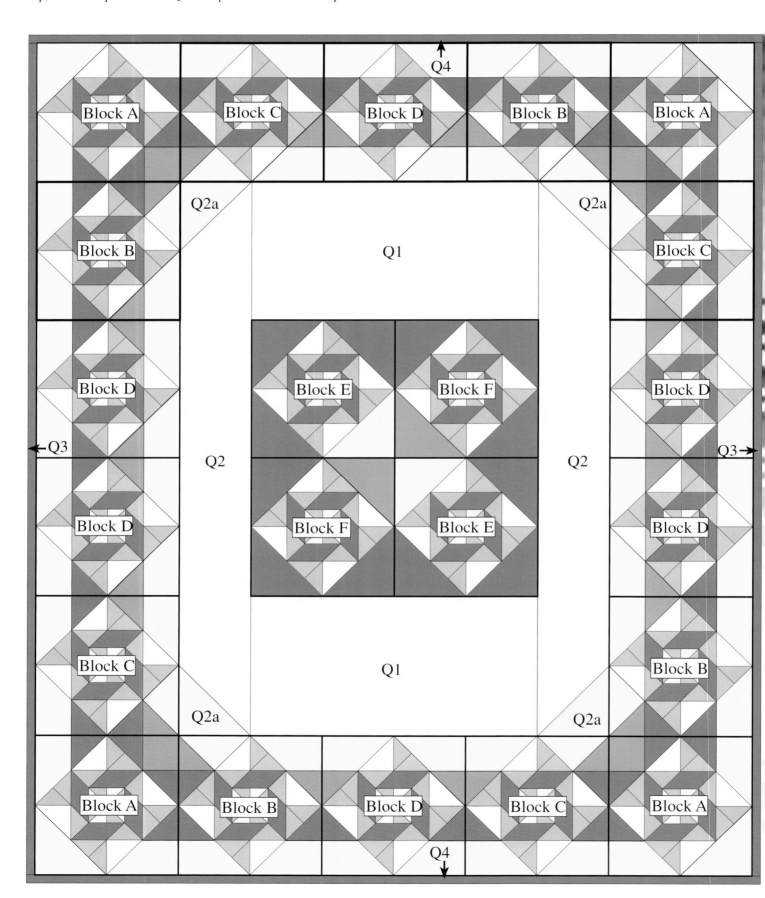

☐	Fabric I (ivory print) 7/8 yard	Need 25 1/2"
☐	Fabric II (light yellow print) 3/4 yard	Need 21"
☐	Fabric III (light green print) 3/4 yard	Need 23"
☐	Fabric IV (medium green print) 1/2 yard	Need 15"
☐	Fabric V (light lavender print) 3/4 yard	Need 22 1/2"
☐	Fabric VI (medium lavender) 1/4 yard	Need 5"
☐	Fabric VII (dark purple print) 1 1/4 yards	Need 40"

12" wide Steam-A-Seam 2   Need 20"   1 yard
Backing   2 3/4 yards

Cutting For Table Topper

☐ **From Fabric I, cut: (ivory print)**
- One 15 1/2" wide strip. From this, cut:
  * One - 15 1/2" square (Q1)
  * Four - 3 1/2" x 21 1/2" (Q5)
- One 6 1/2" wide strip. From this, cut:
  * Twelve - 3 1/2" x 6 1/2" (A1, B1)
- One 3 1/2" wide strip. From this, cut:
  * Four - 3 1/2" x 6 1/2" (add to A1, B1)

☐ **From Fabric II, cut: (light yellow print)**
- Six 3 1/2" wide strips. From these, cut:
  * Forty-four - 3 1/2" squares (A2b, B2b, and prairie points)
  * Two - 3 1/2" x 21 1/2" (Q3)
  * Two - 3 1/2" x 15 1/2" (Q2)
  * One - 2 1/2" x 4 1/2" (flower centers)

From Fabric III, cut: (light green print)
- Five 3 1/2" wide strips. From these, cut:
  * Four - 3 1/2" x 21 1/2" (Q4)
  * Thirty-two - 3 1/2" squares (A2a, A2b, B2a, B2b)
- One 5 1/2" square (leaves)

From Fabric IV, cut: (medium green print)
- Three 3 1/2" wide strips. From these, cut:
  * Twenty-eight - 3 1/2" squares for prairie points
- One 4 1/2" wide strip. From this, cut:
  * One - 4 1/2" x 12 1/2" for stems

From Fabric V, cut: (light lavender print)
- One 5" wide strip. From this, cut:
  * One - 5" x 11 1/2" (flower petals)
- Five 3 1/2" wide strips. From these, cut:
  * Four - 3 1/2" x 21 1/2" (Q6)
  * Thirty-two - 3 1/2" squares (A1a, B1a)

From Fabric VI, cut: (medium lavender print)
- One 5" x 11 1/2" (flower petals)

From Fabric VII, cut: (dark purple print)
- One 5" wide strip. From this, cut:
  * One - 5" x 11 1/2" (flower petals)
  * Eight - 3 1/2" squares (prairie points)
- Ten 3 1/2" wide strips. From these, cut:
  * Four - 3 1/2" x 21 1/2" (Q7)
  * Sixteen - 3 1/2" x 6 1/2" (A2, B2)
  * Fifty-two - 3 1/2" squares (add to 3 1/2" sq. above)

Flower Appliqué

1. All of the appliqués for the flowers are on page 38. Refer to the placement diagram above. We used Steam-A-Seam Lite and Steam-A-Seam 2 for all of the appliqués. Follow manufacturers instructions for using the Steam-A-Seam. Lay flowers and stems in place with the quilt top on a flat surface. Pin if necessary. Refer to the diagram above, and place the flowers as shown. We used an "over and under" effect for the flower petals that was very effective.

2. We recommend Robison Anton's rayon thread, which was used for a machine blanket stitch around all of the flowers, stems and leaves. Use a good iron on, tear away stabilizer behind the appliqués when you stitch. Pull it away upon completion of the stitching.

Quilting

Mary quilted a lovely feather design in all of the large yellow spaces and carried a similar design in the block centers. She "ditched" the patchwork, and put vein lines in the flowers to give them more of a dimensional look.

Refer to page 12 for instructions on making straight-grain binding. Use the ten 2 1/2" wide strips from Fabric VII for the binding, and bind your quilt.

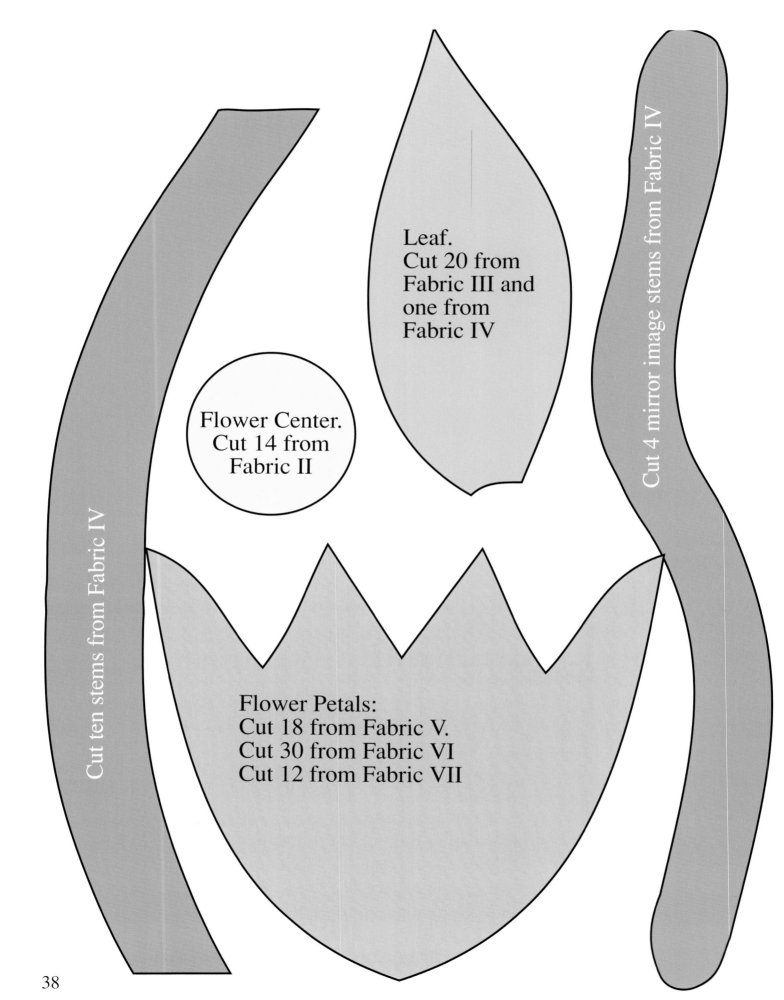

Leaf.
Cut 20 from
Fabric III and
one from
Fabric IV

Cut 4 mirror image stems from Fabric IV

Flower Center.
Cut 14 from
Fabric II

Cut ten stems from Fabric IV

Flower Petals:
Cut 18 from Fabric V.
Cut 30 from Fabric VI
Cut 12 from Fabric VII

Table Topper Assembly

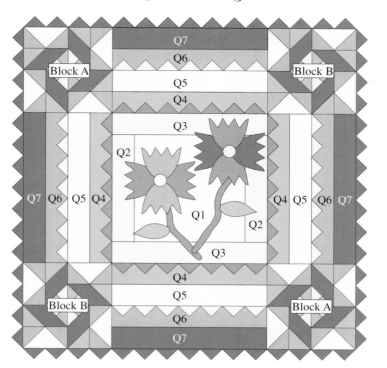

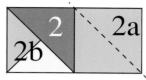

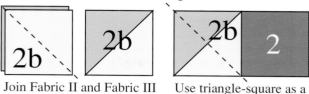

Making Unit 2 for blocks A and B. Triangle-Squares used as diagonal corners.

Join Fabric II and Fabric III together for triangle-square.

Use triangle-square as a diagonal corner. Stitch.

Press 2b corner; then add diagonal corner 2a.

Press 2a corner.

1. Refer to diagram above to make Unit 2b triangle-square, and then use it as a diagonal corner on Unit 2. Make four for each block. Use diagonal corner technique to make four of Unit 1 for each block.

2. To assemble Block A, begin at top left corner and join units 1 and 2 as shown. For bottom left corner, join units 1 and 2 as shown. Join the two combined 1/2 units together. For right side of block, refer to block diagram and join the remaining 1 and 2 units together. Join these combined units together for right side of block. Join the two sections together to complete Block A. Make 2.

3. Block B is assembled the same as Block A, only the position of the 1/2 units are different. Refer to Block B diagram and join the units as in Step 2 to complete the block. Make 2.

4. Refer to illustration below showing how to fold the 3 1/2" squares for Prairie Points. The long bias edge of each prairie point will be sewn into the seams. Fold all of the prairie points from fabrics II, IV, and VII.

5. Join units Q6 and Q7 as shown. Make 4. A tip that works for placing the prairie points so that they don't shift is to cut a small strip of Steam-A-Seam 2 (approx. 1/4") and press one side down along the raw edge of Unit Q6. Remove the paper from the other side and begin to place your prairie points. They should overlap 1/4". Be careful when handling them so that they do not stretch because of the bias edge. When all of the Fabric II prairie points are in position, lay a press cloth over them, and with your iron on a hot, steam setting, press them in place. This will hold them securely until they are sewn into the seam.

6. Join Unit Q5 to top of Unit Q6, catching the prairie points in the seam; then add Unit Q4 to top of Unit Q5 as shown. Make 4. Refer to Step 5, and place prairie points from Fabric IV the same as you did with Fabric II prairie points. Set aside.

7. Join Unit Q2 to opposite sides of Unit Q1; then add Unit Q3 to top and bottom of center section. Join two sets of the prairie point stripes to top and bottom of center section, catching the Fabric IV prairie points in the seam. Refer to the left side of the table topper diagram, and join Block A to top of one prairie point stripe set; then add Block B to the bottom. Repeat this procedure for the stripe set on the right, only reverse the position of the A and B blocks. Join these two sections to left and right side of table topper as shown.

8. Place and then press the prairie points along bottom raw edges of the table topper. The Steam-A-Seam 2 will hold them in place when you quilt.

9. Follow instructions for the appliqué flowers as for the quilt top. Press them in place and blanket stitch around them by machine or hand.

10. Mary "ditched" the patchwork in her quilting and repeated smaller versions of the feather design in open stripe areas.

11. Trim the batting and backing for the quilting to the edge of the table topper. Cut two 23" x 45 1/2" pieces from the backing fabric of your choice and piece them together to form a 45 1/2" square. If there has been take-up in the table topper because of the quilting, trim the backing you have chosen if necessary. Place the backing fabric right sides together on the table topper top and pin all the way around. Prairie points must be pinned so that they are facing in towards the table topper center. Stitch around the table topper, leaving a 8" opening to turn. Turn right side out, pull the prairie point out, and slip stitch the opening closed. Press the prairie points flat.

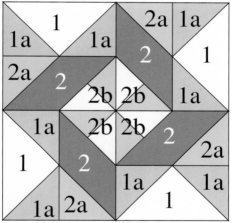

Block A. Make 2. When block is completed it should measure 12 1/2" square

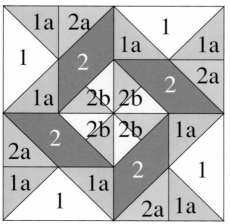

Block B. Make 2. When block is completed it should measure 12 1/2" square

Folding Prairie Points

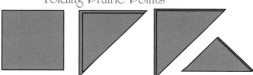

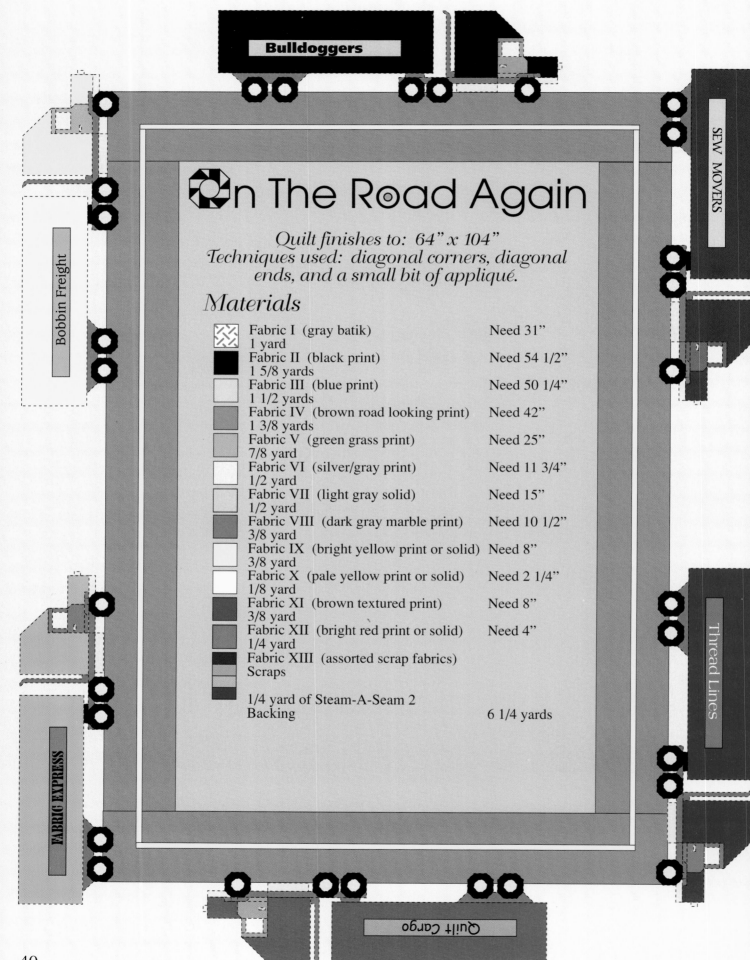

On The Road Again

Quilt finishes to: 64" x 104"
Techniques used: diagonal corners, diagonal
ends, and a small bit of appliqué.

Materials

Fabric I (gray batik) 1 yard	Need 31"	
Fabric II (black print) 1 5/8 yards	Need 54 1/2"	
Fabric III (blue print) 1 1/2 yards	Need 50 1/4"	
Fabric IV (brown road looking print) 1 3/8 yards	Need 42"	
Fabric V (green grass print) 7/8 yard	Need 25"	
Fabric VI (silver/gray print) 1/2 yard	Need 11 3/4"	
Fabric VII (light gray solid) 1/2 yard	Need 15"	
Fabric VIII (dark gray marble print) 3/8 yard	Need 10 1/2"	
Fabric IX (bright yellow print or solid) 3/8 yard	Need 8"	
Fabric X (pale yellow print or solid) 1/8 yard	Need 2 1/4"	
Fabric XI (brown textured print) 3/8 yard	Need 8"	
Fabric XII (bright red print or solid) 1/4 yard	Need 4"	
Fabric XIII (assorted scrap fabrics) Scraps		

1/4 yard of Steam-A-Seam 2
Backing   6 1/4 yards

Bulldoggers

SEW MOVERS

Bobbin Freight

Thread Lines

FABRIC EXPRESS

Quilt Cargo

Robert had a great time designing these 18 wheelers. We all enjoyed giving them quilting names. The interesting thing about the quilting on this piece is what Mary did with the trucks, and what can not be seen in the photo as she quilted it with metallic colors that match each truck.

Each cab has a logo. Quilt Cargo has a 9 patch, Bobbin Freight has a bobbin, Sew Movers has a sewing machine, and Thread Lines has woven lines. We hope you enjoy putting your special touches on these *Kings Of The Road!*

Cutting

From Fabric I, cut: (gray batik)
- Ten 2 3/4" wide strips. From this, cut:
  * Ten - 2 3/4" x 22" (Q2) Piece two together
    to = five 43 1/2" lengths.
- Two 1 3/4" wide strips. From these, cut:
  * Two - 1 3/4" x 22" (Q1) Piece together to
    = one 43 1/2" length.

From Fabric II, cut: (black print)
- Two 3 1/2" wide strips. From these, cut:
  * Sixty - 1 1/4" x 3 1/2" (A7, A15, A31, A36, A39, A42)
  * Four - 1" x 3 1/2" (B22, C22)
- Fourteen 2 1/2" wide strips. Nine strips for straight-grain binding.
  From remaining five strips, cut:
  * 128 - 1 1/2" x 2 1/2" (D2, D4)
  * Twenty - 1" x 1 1/4" (B14, B17, C14, C17)
    Stack this cut.
- Two 2" wide strips. From these, cut:
  * Sixty - 1 1/4" x 2" (A13, A32, A40)
- Three 1 1/2" wide strips. From these, cut:
  * Sixty-four - 1 1/2" squares (D1b)
- Four 1" wide strips. From these, cut:
  * Six - 1" x 2 3/4" (A35)
  * 120 - 1" squares (A14a, A33a, A41a)

From Fabric III, cut: (blue print)
- One 4 1/4" wide strip. From this, cut:
  * Four - 4 1/4" x 5 1/2" (B27, C27)
  * Four - 2" squares (B11a, C11a) Stack this cut.
  * Twelve - 1" x 1 1/2" (A34) Stack this cut.
- Three 4" wide strips. From these, cut:
  * Six - 4" x 12" (A43)
  * Six - 3 1/4" x 4" (A45)
  * Four - 1 1/4" x 4 1/2" (B24, C24) Stack this cut
  * Eight - 1 1/4" x 2" (B13, C13) Stack this cut.
  * Eight - 1" x 8" (B25, C25) Stack this cut.
  * Six - 1" squares (A30b)
- Two 3 3/4" wide strips. From these, cut:
  * Six - 3 3/4" x 8 1/4" (A27)
  Stack the following cuts:
  * Sixty - 1 1/4" squares (A15a, A31b, A36b, A42a)
  * Fourteen - 1" x 1 1/4" (A9, B18, C18)
- Three 2 3/4" wide strips. From these, cut:
  * Four - 2 3/4" squares (B16, C16)
  * Six - 2 3/4" x 5" (A22)
  * Six - 2 3/4" x 3" (A12)
  * Six - 2 1/2" x 2 3/4" (A17)
  * Ten - 1 3/4" x 2 3/4" (A18, B15, C15)
  * Twelve - 1" x 2 3/4" (A38)
  * Six - 2 1/4" x 2 1/2" (A24)
  * Four - 1 1/2" x 2 1/4" (B20, C20)
- Six 2" wide strips. From these, cut:
  * Two - 2" x 22" (Q3) Piece
    together to = 43 1/2" length.
  * Twelve - 2" x 11 1/2" (A50)
  * Six - 1 3/4" x 4 1/2" (A20)
  * Six - 1" x 2 1/4" (A11)
- Two 1 3/4" wide strips. From these, cut:
  * Six - 1 3/4" x 8 1/2" (A30)
- Two 1" wide strips. From these, cut:
  * Six - 1" x 7 3/4" (A28)

From Fabric IV, cut: (brown road looking print)
- Twelve 3 1/2" x 40 1/2" strips. From these, piece:
  * Piece eight together to = four 80 1/2" lengths. (Q4)
  * Remaining four strips are for (Q7)

From Fabric V, cut: (green grass print)
- Four 4 1/2" wide strips. From these, cut:
  * Eight - 4 1/2" x 5 1/2" (Q9)
  * Sixteen - 4 1/2" squares (Q5)
  * Four - 2 1/2" x 4 1/2" (Q6)
  * Seventy-eight - 1 1/2" squares (D1a, D4a)
- Two 2" wide strips. From these, cut:
  * Two - 2" x 40 1/2" (Q8)
- Two 1 1/2" wide strips. From these, cut:
  * Fifty - 1 1/2" squares (add to 1 1/2" squares above)

From Fabric VI, cut: (silver/gray print)
- Two 2 1/2" wide strips for applique tire centers (Block D, Unit 5)
- Two 2" wide strips. From these, cut:
  * Thirty - 2" squares (A14, A33, A41)
  * Six - 1 1/4" x 2 1/2" (A6)
  * Six - 1" x 1 1/4" (A10)
- One 1 1/2" wide strip. From this, cut:
  * Six - 1 1/2" x 4 1/2" (A19)
- One 1 1/4" wide strip. From this, cut:
  * Six - 1 1/4" squares (A7a)

From Fabric VII, cut: (light gray solid)
- Ten 1 1/2" wide strips. From these, cut:
  * 128 - 1 1/2" x 2 1/2" (D1, D3)
  * Sixty-four - 1 1/2" squares (D4a)

From Fabric VIII, cut: (dark gray marble print)
- One 2" wide strip. From this, cut:
  * Eight - 1 1/2" x 2" (B19, C19)
  * Twelve - 1" x 2" (A2a, A4)
  * Eighteen - 1" x 1 1/4" (A29, A37)
- One 1 3/4" wide strip. From this, cut:
  * Twelve - 1 3/4" squares (A43a, A45a)
  * Six - 1 1/2" squares (A30a)
  * Nine - 1 1/4" squares (A7b, A31a, A36a, A39a)
- Three 1 1/4" wide strips. From these, cut:
  * Six - 1 1/4" x 5 3/4" (A21)
  * Six - 1 1/4" x 2 1/2" (A16)
  * Forty-five - 1 1/4" squares (add to 1 1/4" sq. above)
- Three 1" wide strips. From these, cut:
  * Six - 1" x 8 1/2" (A30)
  * Six - 1" x 7" (A44)

From Fabric IX, cut: (bright yellow print or solid)
- One 2" wide strip. From this, cut:
  * Four - 2" x 4" (B12, C12)
- Six 1" x 40 1/2 strips. From these, piece:
  * Piece four together to = two 80 1/2" lengths. (Q4)
  * Remaining two strips are for (Q7)

From Fabric X, cut: (pale yellow print or solid)
- One 2 1/4" wide strip. From this, cut:
  * Four - 2 1/4" x 4" (B4, C4)
  * Four - 2 1/4" x 2 1/2" (B7, C7)

From Fabric XI, cut: (brown textured print)
- Two 3" wide strips. From these, cut:
  * Four - 3" x 7 1/2" (B10, C10)
  * Four - 3" x 4 1/4" (B9, C9)
  * Four - 1 1/4" x 5 1/2" (B26, C26)
  * Twelve - 1 1/4" x 3 3/4" (B1, B8, C1, C8)
- One 2" wide strip. From this, cut:
  * Four - 2" x 4 1/2" (B5, C5)
  * Four - 1 3/4" x 2 1/4" (B6, C6)
  * Four - 1" x 2 1/4" (B3, C3)

 **From Fabric XII, cut: (bright red print or solid)**
- Two 2" wide strips. From these, cut:
  - * Four - 2" x 7 1/2" (B11, C11)
  - * Four - 2" x 3 3/4" (B2, C2)
  - * Eight - 1" squares (B21, C21)

 **From Fabric XIII, cut: (scraps)**
Note: Requirements are listed for one block.
Referring to photo, make blocks with as many scrap fabrics as desired.
- One - 5 1/4" x 5 3/4" (A26 sleeper)
- Two - 4 1/4" x 8" (A49 trailer)
- One - 4" x 18" (A46 trailer)
- One - 3 3/4" x 8 3/4" (A27a cab top)
- One - 2 1/2" x 18" (A48 trailer)
- One - 2 1/2" x 3" (A5 hood)
- One - 2" x 2 1/2" (A3 hood)
- One - 1" square (A1a hood)
- One - 2 1/2" x 18" (A47 trailer name plate)
- One - 2 1/2" x 4" (A1 door)
- One - 1" x 3" (A2 door)
- One - 1" x 3 1/2" (A25 door)
- Two - 1" x 2 1/4" (A23 door)

Block A Assembly

1. Please note that trucks are mirror images. Three are facing right, and three are facing left. Refer to the mirror image diagram on page 44 for correct positioning of mirror image units. The wheels and bottom parts of the trucks will remain the same, however we have given you correct sizes for the cab, and trailer so that you may use scrap fabrics for those areas if you choose to do so.

2. Use diagonal corner technique to make one each of units 1, 7, 14, 15, 30, 31, 33, 36, 43, and 45.. Use this technique to make three each of units 39, 41, and 42. Use diagonal end technique to make one of units 2 and 27 as shown at right.

3. To assemble the front of the truck, begin by joining units 1 and 2. Join units 3 and 4. Join the 1/2 combined units with the 3/4

combined units, matching seams; then add Unit 5 to left side of combined units as shown above. Join units 6, 7 and 16 in a horizontal row and add them to the bottom of the other combined units, matching seams. Join units 9, 10 and 11 in a vertical row. Add them to the front of the truck cab combined units. Join

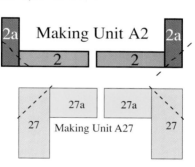

Front of Block A. Make 6 with mixed colors. When completed, truck front should measure 11 1/2" x 17".

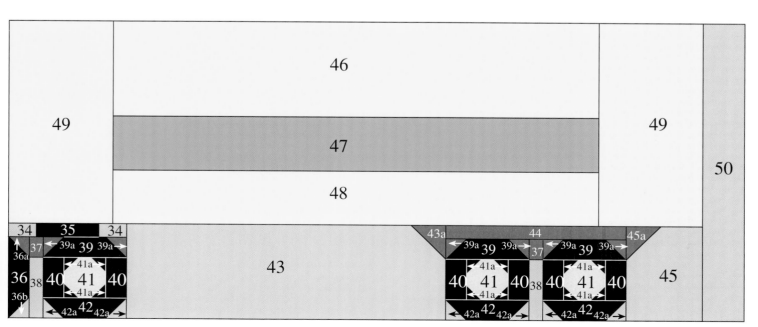

Back of Block A. Make 6 with mixed colors. When completed, truck back should measure 11 1/2" x 27"
When entire Block A truck is pieced together, it should measure 11 1/2" x 43 1/2".

units 13, 14 and 13 in a row as shown. Add Unit 15 to bottom of these combined units. Join Unit 12 to left side of combined units and Unit 17 to right side. Add these units to bottom of other combined cab units. Note that the placement of these units will be reversed for the mirror image trucks.

4. Join units 23, 24, and 23 as shown; then add Unit 25 to top of these combined units. Join Unit 22 to left side of combined units; then join these combined units to the top of the truck cab. Join units 19 and 20; then add Unit 18 to right side of combined units. Join units 26 and 21; then join them to top of combined units 18-20. Add these combined units to the right of other combined units . Join Unit 27 to top of cab as shown, matching seams. Add Unit 50 to front of cab as shown. Join units 32, 33, and 32 in a row; then join Unit 31 to left side of wheel combined units.

5. Join units 28 and 29. Join the 1" x 8 1/2" strip of Fabric VIII and the 1 3/4" x 8 1/2" strip of Fabric III together, forming Unit 30. Join diagonal corner 30a to top left corner of

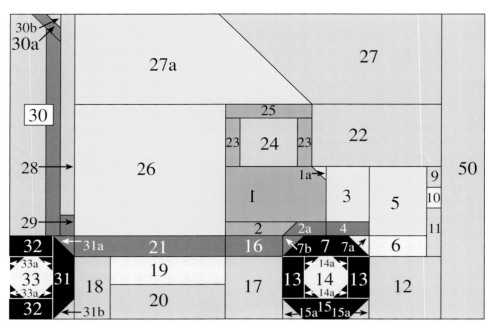

Front of Block A mirror image.

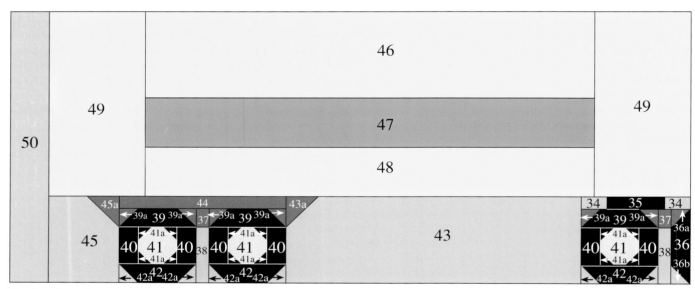

Back of truck mirror image.

Unit 30; then add diagonal corner 30b as shown. Join combined units 28/29 to Unit 30; then add the combined wheel units to bottom. Add this section to back of truck cab to complete the front of the truck.

6. To assemble the back of the truck, begin by joining units 46, 47 and 48 in a row; then join Unit 49 to opposite ends of the combined units. Join Unit 40 to opposite sides of Unit 41 as shown. Add Unit 39 to top of wheel centers and Unit 42 to bottom. Make 3. Join units 37 and 38. Make 2. For the back of the truck, join a wheel to each long side of combined units 37/38. Add Unit 44 to top of wheels; then join units 43 and 45 to opposite sides of wheels as shown.

7. For the front wheels, join remaining wheel to one side of remaining combined units 37/38; then add Unit 36 to other side of combined units. Join units 34, 35, and 34 in a horizontal row and add them to top of front wheel section; then join to Unit 43. Join the wheel section to the trailer; then add Unit 50 to back to complete the back of the truck. Join the front and back of the truck to complete Block A. Make a total of 6 trucks.

8. Name your trucks and if you have an embroidery machine ,stitch

the name on Unit 47. If you don't have an embroidery machine, fabric paint will work nicely.

Blocks B and C Assembly

1. Use diagonal corner technique to make one of Unit 11.

2. To assemble the mirror image blocks, refer to the block diagrams on page 45 for correct positioning of all units. To begin, join Unit 1 to opposite sides of Unit 2. Join units 3 and 4; then add Unit 5 to bottom of these combined units. Join units 6 and 7; then add Unit 8 to bottom. Join Unit 9 to side of combined 6-8 units as shown. Join this row to top of combined 1-5 unit row.

3. Join units 10 and 11 and add them to top of other combined units. Join units 13, 14, and 13 in a horizontal row as shown; then add Unit 12 to top. Join units 15 and 16 to opposite sides of the combined 12-14 units, checking block diagrams for correct positioning of units.

4. Join units 17, 18 and 17 in a row. Make two for each block. Add Unit 19 to top of combined units. Join the combined units to opposite sides of Unit 20. Join units 21, 22, and 21 in a row; then add this row to the top of the other combined units. Join units 23

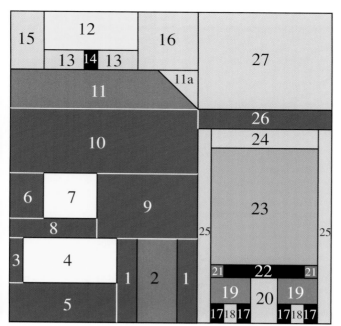

Block B. Make 2 with mixed colored trucks. When complete, block should measure 12 1/2" square.

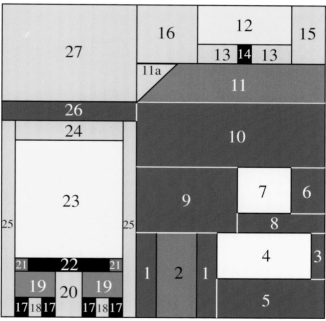

Block C. Make 2 with mixed colored trucks. When complete, block should measure 12 1/2" square.

and 24 and add them to the top of the other combined units. Join Unit 25 to opposite sides as shown. Join Unit 26 and Unit 27. Join them to the top of the truck.

5. Join the two sections together to complete blocks B and C.

6. If you are going to machine embroider the sign and building, we suggest doing it before you piece the blocks.

Block D Assembly

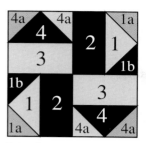
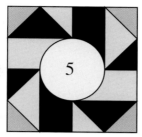

Block D. Make 32. When complete, block should measure 4 1/2" square

1. To assemble Block D, use diagonal corner technique to make two each of units 1 and 4.

2. Begin in the top left corner, and join units 3 and 4 as shown. Join units 1 and 2 and join them to bottom of combined units 3/4. Make two of these rows. Turn the second row around referring to block diagram for correct positioning of the units; then join the two sections together, forming the border wheel.

3. We used Steam-A-Seam 2 to press the wheel centers in the center of the wheel as shown in illustration above. Use a good press on tear away stabilizer behind the wheels. Using a light gray thread, or silver metallic, blanket stitch or satin stitch around the wheel centers. Tear the stabilizer away.

> Cut 32 for Block D appliqué tire centers.

Quilt Assembly

1. To assemble the quilt top, refer to quilt top illustration on page 46, and begin by joining five truck blocks together with pieced Unit Q2 between them. Join another Unit Q2 to bottom of fifth truck; then add the sixth truck. Join Unit Q3 to the top of the truck blocks and Unit Q1 to the bottom as shown.

2. To make the road, begin with Unit Q7. Join Fabric IV strips to opposite sides of Fabric IX strip. Make 2. Join Unit Q8 to each completed road section. Make two of pieced Unit Q4 for the side road. Join five of Block D, with Unit Q9 between them. Refer to quilt illustration for correct placement. Referring to quilt diagram, join Block B to left side of combined road and tire border, and Block C to right side as shown. Make two and set aside.

3. Join five Block D tires with Unit Q5 between them. Make four of these rows. Join Unit Q6 to opposite sides of remaining tire blocks. Make two. Join the tire rows with Unit Q5 between them to opposite ends of Unit Q6. Make two and join them to completed road Unit Q4. Join these rows to opposite sides of quilt, with the Q4 road to the inside.

4. Join the remaining road/truck stop rows to top and bottom of quilt, once again referring to quilt diagram for proper placement.

5. Mary "ditched" the patchwork and quilted clouds in the blue sky.

6. Join the nine 2 1/2" wide strips of Fabric II together to make straight-grain binding, and bind your quilt.

daily bread

Tablecloth finishes to: 59" x 80"
Techniques used: diagonal corners, diagonal ends and triangle-squares. There is also a small bit of blanket stitch appliqué.

Materials For Tablecloth

☐	Fabric I (light tan with gold print)	Need 87 1/4"	2 5/8 yards
■	Fabric II (dark brown batik)	Need 67"	2 yards
▨	Fabric III (dark gold print)	Need 30"	1 yard
▢	Fabric IV (medium gold print)	Need 28"	7/8 yard
▢	Fabric V (light gold print)	Need 14 7/8"	1/2 yard
☐	Fabric VI (ivory with gold check)	Need 10 1/2"	3/8 yard
▨	Fabric VI (medium gold batik)	Need 5 3/4"	1/4 yard
	12" wide Steam-A-Seam II		5/8 yard
	Backing		3 5/8 yards

Cutting

From Fabric I, cut: (light tan with gold print)
- One 10 3/8" wide strip. From this, cut:
  * Eight - 1 1/2" x 10 3/8" (A6)
  * Eight - 1 1/4" x 10 3/8" (A5)
  * Eight - 2" x 5" (C5) Stack this cut.
  * Eight - 1 3/4" x 5" (C7) Stack this cut.
  * Sixteen - 1 1/4" squares (A3a) Stack this cut.
- Two 5 3/4" wide strip. From this, cut:
  * Four - 5 3/4" x 14 3/4" (Q3)
  * Four - 2 7/8" x 4 1/2" (Q5) Stack this cut.
  * Eight - 2 7/8" x 3 1/8" (A8) Stack this cut.:
- Two 4 1/2" wide strips. From these, cut
  * Eight - 2 5/8" x 4 1/2" (A13)
  * Eight - 1 7/8" x 4 1/2" (A10)
  * Eight - 1 3/8" x 4 1/2" (A7)
  * Eight - 4 1/8" x 4 1/4" (A15)
- One 4 1/4" wide strip. From this, cut:
  * Eight - 3 7/8" x 4 1/4" (A14)
  * Fourteen - 1 1/2" squares (A9a, A11b) Stack this cut.
- Four 3 1/2" wide strips. From these, cut:
  * Four - 3 1/2" x 20 1/2" (Q11)
  * Four - 3 1/2" x 15 1/4" (Q14)
  * Twenty-four - 1 3/4" squares (A8b, A12a, C4d) Stack this cut.
- Two 3" wide strips. From these, cut:
  * Sixteen - 2 7/8" x 3" (A2)
  * Four - 1 1/2" x 8 3/4" (Q6) Stack this cut.
  * Eighteen - 1 1/2" squares (add to A9a, A11b above)
- Four 2 5/8" wide strips. From these, cut:
  * Four - 2 5/8" x 20" (Q4)
  * Sixteen - 2 5/8" x 3 1/8" (A11)
  * Eight - 2 3/8" squares (A12b)
- One 2 1/2" wide strip. From this, cut:
  * Sixteen - 2 1/2" squares (C1c)
- One 2 1/8" wide strip. From this, cut:
  * Sixteen - 2 1/8" squares (A9b)
- Five 2" wide strips. From these, cut:
  * 104 - 2" squares (A1a, C4c)
- One 1 5/8" wide strip. From this, cut:
  * Sixteen - 1 5/8" squares (A3b, A3c)
- One 1 3/8" wide strip. From this, cut:
  * Two - 1 3/8" x 8 3/4" (Q2)
- Four 1" wide strips for Strip Set 1.

From Fabric II, cut: (dark brown batik)
- One 10" wide strip. From this, cut:
  * Four - 2 5/8" x 10" (B12)
  * Four - 2 1/2" x 10" (B13)
  * One - 8 3/4" square (Q1)
  * Four - 1 1/2" x 4 7/8" (B2) Stack this cut vertically.
  * Four - 1" x 4" (B6) Stack this cut vertically
  * Four - 2 5/8" squares (B9) Stack this cut.

* Four - 1 3/4" squares (B11a) Stack this cut.
- Two 3 1/2" wide strips. From these, cut:
  * Four - 3 1/2" x 9 1/4" (Q15)
  * Four - 3 1/2" x 6" (Q12)
  * One - 3 1/4" x 14 3/4" (B15)
- Two 3 1/4" wide strips. From these, cut:
  * Three - 3 1/4" x 14 3/4" (add to B15 above)
  * Two - 1 1/2" x 25" (Q8) Join two together to
    = two 49 1/2" lengths.
- Nine 2 1/2" wide strips. Seven for straight-grain binding.
  From remaining strips, cut:
  * Four - 2 1/2" x 14 3/4" (B14)
  * Four - 2 1/8" squares (B5)
- Fourteen 1 1/2" wide strips. From these, cut:
  * Four - 1 1/2" x 40 1/2" (Q17) Join two together
    to = two 80 1/2" lengths.
  * Four - 1 1/2" x 36 1/2" (Q9) Join two together
    to = two 72 1/2" lengths.
  * Four - 1 1/2" x 29" (Q16) Join two together
    to = two 57 1/2" lengths.
  * Two - 1 1/2" x 25" (add to Q8 above)

From Fabric III, cut: (dark gold print)

- Two 3 5/8" wide strips. From these, cut:
  * Two - 3 5/8" x 41 1/2" (Q7)
- Four 3 1/2" wide strips. From these, cut:
  * Two - 3 1/2" x 21 1/2" (Q10)
  * Two - 3 1/2" x 10 1/2" (Q13)
  * Eight - 3 1/2" squares (C1b)
  * Eight - 3 1/4" x 3 1/2" (C4)
  * Eight - 2 1/2" x 3 1/2" (C3)
  * Eight - 1 3/4" x 5" (C6) Stack this cut.
- One 2 1/2" wide strip. From this, cut:
  * Eight - 2 1/2" squares (C2a)
  * Eleven - 2" squares (A11a)
- One 2 1/4" wide strip. From this, cut:
  * Eight - 2 1/4" squares (A8a)
  * Five - 2" squares (add to A11a above)
- Four 1" strips. Two for Strip Set 1. From remainder, cut:
  * Eight - 1" x 10 1/8" (A16)

From Fabric IV, cut: (medium gold print)

- One 4 7/8" wide strip. From this, cut:
  * Four - 3 1/8" x 4 7/8" (B3)
  * Four - 2 5/8" x 4" (B11)
  * Four - 1" x 8" (B8) Stack this cut.
- Two 3 1/2" wide strips. From these, cut:
  * Eight - 3 1/2" x 4 1/2" (C1)
  * Sixteen - 2 1/2" x 3 1/2" (C2, C3b)
- Four 3" wide strips. From these, cut:
  * Forty-eight - 3" squares (A1)
  * Eight - 2 1/2" squares (C4a)
- One 2 1/8" wide strip. From this, cut:
  * Eight - 2 1/8" squares (B5, B10)
- One 2" wide strip. From this, cut:
  * Eight - 2" x 4 3/8" (A3)

From Fabric V, cut: (light gold print)

- Two 3 1/2" wide strips. From these, cut:
  * Eight - 3 1/2" squares (C1a)
  * Eight - 2 1/2" x 3 1/2" (C2b)
  * Eight - 3 1/4" x 4 1/4" (C4b)
- Two 3 1/8" wide strips. From these, cut:
  * Eight - 2 3/8" x 3 1/8" (A12)
  * Sixteen - 2 1/8" x 3 1/8" (A9)
  * Eight - 2 1/2" squares (C3a)
- One 1 5/8" wide strip. From this, cut:
  * Twenty-four - 1 5/8" squares (A8c, A11c)

From Fabric VI, cut: (ivory with gold check)

- One 9" wide strip. From this, cut:
  * Four - 2 1/8" x 9" (B4)
  * Four - 3 1/2" x 8" (B7)
  * Four - 4 7/8" x 7" (B1)
- One 1 1/2" wide strip. From this, cut:
  * Eight - 1 1/2" squares (B2b, B3b)
  * Eight - 1" squares (B2a, B3a)

From Fabric VII, cut: (medium gold batik)

- One 5 3/4" strip for appliqué leaves.

Block A Assembly

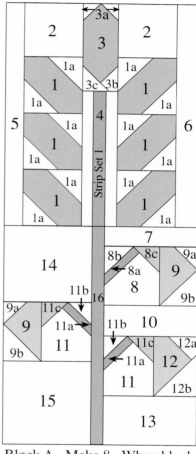

Block A. Make 8. When block is complete, it should measure 8 3/4" X 20".

Strip Set 1. Make 2. Cut into eight 6 1/2" segments for Unit A4

1. Use diagonal corner technique to make six of Unit 1, two of units 9 and 11, and one each of units 3, 8, and 12.

2. Refer to Strip Set 1 below and instructions for strip piecing on page 7. Piece the strip set and cut into required segments as directed.

3. Unit 3 is made by joining diagonal corners in alphabetical order. Do not trim center seam for the diagonal corners used in Unit 3.

4. Refer to diagram below of Unit 8. Make one Unit 11 the same as Unit 8, the other Unit 11 is mirror imaged. When making mirror image Unit 11, check Block A illustration for correct positioning of units. To make Unit 8, begin by joining Unit 8a diagonal corner as shown. Trim seam and press. Join diagonal corner 8b, however since it is a lighter fabric we do not suggest trimming seam as the darker fabric beneath it will show through. Join diagonal corner 8c as shown. Trim seam and press.

5. To assemble the block, begin by joining units 3 and 4 (strip set 1). Join Unit 1 in a row as shown. Make two, being careful to turn them in the right direction. Join Unit 2 to top of each row. Join Unit 5 to left row, and

Making units A8 and A11.

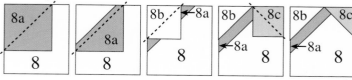

Unit 6 to side of right row. Join the two rows to opposite sides of combined units 3 and 4, completing the top section.

6. For bottom section, join units 8 and 9 together; then add Unit 7 to top of combined units and Unit 10 to the bottom. Join units 11 and 12; then add Unit 13 to bottom of these combined units. Join the two leaf combined units together. Join units 9 and 11 as shown on left side of stalk. Add Unit 14 to the top of 9/11 combined units, and Unit 15 to the bottom. Join stalk Unit 16 to right side of these combined units; then join the right side leaves to remaining raw edge of Unit 16 to complete the bottom section.

7. Join the two sections together, matching the stalk carefully. Make 8.

Block B Diagrams

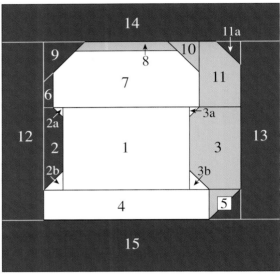

Block B. Make 4. When block is complete, it should measure 14 3/4" square.

5 Place 2 1/8" squares of Fabrics II and IV right sides together, raw edges matching, and stitch a diagonal as shown. Trim seam and press open for Unit B5.

Block B Assembly

1 Use diagonal corner technique to make one each of units 1, 2, 3, and 11. Refer to diagram and instructions below left for making Unit 5.

2. To assemble the bread, begin by joining units 1, 2, and 3. Join units 4 and 5 in a horizontal row and add them to the bottom of combined units 1-3, matching seams. Join units 7 and 8; then add Unit 6 to left side of the 7/8 combined units. Join diagonal corner, Unit 9 to top left side of bread and diagonal corner Unit 10 to top right as shown. Join Unit 11 to right side of the 6-10 combined units; then add it to top of other combined units. Join Unit 12 to left side of bread; then add Unit 13 to right side. Join Unit 14 to top and Unit 15 to bottom to complete the bread. Make 4.

Block C Assembly

1. Refer to the diagram of Block C, and join units 5, 6, and 7 together as shown. Refer to the diagrams below and at the top of page 51 for construction of the combined diagonal corner/diagonal end units. Follow the illustrations closely and read the instructions. Unit C1 is comprised of all diagonal corners, joined in alphabetical order. C2, C3, and C4 utilize both diagonal corners and diagonal ends.

2. Complete the units, and join them in rows shown at left. Make 8.

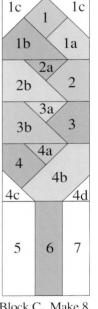

Block C. Make 8. When block is complete it should measure 4 1/2" x 14 3/4"

Making units C2 and C3

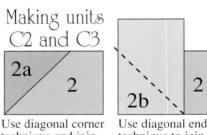

Use diagonal corner technique and join Unit 2a. Trim seam and press.

Use diagonal end technique to join Unit 2b.

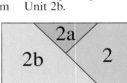

Trim seam and press.

Making Unit C1.

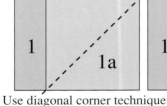

Use diagonal corner technique and join Unit 1a.

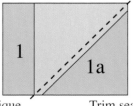

Trim seam and press.

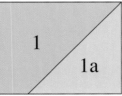

Use diagonal corner technique and join Unit 1b.

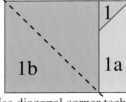

Trim seam and press.

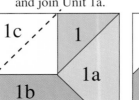

Use diagonal corner technique and join Unit 1c.

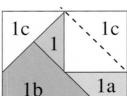

Do not trim this seam. Press towards corner

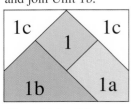

Repeat for second 1c unit.

Do not trim this seam. Press towards corner

50

Making Unit C4

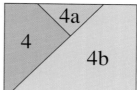
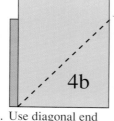

Use diagonal corner technique and join Unit 4a

Trim seam and press.

Use diagonal end technique and join Unit 4b.

Trim seam and press.

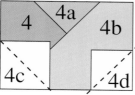
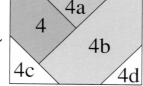

Tablecloth Assembly

1. To assemble the tablecloth, refer to the tablecloth diagram below. Begin by joining two of wheat Block A, tip to tip as shown; then add Unit 6 to opposite short ends. Join Unit 7 to one side of combined wheat blocks an Unit 6. Make two.

2. Again referring to tablecloth diagram for correct positioning of bread, join Unit 3 to bread Block B as shown. Note that Unit 3 will be joined in different places. Two at the bottom of the bread, and two on the sides.

3. Join two bread blocks to opposite sides of one wheat Block A as shown; then add Unit 4 to to opposite sides as shown. Make two, and join them to the wheat combined units. Set aside.

4. Refer to diagram, and join two C blocks to opposite ends of Unit 5 as shown. Tips of wheat will be facing Unit 5. Make four and join them to opposite sides to the two bread/wheat sections.

5. For the center row of the tablecloth, join Unit 2 to short ends of wheat Block A. Unit 2 will be next to points of wheat. Join this combination to opposite sides of Unit 1. Join the two bread/wheat sections to opposite long ends of center section.

6. Join pieced Unit 8 to top and bottom of tablecloth as shown; then add pieced Unit 9 to opposite sides. Join units 12, 11, 10, 11, and 12 in a long vertical row. Make two and join them to opposite sides of tablecloth. Join units 15, 14, 13, 14, and 15 in a long horizontal row. Make two and join them to top and bottom of tablecloth.

7. Join pieced sashing Unit 16 to top and bottom of tablecloth; then join pieced Unit 17 to opposite sides to complete tablecloth top.

8. We used Steam-A-Seam 2 for the final leaves on wheat Block C. Follow manufacturers instructions, and use the pattern supplied on page 52. Press the leaves in place and place a good press on tear-away stabilizer behind the leaves. Use a blanket stitch to appliqué the leaves in place.

9. Mary did some wonderful things with this tablecloth as you can see in the photo. She quilted wheat with brown thread and I love what she did with the center of the bread to give it texture. She "ditched" the patchwork and used her swirl fill behind the wheat.

10. Use the seven 2 1/2" wide strips of Fabric II and make straight-grain binding. Refer to page 12 for binding instructions, and bind the tablecloth.

Cut 4 for tablecloth from Fabric VII.

Turn pattern over and cut 4 more from Fabric VII.

daily bread place mats

Place mats finish to: 14 1/4" x 18 1/4"

I love this tablecloth and place mat set. The brown and gold tones are so warm and inviting. They make you feel comfortable before you sit down to the table. A simple color combination, yet rich, elegant and pleasing, shows that you can stay with the same tones and achieve some wonderful effects. I guarantee this one is going on my table this fall!

Materials For Two Place Mats

☐ Fabric I (light tan with gold print) Need 7 5/8" 1/4 yard

☐ Fabric II (light gold print) Need 3" 1/4 yard

☐ Fabric III (medium gold batik) Need 3 3/8" 1/4 yard

☐ Fabric IV (dark gold print) Need 3 3/4" 1/4 yard

☐ Fabric V (dark rust print) Need 22 1/2" 3/4 yard
  Backing 1/2 yard

Cutting For Two Place Mats

☐ **From Fabric I, cut: (ivory with gold check)**
- One 3 3/8" wide strip. From this, cut:
  * Two - 2 3/8" x 3 3/8" (A12)
  * Two - 1 3/4" x 3 3/8" (A13)
  * Four - 1 1/8" x 3 3/8" (A7)
  * Four - 2 1/8" x 2 5/8" (A8)
  * Two - 2 1/8" x 2 3/8" (A10)
  * Four - 2 3/8" squares (A4)
- One 1 3/4" wide strip. From this, cut:
  * Six - 1 3/4" squares (A9b, A11b)
  * Twenty-one - 1 1/2" squares (A5a)
- One 1 1/2" wide strip. From this, cut:
  * Three - 1 1/2" squares (add to A5a above)
  * Six - 1 3/8" squares (A9a, A11a)
  * Fourteen - 1 1/4" squares (A3a, A8b, A10b)
  * Two - 1" x 5 1/8" (A2)
- One 1" wide strips. From this and scrap, cut:
  * Four - 1" x 8" (A6)
  * Two - 1" x 5 1/8" (add to A2 above)

☐ **From Fabric II, cut: (light gold print)**
- One 1 3/4" wide strip. From this, cut:
  * Four - 1 3/4" x 2 5/8" (A9)
  * Two - 1 3/4" x 2 3/8" (A11)
  * Six - 1 3/8" squares (A8c, A10c)
- One 1 1/4" wide strip. From this, cut:
  * Two - 1 1/4" x 12 1/2" (Q2)

☐ **From Fabric III, cut: (medium gold batik)**
- One 3 3/8" wide strip. From this, cut:
  * Two - 2" x 3 3/8" (A3)
  * Twelve - 2 3/8" squares (A5)

☐ **From Fabric IV, cut: (dark gold print)**
- One 2" wide strip. From this, cut:
  * Two - 2" x 15 3/8" (Q5)
  * Two - 2" x 3 3/8" (Q3)
- One 1 3/4" wide strip. From this, cut:
  * Six - 1 3/4" squares (A8a, A10a)

☐ **From Fabric V, cut: (dark rust print)**
- One 12 1/2" wide strip. From this, cut:
  * Two - 12 1/2" squares (Q1)
- Stack these cuts:
  * Two - 1" x 5 3/4" (A14)
  * Two - 1" x 5 1/8" (A1)
  * Two - 1" x 2" (Q4)
- Four 2 1/2" wide strips for straight-grain binding.

Assembly

1. To assemble Block A, refer to instructions for tablecloth, Block A assembly. Although the units numbers and colors are different for place mats, the assembly is the same.

2. Use diagonal corner technique to make six of Unit 5, two of units 8 and 9, and one each of units 3, 10, and 11. Refer to diagram below to make units 8 and 10. Join the block as described for tablecloth. Make 2.

3. To assemble the place mat, join units 1 and 2; then add Block A to left side as shown. Join units 3, 4, and 5 in a row. Join to bottom of place mat, matching Unit Q4 seam.

4. Quilt as desired, and use the four 2 1/2" wide strips of Fabric V to make straight-grain binding, and bind the place mats.

Block A. Make 2. When block is complete, it should measure 6 3/4" X 13 1/4".

Making units A8 and A10.

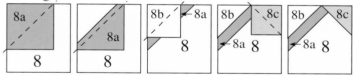

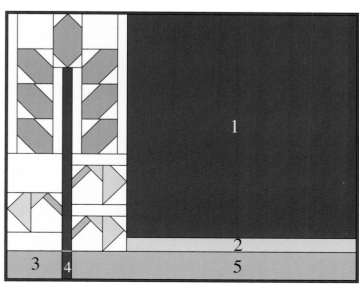

53

Quilt finishes to: 96" x 105"

Rambling rose

Large multiple rose blocks should measure 36 1/2" square when pieced.

Techniques used: diagonal corners, diagonal ends, triangle squares, and strip sets used as diagonal corners.

Materials For Quilt

☐	Fabric I (white with pink print) 4 7/8 yards	Need 166"
☐	Fabric II (white on white print) 5 yards	Need 168"
■	Fabric III (dark burgundy print) 1/4 yard	Need 5 5/8"
■	Fabric IV (dark rose print) 1/4 yard	Need 5 1/8"
■	Fabric V (medium rose batik) 2 3/4 yards	Need 92 3/8"
■	Fabric VI (light rose print) 3 1/8 yards	Need 108 1/2"
☐	Fabric VII (light pink print) 1 1/4 yards	Need 39 3/4"
☐	Fabric VIII (pale pink print) 1/2 yard	Need 12 1/4"
■	Fabric IX (dark green print) 3/4 yard	Need 21 3/8"
☐	Fabric X (light green print) 7/8 yard	Need 26 1/2"
	Backing	8 5/8 yards

When we began scouting photo locations, one of the first homes we were privileged to see was the home of Joe and Carol Davis. Carol had grown up with Victorian antiques, which was a passion of her mothers. Although their home is filled with the most incredible collection of colonial antiques that I have ever seen, one room is decorated with beautiful Victorian antiques, in honor of Carol's mother. The authenticity of the decor was so fascinating that I asked Chris to shoot some extra small shots of the lovely memorabilia that adorned the tables and dressers. The photo below is a collection of Carol's mother's hat pins.

The truck quilt photo on page 41 was shot on a rope bed in the Davis home. The trunk next to the bed on the right is the quilt trunk that accompanied Carol's father when he, at the age of one year, along with his parents, sister, and other relatives journeyed in a covered wagon from Nevada, Missouri to Anadarko, Oklahoma Territory in 1901. Anadarko was still Indian territory at that time. Oklahoma did not become a state unit 1906. As this is being written in 2003, Carol's father is living in his 102nd year, and about to celebrate his 103rd birthday. The Davis' have a number of wood carvings that Carol's dad created over the years.

Cutting For Quilt

☐ **From Fabric I, cut: (white with pink print)**
- Three 8 1/2" wide strips. From these, cut:
  * Eight - 8" x 8 1/2" (Q5)
  * Eight - 6 1/2" x 8 1/2" (Q3)
  * Forty-nine - 1 1/8" squares (A6a, A8b, A12a, A13a, A14a, A17, A21a, A26a, A30a, B6a, B8b, B12a, B13a, B14a, B17, B21a, B26a, B30a)
- Three 8" wide strips. From these, cut:
  * Sixteen - 6 1/2" x 8" (Q4)
  * 126 - 1 1/8" squares (add to 1 1/8" squares above)
- Four 3 1/2" wide strips. From these, cut:
  * Eight - 3 1/2" x 16 1/2" (Q1)
  * Ninety-six - 1 1/8" squares (add to 1 1/8" squares above)
- Seventeen 2 1/2" wide strips. From these, cut:
  * Eight - 2 1/2" x 21 1/2" (Q2)
  * Forty-six - 2 1/2" x 4 1/2" (Q11)
  * Ninety-six - 2 1/2" x 3" (Q13, Q14)
  * Four - 2 1/2" squares (Q12)
  * Fifty-eight 1 1/8" squares (add to 1 1/8" squares above)
- Ten 2 3/8" wide strips. From these, cut:
  * Forty-eight - 2 3/8" x 3" (A32, B32)
  * Forty-eight - 1 3/4" x 2 3/8" (A29, B29)
  * 144 - 1 1/8" x 2 3/8" (A8, A25, A31, B8, B25, B31)
  * Forty-eight - 1 1/8" squares (add to 1 1/8" squares above)
- Fifteen 1 3/4" wide strips. From these, cut:
  * Forty-eight - 1 3/4" x 4 3/4" (A20, B20)
  * 144 - 1 3/4" squares (A11, A24, A27a, B11, B24, B27a)
  * Ninety-six - 1 1/8" x 1 3/4" (A19, A28, B19, B28)
  * Thirty-three - 1 1/8" squares (add to 1 1/8" sq. above)
- Two 1 5/8" wide strips. From these, cut:
  * Forty-eight - 1 5/8" squares (A12b, B12b)
- Six 1 1/8" wide strips. Four for Strip Sets 1 and 2.
  From remainder, cut:
  * Seventy - 1 1/8" squares (add to 1 1/8" sq. above)

☐ **From Fabric II, cut: (white on white print)**
- Twelve 6 1/2" wide strips. From these, cut:
  * 180 - 2 1/2" x 6 1/2" (E3, E4) Make E4 the same.
- Thirty-six 2 1/2" wide strips. From these, cut:
  * Thirty-six - 2 1/2" x 36 1/2" (E2)

■ **From Fabric III, cut: (dark burgundy print)**
- Five 1 1/8" wide strips. Two for Strip Set 4.
  From remainder, cut:
  * Forty-eight - 1 1/8" x 2 3/8" (A5, B5)
  * Nine - 1 1/8" squares (C2a, D2a)

■ **From Fabric IV, cut: (dark rose print)**
- Two 1 3/4" wide strips for Strip Set 4.
- One 1 5/8" wide strip. From this, cut:
  * Nine - 1 5/8" squares (C2, D2)

▨ **From Fabric V, cut: (medium rose batik)**
- Twelve 6 1/2" wide strips. From these, cut:
  * Twelve - 6 1/2" x 36 1/2" (E1)
- From scrap, cut
  * Forty-eight - 1 3/4" x 2 7/8" (A18, B18)
  * Thirty-six - 1 3/4" squares (A4, A12c, A13, B4, B12c, B13)
- Five 1 3/4" wide strips. From these, cut:
  * 108 - 1 3/4" squares (add to 1 3/4" squares above)
- Five 1 1/8" wide strips. Two for Strip Set 3. From two remaining strips, cut:
  * Ninety-six - 1 1/8" squares (A9a, A17, B9a, B17)

▨ **From Fabric VI, cut: (light rose print)**
- Two 3" wide strips. From these, cut:
  * Forty-eight - 1 5/8" x 3" (A6, B6)
- Ten 2 1/2" wide strips for straight-grain binding
- One 1 7/8" wide strip. From this, cut:
  * Nine - 1 7/8" squares (C8a, D8a)
  * Sixteen - 1 1/2" squares (Q11a, Q12a, Q13b, Q14b)
- Seven 1 3/4" wide strips. From these, cut:
  * Nine - 1 3/4" x 3 1/4" (C1, D1)
  * Forty-eight - 1 3/4" x 3" (A26, B26)
  * Forty-eight - 1 3/4" squares (A9, B9)
  * Twenty-three - 1 1/2" squares (add to 1 1/2" sq. above)
- Thirty-four 1 1/2" wide strips. From these, cut:
  * Four - 1 1/2" x 42" (Q10)
  * Twelve - 1 1/2" x 40 1/2" (Q8, Q9) Piece two together to = six 80 1/2" lengths.
  * Four - 1 1/2" x 36 1/2" (Q6)
  * Eight - 1 1/2" x 27 3/4" (Q10) Join two to opposite ends of (Q10) 42" strips to = four 96 1/2" lengths.
  * Eighteen - 1 1/2" x 6 1/2" (Q7)
  * 153 - 1 1/2" squares (add to 1 1/2" squares above)
- Eleven 1 1/8" wide strips. Two for Strip Set 3.
  From remainder, cut:
  * Forty-eight - 1 1/8" x 2 3/8" (A3, B3)
  * 201 - 1 1/8" squares (A1a, A5a, A10a, A21b, B1a, B5a, B10a, B21b, C4a, D4a)

▨ **From Fabric VII, cut: (light pink print)**
- Two 3 1/2" wide strips. From these, cut:
  * Forty-eight - 1 3/4" x 3 1/2" (A7, B7)
- Two 3" wide strips. From these, cut:
  * Forty-eight - 1 3/4" x 3" (A10, B10)
- Two 2 7/8" wide strips. From these, cut:
  * Forty-eight - 1 3/4" x 2 7/8" (A12, B12)
- Four 1 3/4" wide strips. From these, cut:
  * Ninety-six - 1 3/4" squares (Q13a, Q14a)
- One 1 5/8" wide strip. From this, cut:
  * Nine - 1 5/8" x 2 1/8" (C3, D3)
- Eleven 1 1/8" wide strips. From these, cut:
  * Forty-eight - 1 1/8" x 3" (A8a, B8a)
  * Forty-eight - 1 1/8" x 1 3/4" (A15, B15)
  * 201 - 1 1/8" squares (A5b, A6b, A14b, A18a, B5b, B6b, B14b, B18a, C1a, D1a)

☐ **From Fabric VIII, cut: (pale pink print)**
- One 5 1/4" strip. From this, cut:
  * Nine - 1" x 5 1/4" (C13, D13)
  * Nine - 1 3/4" x 5 1/8" (C14, D14)
  * Nine - 1 3/4" x 2 1/4" (C12, D12) Stack this cut.
  * Nine - 1 5/8" x 2 1/4" (C11, D11) Stack this cut.
- One 1 7/8" wide strip. From this, cut:
  * Nine - 1 7/8" squares (C8a, D8a)
  * Nine - 1 3/4" x 1 7/8" (C15, D15)
- One 1 1/2" wide strip. From this, cut:
  * Nine - 1 1/2" x 2" (C7, D7)
  * Nine - 1 3/8" squares (C4c, D4c)
  * Nine - 1 1/8" squares (C10b, D10b)
- One 1 3/8" wide strip. From this, cut:
  * Nine - 1 3/8" x 2 7/8" (C5, D5)
  * Twelve - 1 1/4" squares (C3a, C4b, D3a, D4b)
- One 1 1/4" wide strip. From this, cut:
  * Six - 1 1/4" squares (add to 1 1/4" sq. above)
  * Nine - 1" x 2 3/4" (C9, D9)
- One 1" wide strip. From this, cut:
  * Twenty-seven - 1" squares (C2b, C4d, C10a, D2b, D4d, D10a)

From Fabric IX, cut: (dark green print)
- Two 2 3/8" wide strips. From these, cut:
  * Forty-eight - 1 3/4" x 2 3/8" (A30, B30)
- Five 1 3/4" wide strips. From these, cut:
  * 105 - 1 3/4" squares (A14, A20a, B14, B20a, C12a, D12a)
  * Twenty-three - 1 1/8" squares (A16, A19a, A26b, A27b, A31a, B16, B19a, B26b, B27b, B31a, C10c, D10c)
- Seven 1 1/8" wide strips. From these, cut:
  * 226 - 1 1/8" squares (add to 1 1/8" squares above)

From Fabric X, cut: (light green print)
- Two 3" wide strips. From these, cut:
  * Forty-eight -1 3/4" x 3" (A27, B27)
- Four 2 3/8" wide strips. From these, cut:
  * Nine - 2 3/8" x 2 7/8" (C4, D4)
  * Nine - 2 3/8" x 2 3/4" (C10, D10)
  * Forty-eight - 2 3/8" squares (A21, B21)
- One 1 7/8" wide strip. From this, cut:
  * Nine - 1 7/8" x 2" (C8, D8)
  * Twenty-one - 1 1/8" squares (A20b, A28a, B20b, B28a, C14a, D14a)
- Two 1 3/4" strips for Strip Set 2.
- Five 1 1/8" strips. Two for Strip Set 1. From remainder, cut:
  * Eighty-four - 1 1/8" squares (add to 1 1/8" squares above)

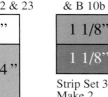
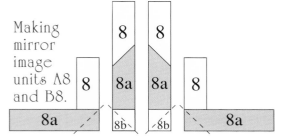

Units A & B 18b — 1 1/8" / 1 1/8" — Strip Set 1. Make 2. Cut into 48 1 3/4" segments.

Combined units A and B22 & 23 — 1 1/8" / 1 3/4" — Strip Set 2. Make 2. Cut into 48 - 1 1/8" segments.

Units A & B 10b — 1 1/8" / 1 1/8" — Strip Set 3. Make 2. Cut into 48 1 3/4" segments.

Combined units A and B 1 and 2 — 1 3/4" / 1 1/8" — Strip Set 4. Make 2. Cut into 48 1 3/4" segments.

Assembly of Blocks A and B

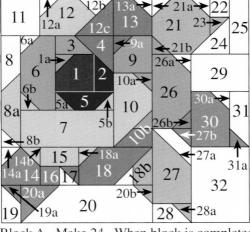

Block A. Make 24. When block is completed, it should measure 8" x 8 1/2"

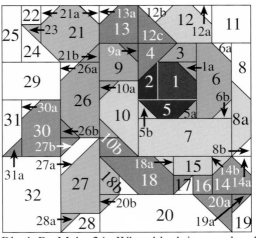

Block B. Make 24. When block is completed, it should measure 8" x 8 1/2"

1. Please note that A and B blocks are mirror images. Refer frequently to block diagrams for correct placement of units. Instructions are for one block.

2. Use diagonal corner technique to make one of unit 5, 6, 9, 10, 12, 13, 14, 18, 19, 20, 21, 26, 27, 28, 30, and 31. Units 1 and 2 are a Strip Set 4 segment. Join diagonal corner 1a to Fabric III corner as shown.

3. Use diagonal end technique to make one of Unit 8. Refer to diagram at the top of the page. Make diagonal

Making mirror image units A8 and B8.

end first; then add diagonal corner 8b.

4. Refer to page 7 for strip piecing, and piece the strip sets shown at top of page. Each is marked with the size strip to be pieced, the segments to be cut, and the units that the strip sets are used for. Store them in zip top marked bags as you would for other units.

5. Unit 10b is a segment of Strip Set 3. Refer to the diagram at left, and place the segment on Unit 10 as shown. Refer to both drawings for mirror image units. When making a strip set diagonal corner, if the stripes are to finish vertically, the unit must be placed horizontally. If the stripes are to finish horizontally, the unit must be placed vertically. Stitch diagonal corner 10b in place. Trim seam as shown and press. Join diagonal corner 10a to complete the unit.

Making mirror image units A10 and B10.

6. Refer to the diagram on page 58 for making mirror image units A12 and B12. Begin by joining diagonal corner 12a. Do not trim the seam as it is a lighter fabric than the fabric beneath it. If seam is trimmed, the darker fabric may show through. Join diagonal corner 12b. Do not trim seam. Press as shown. Join diagonal corner 12c. Trim seam and press to complete the unit.

Making units A17 and B17

Place 1 1/8" squares of Fabrics I and V right sides together, raw edges matching, and stitch a diagonal as shown. Do not trim Fabric I seam. Press

7. Refer to the diagram above for Unit 17. Follow graphics and instructions to complete the unit.

Making mirror image units A18 and B18.

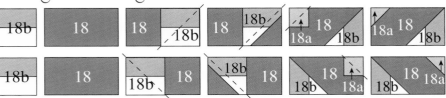

Making mirror image units A12 and B12.

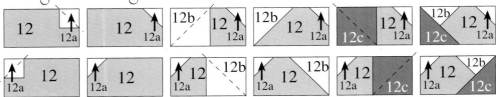

8. To make Unit 18, refer to the diagram at the bottom of page 57. This unit is basically the same as units A and B 12 above. Diagonal corner 18b is a segment cut from Strip Set 1. Refer to Step 6 and read the instructions.

9. The diagram at right shows how to make combined units 21-24 for blocks A and B. Units 22 and 23 are cut from Strip Set 2. Read the instructions, and follow the graphics to complete the combined units. Unit 27 is made by joining diagonal corners in alphabetical order.

10. Now that all units have been completed, the following instructions are for assembly of A and B blocks which are shown on page 57. Begin by joining Unit 3 to top of strip set 4 combined units 1 and 2; then add Unit 5 to the bottom. Join diagonal corner, Unit 4 to top of combined units as shown. Join Unit 6 to side of combined units; then add Unit 7 to bottom. Join Unit 8 to side. Join units 9 and 10, and add them to other side of combined units as shown in illustration.

11. Join units 11, 12 and 13 in a row as shown. Add them to rose center units. Join units 16 and 17; then add Unit 15 to top of the 16/17 combined units. Join Unit 14 to one side as shown and Unit 18 to the other side. Join units 19 and 20. Join these combined units to combined units 14-18, matching seams. Add this section to bottom of rose section.

12. Join Unit 25 to combined units 21-24. Join units 26, 27, and 28 in a vertical row. Join units 30 and 31; then add Unit 29 to top of these combined units and Unit 32 to bottom. Add the vertical row of combined units 26-28 to side of combined units 29-32, matching leaf seam. Add combined units 21-25 to top to complete the leaf section. Join the leaf and rose sections as shown, matching seams to complete the blocks. Make 24 of Block A, and 24 of Block B.

Making combined units 21-24 for A and B blocks.

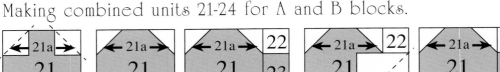

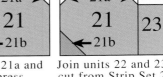
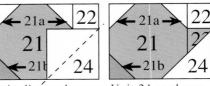

Join diagonal corners 21a and 21b as shown and press.

Join units 22 and 23, cut from Strip Set 2.

Join diagonal corner Unit 24 as shown.

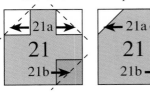
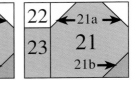
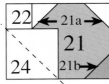
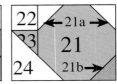

Making mirror image units C8 and D8

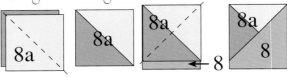

Place 1 7/8" squares of Fabrics VI and VIII right sides together, raw edges matching, and stitch a diagonal as shown. Trim seam and press open for Unit D8a. To complete the unit, place the triangle-square on 1 7/8" x 2" piece of Fabric X, right sides facing, and raw edges matching. Stitch diagonal, trim seam and press for Unit D8. Reverse the position of D8a for mirror image unit.

Assembly of Blocks C and D

1. Use diagonal corner technique to make one each of units 1, 2, 3, 4, 10, 12, and 14. Refer to the diagram at right for making the triangle-square diagonal corner C8 and D8. Keep in mind that they are mirror images. Refer to Block C diagram for correct placement of Unit 8.

2. To assemble the bud blocks, begin by joining units 2 and 3; then add Unit 1 to side. Join units 4 and 5. Add these combined units to bottom of 1-3 combined units. Join units 7 and 8. Join units 9 and 10, and add them to the bottom of combined units 7/8. Join units 11 and 12. Join these combined units to bottom of combined units 7-10 as shown. Add this section to bud section, matching seams where necessary. Join unit 13 to top of the combined units. Join units 14 and 15. Add them to the side of the bud, to complete the block.

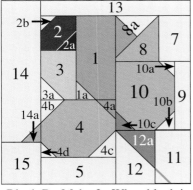

Block C. Make 6. When block is completed, it should measure 6 1/2" square.

Block D. Make 3. When block is completed, it should measure 6 1/2" square.

Assembly of Trellis Block E

Folding For Trellis

3/4" Fold Line
1"
3/4" Fold Line

1. After all of the trellis strips have been cut, they must be folded. Twenty-four of the 2 1/2" x 36 1/2" strips will be folded in half, wrong sides together. The remaining twelve will be folded as shown on the left. To do so, fold under 3/4" on both sides of the strip. Press each one as they are folded so that exactly 1" is showing on top. Twenty-four of Unit 3

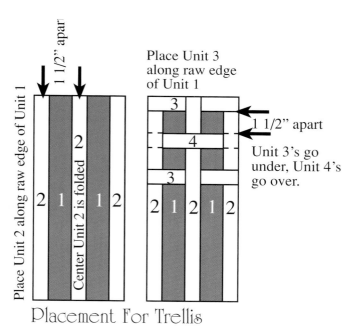

1 1/2" apart

Place Unit 3 along raw edge of Unit 1

Place Unit 2 along raw edge of Unit 1

Center Unit 2 is folded

2 1 2 1 2

3
2 1 2 1 2
3
4

1 1/2" apart

Unit 3's go under, Unit 4's go over.

Placement For Trellis

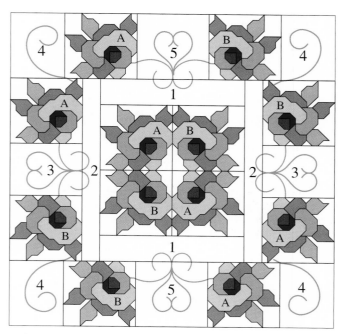

This block, when assembled measures 36 1/2" square. Make 4 for quilt top.

will be folded in half, with the remainder folded as shown in the folding illustration on page 58.

2. The diagram above shows how to place the strips. The 36 1/2" strips are placed first on the 6 1/2" x 36 1/2" pieces of Fabric V. Two of the long strips that are folded in half are placed along raw edges of Unit 1, with raw edges matching. Pin in place securely. A long strip that is folded under as in the illustration, is placed in the center as shown . There should be 1 1/2" between the Unit 2 strips. Pin securely in place.

3. Beginning at the top short end of the trellis, place one Unit 3 strip that is folded in half, raw edges matching, along the short end of Fabric V. The Unit 3 strip will always be under the center strip. All other Unit 3 strips will be folded under the 3/4". All Unit 3's that are folded in half will be along raw edges only. Next, place folded strip, Unit 4, 1 1/2" below Unit 3. Unit 4 will always weave over the Unit 2 center strip, and go under the outer Unit 2 strips as indicated by the dashed lines in the diagram. The trick to placing these strips so that they remain in place is to cut small pieces of Steam-A-Seam 2, remove the paper on both sides, and press the pieces down in several places when you are certain that they are placed correctly.. Place the Unit 2 center strip first, so that weaving the shorter strips is easier. It also allows you to use the Steam-A-Seam 2 placed under Unit 4 to hold the strips in place. Continue this procedure until you have reached the bottom of the trellis, then place a Unit 3 piece that is folded in half along the raw edge. When you are certain that all strips are in their proper position, run a basting stitch around Unit 1, 1/8" from raw edge. This holds the outer Unit 2 strips in place as all raw edges will be encased in the seams.

4. We placed a piece of tear-away stabilizer behind the trellis. Top stitch the strips in place with white thread along the edge of each strip.

Block E. Make 12. When block is completed,it should measure 6 1/2" x 36 1/2"

1. Refer to the diagram above. The effect that is achieved with the rose blocks is because of the way they are turned. Check the diagram frequently when joining the blocks and "Q" units.

2. For the large block center, begin by joining Block A and Block B so that they are facing each other. Make 2, and join them together as pictured. Add Unit Q1 to top and bottom of this center section; then join Unit Q2 to opposite sides. For left side row, join rose Block A, Unit Q3, and rose Block B together as shown. Join to left side of center section. For right side row, join rose Block B, Unit Q3, and rose Block A together. Add to right side of center section.

3. For top row, join Unit Q4, Block A, Unit Q5, Block B, and Unit Q4. Make two. One for the top of the block and one for the bottom. Join the two rows to top and bottom of center section to complete the block. Make 4.

4. The swirls and hearts add a lot to the quilt. Mary quilted them with dark green thread when the quilt was complete. They can be satin stitched or triple stitched, which ever you prefer.

Blow up of lace for top and bottom of quilt.

13a	14a	14a	14a	14a	14a	14a	14a	14a	14a	14a	14a
13	**14**	**14**	**14**	**14**	**14**	**14**	**14**	**14**	**14**	**14**	**14**
13b	14b	14b	14b	14b	14b	14b	14b	14b	14b		
12a		11a		11a		11a		11a		11a	
12	**11**		**11**		**11**		**11**		**11**		**11**

5. To make the lace for the top and bottom of the quilt, use diagonal corner technique to make ninety-six of units Q13 and Q14, forty-six of Unit Q11, and four of Unit Q12. Join units 12 and 13 together, matching seams. Make two. The second one will be a mirror image. Join two of Unit 14 together as shown above. Make a total of twenty-three Unit 14 pairs. Join Unit 11 to bottom of each pair. Join the twenty-three combined sections together. Join the mirror imaged, combined 12/13 units to opposite ends. Make two lace borders, one for the top of the quilt, and one for the bottom.

Quilt Assembly

1. To assemble the quilt top with the blocks and sashing, begin in the top left corner and make a long vertical row. Join Unit Q7, Block C, Q7, Block E, Q7, Block C, Q7, Block E, Q7, Block C, and Unit Q7. Make two of these rows, the second one for the right side of the quilt top,

substituting Block D for Block C in the right row.

2. Join Unit Q6 to opposite long ends of Block E. Join the large rose block to opposite long ends of the Q6/Block E combined section. Make two. Join Unit Q8 to the right side of one of the rose/trellis sections, and join another Q8 unit to the left side on the remaining rose/trellis section. Make a center trellis row by joining Unit Q7 to top and bottom of one Block C; then add a trellis to top and bottom of Unit Q7. Join the two rose/trellis sections to opposite sides of the center row, matching seams. Join sashing Unit Q9 to top and bottom of the quilt top as shown.

3. Make two horizontal rows as follows: Join sashing Unit Q7 to opposite sides of remaining Block C; then add trellis Block E to opposite sides of Unit Q7. Make 2 rows. Join rows to top and bottom of quilt top; then add sashing Unit Q9 to top and bottom as shown. Join sashing Unit Q10 to opposite sides of quilt top. Add the two side rows, previously made to opposite sides of the quilt. Join another Q10 sashing strip to opposite sides of quilt. Join the lace rows, previously made to top and bottom of quilt.

4. Mary "ditched" the patchwork and made leaves with veins inside of the pieced leaves. She did a swirl stipple behind the roses.

    5. Join the ten 2 1/2" wide strips of Fabric VI to make straight-grain binding and referring to page 12 for instructions, bind your quilt.

60

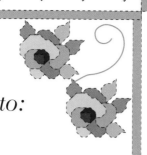

Rambling rose tablecloth

Tablecloth finishes to:
61" square.

Materials For Tablecloth

☐	Fabric I (white with pink print) 2 5/8 yards	Need 87 3/8"
■	Fabric II (dark burgundy print) 1/4 yard	Need 3 3/8"
■	Fabric III (dark rose print) 1/4 yard	Need 3 3/8"
■	Fabric IV (medium rose batik) 3/8 yard	Need 8 7/8"
▨	Fabric V (light rose print) 1 1/4 yards	Need 38"
☐	Fabric VI (light pink print) 5/8 yard	Need 19"
☐	Fabric VII (pale pink print) 1 1/4 yards	Need 38 7/8"
▨	Fabric VIII (dark green print) 1/4 yard	Need 7 1/2"
▨	Fabric IX (light green print) 1/2 yard	Need 14 3/4"
	Backing	3 3/4 yards

Cutting For Tablecloth

From Fabric I, cut: (white with pink print)
- Three 5" wide strips. From these, cut:
  * Four - 5" x 11 1/2" (Q5)
  * Eight - 5" x 6 1/2" (Q6)
  * Four - 2 1/2" x 8" (Q1) Stack this cut.
- Five 3 1/2" wide strips. From these, cut:
  * Four - 3 1/2" x 12" (Q4)
  * Six - 2 1/2" x 18 1/2" (Q2)
  * Twelve - 1 3/4" x 2 3/8" (A29, B29) Stack this cut.
  * Thirty-six - 1 3/4" squares (A11, A24, A27a, B11, B24, B27a) Stack this cut.
- Eight 3" wide strips. From these, cut:
  * 104 - 2 1/2" x 3" (Q15, Q16)
  * Twelve - 2 3/8" x 3" (A32, B32)
  * Four - 1 1/2" x 13 1/2" (Q8) Stack this cut.
- Six 2 1/2" wide strips. From these, cut:
  * Forty-eight - 2 1/2" x 4 1/2" (Q14)
  * Eight - 2 1/2" squares (Q13)
- One 2" wide strip. From this, cut:
  * Two - 2" x 18 1/2" (Q3)
- Three 1 3/4" wide strips. From these, cut:
  * Twelve - 1 3/4" x 4 3/4" (A20, B20)
  * Twenty-four - 1 1/8" x 1 3/4" (A19, A28, B19, B28)
  * Twelve - 1 5/8" squares (A12b, B12b)
  * Nineteen - 1 1/8" squares (A6a, A8b, A12a, A13a, A14a, A17, A21a, A22, A26a, A30a, B6a, B8b, B12a, B13a, B14a, B17, B21a, B22, B26a, B30a)
- Two 1 1/2" wide strips. From these, cut:
  * Four - 1 1/2" x 11" (Q7)
  * Thirty-five - 1 1/8" squares (add to 1 1/8" squares above)
- Five 1 1/8" wide strips. One for Strip Set 1. From remainder, cut:
  * Thirty-six - 1 1/8" x 2 3/8" (A8, A25, A31, B8, B25, B31)
  * Seventy-eight - 1 1/8" squares (add to 1 1/8" squares above)

From Fabric II, cut: (dark burgundy print)
- Three 1 1/8" wide strips. One for Strip Set 3. From remaining strip, cut:
  * Twelve - 1 1/8" x 2 3/8" (A5, B5)
  * Sixteen - 1 1/8" squares (C2a, D2a)

From Fabric III, cut: (dark rose print)
- One 1 3/4" wide strip for Strip Set 3.
- One 1 5/8" wide strip. From this, cut:
  * Sixteen - 1 5/8" squares (C2, D2)

From Fabric IV, cut: (medium rose batik)
- One 2 1/2" wide strip. From this, cut:
  * Four - 2 1/2" x 6 1/2" (Q9)
- Three 1 3/4" wide strips. From these, cut:
  * Twelve - 1 3/4" x 2 7/8" (A18, B18)
  * Thirty-six - 1 3/4" squares (A4, A12c, A13, B4, B12c, B13)
  * Twenty-four - 1 1/8" squares (A9a, A17, B9a, B17)
- One 1 1/8" wide strip for Strip Set 2.

From Fabric V, cut: (light rose print)
- One 6 1/2" wide strip. From this, cut:
  * Four - 6 1/2" squares (Q10)
  * Twelve - 1 3/4" x 3" (A26, B26)
  * Twelve - 1 1/2" squares (Q13a, Q14a, Q15b, Q16b)
- One 5" wide strip. From this, cut:
  * Four - 5" squares (Q17)
  * Forty-two - 1 1/2" squares (add to 1 1/2" sq. above)
- One 1 7/8" wide strip. From this, cut:
  * Sixteen - 1 7/8" squares (C8a, D8a)
  * Eight - 1 1/2" squares (add to 1 1/2" squares above)
- Two 1 3/4" wide strips. From these, cut:
  * Sixteen - 1 3/4" x 3 1/4" (C1, D1)
  * Twelve - 1 3/4" squares (A9, B9)
- One 1 5/8" wide strip. From this, cut:
  * Twelve - 1 5/8" x 3" (A6, B6)
- Ten 1 1/2" wide strips. From these and scrap, cut:
  * Four - 1 1/2" x 26 1/2" (Q12) Join two together to = two 52 1/2" lengths.
  * Four - 1 1/2" x 25 1/2" (Q11) Join two together to = two 50 1/2" lengths.
  * 146 - 1 1/2" squares (add to 1 1/2" squares above)
- Four 1 1/8" wide strips. One for Strip Set 2. From remainder, cut:
  * Twelve - 1 1/8" x 2 3/8" (A3, B3)
  * Sixty-four - 1 1/8" squares (A1a, A5a, A10a, A21b, B1a, B5a, B10a, B21b, C4a, D4a)

From Fabric VI, cut: (light pink print)
- Eight 1 3/4" wide strips. From these, cut:
  * Twelve - 1 3/4" x 2 7/8" (A12, B12)
  * Twelve - 1 3/4" x 3 1/2" (A7, B7)
  * Twelve - 1 3/4" x 3" (A10, B10)
  * 104 - 1 3/4" squares (Q15a, Q16a)
  * Twelve - 1 1/8" x 1 3/4" (A15, B15)
- One 1 5/8" wide strip. From this, cut:
  * Sixteen - 1 5/8" x 2 1/8" (C3, D3)
- Three 1 1/8" wide strips. From these, cut:
  * Twelve - 1 1/8" x 3" (A8a, B8a)
  * Sixty-four - 1 1/8" squares (A5b, A6b, A14b, A18a, B5b, B6b, B14b, B18b, C1a, D1a)

From Fabric VII, cut: (pale pink print)
- One 6 1/2" wide strip. From this, cut:
  * Eight - 1" x 6 1/2" (CB, DB extension)
  * Eight - 3/4" x 6 1/2" (CA, DA extension)
  * Sixteen - 1" x 5 1/4" (C13, D13)
  * Sixteen - 1" x 2 3/4" (C9, D9) Stack this cut.
- One 5 1/4" wide strip. From this, cut:
  * Sixteen - 1 3/4" x 5 1/4" (C14, D14)
  * Sixteen - 1 3/4" x 2 1/4" (C12, D12) Stack this cut.
- Six 2 1/2" wide strips for straight-grain binding.
- One 2" wide strip. From this, cut:
  * Sixteen - 1 1/2" x 2" (C7, D7)
  * Sixteen - 1 1/8" squares (C10b, D10b)

- Two 1 7/8" wide strips. From these, cut:
  * Sixteen - 1 7/8" squares (C8a, D8a)
  * Sixteen - 1 3/4" x 1 7/8" (C15, D15)
  * Sixteen - 1 3/8" squares (C4c, D4c)
- One 1 5/8" wide strip. From this, cut:
  * Sixteen - 1 5/8" x 2 1/4" (C11, D11)
- Two 1 3/8" wide strips. From these and scrap, cut:
  * Sixteen - 1 3/8" x 2 7/8" (C5, D5)
  * Thirty-two - 1 1/4" squares (C3a, C4b, D3a, D4b)
- Two 1" wide strips. From these, cut:
  * Forty-eight - 1" squares (C2b, C4d, C10a, D2b, D4d,

 D10a)

From Fabric VIII, cut: (dark green print)
- Three 1 3/4" wide strips. From these, cut:
  * Twelve - 1 3/4" x 2 3/8" (A30, B30)
  * Forty - 1 3/4" squares (A14, A20a, B14, B20a, C12a, D12a)
  * Twenty-three - 1 1/8" squares (A16, A19a, A26b, A27b, A31a, B16, B19a, B26b, B27b, B31a, C10c, D10c) Stack this cut.
- Two 1 1/8" wide strips. From these, cut:
  * Fifty-three - 1 1/8" squares (add to 1 1/8" squares above)

From Fabric IX, cut: (light green print)
- Three 2 3/8" wide strips. From these, cut:
  * Sixteen - 2 3/8" x 2 7/8" (C4, D4)
  * Sixteen - 2 3/8" x 2 3/4" (C10, D10)
  * Twelve - 2 3/8" squares (A21, B21)
- One 1 7/8" wide strip. From this, cut:
  * Sixteen - 1 7/8" x 2" (C8, D8)
  * Eight - 1 1/8" squares (A20b, A28a, B20b, B28a, C14a, D14a)
- Two 1 3/4" wide strips. From these, cut:
  * Twelve - 1 3/4" x 3" (A27, B27)
  * Twelve - 1 1/8" x 1 3/4" (A23, B23)
- Two 1 1/8" wide strips. One for Strip Set 1. From remainder, cut:
  * Thirty-two - 1 1/8" squares (add to 1 1/8" squares above)

Block Assembly

1. Blocks A, B, C, and D are assembled the same as for the quilt. Refer to instructions and diagrams on pages 57 and 58 for assembly of these blocks Make 6 of each rose block for tablecloth.

2. Below are the strip sets for blocks A and B. Join the strips together as directed and cut the required amount of segments from each strip set. The diagrams of blocks C and D at right show that the center portion of the design requires extensions added to the bud blocks. Read the instructions under each block, and add the required extensions. These extensions are also shown on the tablecloth diagram on page 64.

Units A & B 18b

| 1 1/8" |
| 1 1/8" |

Strip Set 1. Make 1. Cut into 12 1 3/4" segments.

Units A & B 10b

| 1 1/8" |
| 1 1/8" |

Strip Set 2. Make 1. Cut into 12 1 3/4" segments.

Combined units A and B 1 and 2

| 1 3/4" |
| 1 1/8" |

Strip Set 3. Make 1. Cut into 12 1 3/4" segments.

Tablecloth Assembly

1. Referring to the tablecloth diagram on page 64, begin in the center and join blocks A and B as shown. Make two and join them together in a set of four. Once again, referring to the diagram, join bud block with CB exten-

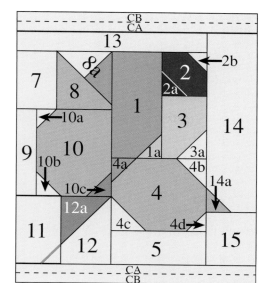

Block C. Make 8. When block is completed, it should measure 6 1/2" square.
Add two CB extensions. You will add (cut size) 1" x 6 1/2" to top and bottom. This block, when completed will measure 6 1/2" x 7 1/2".
Add two CA extensions. You will add 3/4" x 6 1/2" to top and bottom. This block, when completed will measure 6 1/2" x 7".

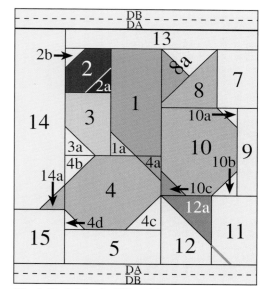

Block D. Make 8. When block is completed, it should measure 6 1/2" square.
Add two DB extensions. You will add (cut size) 1" x 6 1/2" to top and bottom. This block, when completed will measure 6 1/2" x 7 1/2".
Add two DA extensions. You will add 3/4" x 6 1/2" to top and bottom. This block, when completed will measure 6 1/2" x 7".

sion to Unit Q9; then add bud block with DB extension to opposite side of Unit 9. Make two. Join to top and bottom of center section, referring to block illustration for correct placement of bud blocks.

2. Join bud block with DA extension to Unit 9; then add bud block with CA extension to opposite side of Unit 9. Join Unit 10 to opposite sides of this row. Make two. Join them to opposite sides of center section, matching corner seams.

3. Beginning on the left side of center section, join one B block and one A block on opposite sides of Unit Q1 as shown. Join Unit Q3 to left side of combined rose blocks, and Unit Q2 to other side. Add Unit Q5 to opposite short ends as shown. Make two and join them to opposite sides of center section.

4. For the top and bottom of the tablecloth, refer to top left corner of diagram, and join bud Block D with Unit Q6. Join bud block C with another Unit Q6 as shown. Join these two sections together. Join Unit Q7 to left side; then add Unit Q8 to top. Make two. For the top right side of tablecloth, refer to diagram for correct placement of the bud blocks, and begin by once again joining bud Block D with one Unit Q6. Join bud block C with another Unit Q6. Join the two sections together; then add Unit Q7 to right side of this section and Unit 8 to the top. Make 2.

5. For the rose section, join rose Block B to Unit 1; then add rose Block A to opposite side of Unit 1. Join Unit 2 to top and bottom of the combined rose blocks; then join Unit 4 to opposite sides. Make 2. Refer to the diagram, and join the bud sections to opposite sides of the combined rose block sections, making sure that bud blocks are in correct positions. Make two.

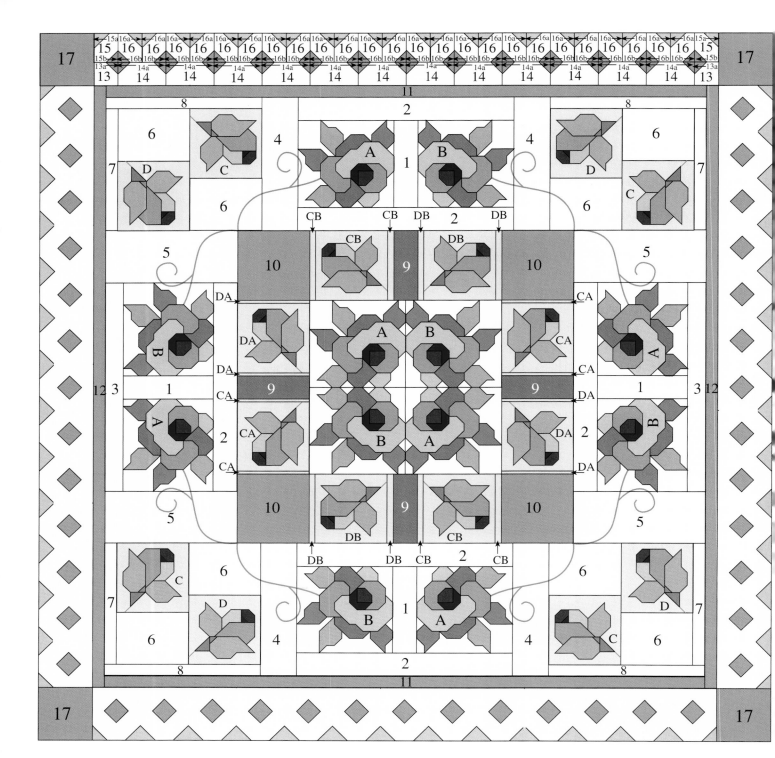

They will be turned when added to tablecloth top. Join them to top and bottom of the center section. Join sashing Unit Q11 to top and bottom of tablecloth; then join sashing Unit Q12 to opposite sides.

Lace Border Assembly

1. To make the lace for the top and bottom of the quilt, use diagonal corner technique to make 104 of units Q15 and Q16, forty-eight of unit Q14, and eight of Unit Q13. Join units 13 and 15, matching seams. Make two, with one being a mirror imaged. Refer to diagram and join two Unit 16's together as shown. Make 12 pairs. Join each pair to the top of Unit 14, matching seams. Join twelve of the combined 14/16 units together with combined units 13/15 on opposite ends. Make 4. Join two to top and bottom of tablecloth. Join Unit Q17 to opposite sides of remaining lace rows; then add to opposite sides to complete the tablecloth.

Blow up of lace.

2. Mary quilted the tablecloth to match the quilt. She "ditched" the patchwork, quilted leaves inside the pieced leaves and quilted the swirls in dark green thread.

    3. Join the six 2 1/2" wide strips of Fabric VI to make straight-grain binding, and bind the tablecloth.

String Of Pearls

Quilt finishes to: 80" x 98"
Techniques used: Strip piecing.

Robert designed this jig saw puzzle that is amazing when it is all pieced together. He used strip sets to accomplish the piecing quickly. The "pearls" are off center, so watch the diagrams closely or it can play tricks on you!

Materials

☐	Fabric I (ivory print)	Need 90 1/2"	2 3/4 yards
■	Fabric II (navy print)	Need 120 1/2"	3 5/8 yards
☐	Fabric III (gold print)	Need 65"	2 yards
☐	Fabric IV (light blue print)	Need 28 1/2"	7/8 yard
☐	Fabric V (medium blue print)	Need 83"	2 1/2 yards
☐	Fabric VI (medium green print)	Need 36"	1 1/8 yards
	Backing		6 yards

Cutting

☐ **From Fabric I, cut: (ivory print)**
- Three 5" wide strips. Two for Strip Sets 10 and 22.
  From remaining strip, cut:
     * Twenty - 1 1/2" x 5" (B6)
- Five 3 1/2" wide strips. From these, cut:
     * Fifty-six - 3 1/2" squares (A4, B4)
- Three 2 1/2" wide strips for Strip Sets 8 and 21.
- Three 2" wide strips for Strip Sets 5 and 16.
- Twenty-one 1 1/2" strips Ten for Strip Sets 1 and 17.
  From remaining eleven strips, cut:
     * Two - 1 1/2" x 42" (Q1)
     * Four - 1 1/2" x 36 1/2" (Q2) Piece two
     together to = two 72 1/2" lengths.
     * Four - 1 1/2" x 25 3/4" (Q1) Piece on opposite sides of 42"
        strips to = two 92 1/2" lengths.
     * Twenty-four - 1 1/2" x 2 1/2" (C3)
- Thirteen 1" wide strips for Strip Sets 2, 4, 15, 18, and 25.

■ **From Fabric II, cut: (navy print)**
- Four 5" wide strips for Strip Sets 11, 12, 26, and 27.
- Eleven 3 1/2" wide strips. From these, cut:
     * Two - 3 1/2" x 42" strips (Q4)
     * Four - 3 1/2" x 37 1/2" (Q3) Piece two
     together to = two 74 1/2" lengths.
     * Four - 3 1/2" x 28 3/4" (Q4) Piece on
     opposite sides of 42" strips to = two 98 1/2" lengths
     * Twenty-four - 3 1/2" squares (C4)
- Thirteen 2 1/2" wide strips. Nine for straight-grain binding, and four for Strip Sets 9 and 13.
- One 2" wide strip for Strip Set 25.
- Eleven 1 1/2" wide strips. Seven for Strip Sets 3, 14, and 23.
  From four remaining strips, cut:

* Fifty-six - 1 1/2" x 2 1/2" (A3, B3)
- Eleven 1" wide strips for Strip Sets 4, 5, 15, 16, and 24.

 From Fabric III, cut: (gold print)
- Four 5 1/2" wide strips for Strip Sets 8 and 9.
- Three 4 1/2" wide strips for Strip Sets 13, and 21.
- Seventeen 1 1/2" wide strips for Strip Sets 1, 2, 6, 7, 14, 15, 16, and 25.
- Four 1" wide strips for Strip Sets 10, 11, 12, and 22.

 From Fabric IV, cut: (light blue print)
- Four 4 1/2" wide strips. Three for Strip Sets 11, 22, and 27.
  From remaining strip, cut:
    * Ten - 1 1/2" x 4 1/2" (B5)
    * Eighteen - 1 1/2" x 3 1/2" (A1, B1, C1)
- Three 3 1/2" wide strips. From these, cut:
    * Sixty-two - 1 1/2" x 3 1/2" (add to A1, B1, C1)

 From Fabric V, cut: (medium blue print)
- Four 6 1/2" wide strips for Strip Sets 7 and 20.
- Four 5 1/2" wide strips for Strip Sets 6 and 19.
- Seven 3 1/2" wide strips. Three for Strip Sets 10, 12, and 26.
  From four remaining strips, cut:
    * Ninety - 1 1/2" x 3 1/2" (A2, B2, B8, C2)
- Seven 1 1/2" wide strips for Strip Sets 8, 9, 13, and 21.

From Fabric VI, cut: (medium green print)
- Twenty-two 1 1/2" wide strips for Strip Sets 3, 4, 5, 17, 18, 19, 20, 23, and 24.
- Three 1" wide strips. Two strips for Strip Sets 26, and 27.
  From remaining strip, cut:
    * Twenty - 1" x 1 1/2" (B7)

The Strip Sets...........

1. Refer to page 7 for strip piecing. Instructions are given under each strip set for the number of segments to cut. Strip sizes are also shown on each strip set illustration. We *strongly* suggest putting them in zip top bags and labeling each strip set with masking tape to avoid confusion.

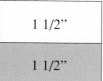
Strip Set 1. Make 6
Cut into 152 - 1 1/2"
segments.

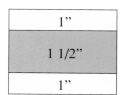
Strip Set 2. Make 2.
Cut into 40 - 1 1/2"
segments.

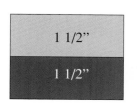
Strip Set 3. Make 2.
Cut into 32 - 1 1/2"
segments.

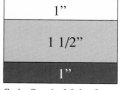
Strip Set 4. Make 2.
Cut into 32 - 1 1/2"
segments.

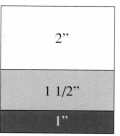
Strip Set 5. Make 2.
Cut into 32 - 1 1/2"
segments.

Strip Set 6. Make 2.
Cut into 32 - 1 1/2"
segments

Strip Set 7. Make 2.
Cut into 32 - 1 1/2"
segments.

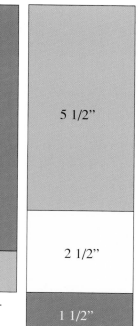
Strip Set 8. Make 2.
Cut into 48 - 1 1/2"
segments.

Strip Set 9. Make 2.
Cut into 32 - 1 1/2"
segments.

Strip Set 10. Make 1.
Cut into 28 - 1 1/2"
segments.

Strip Set 11. Make 1.
Cut into 18 - 1 1/2"
segments.

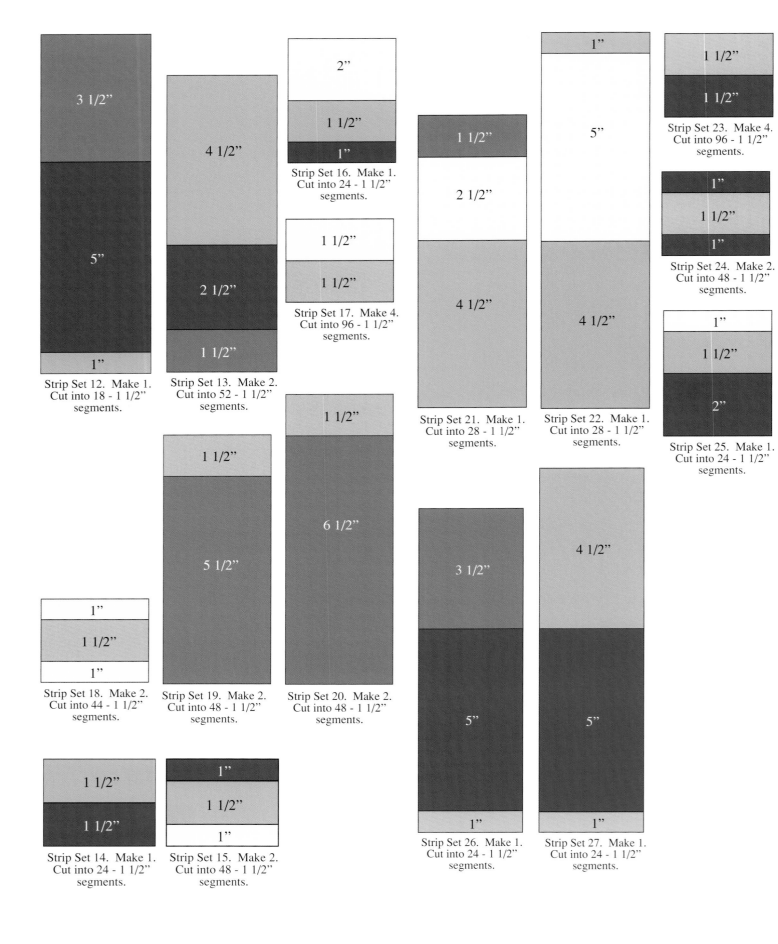

3 1/2"

5"

1"

Strip Set 12. Make 1.
Cut into 18 - 1 1/2"
segments.

4 1/2"

2 1/2"

1 1/2"

Strip Set 13. Make 2.
Cut into 52 - 1 1/2"
segments.

2"

1 1/2"

1"

Strip Set 16. Make 1.
Cut into 24 - 1 1/2"
segments.

1 1/2"

1 1/2"

Strip Set 17. Make 4.
Cut into 96 - 1 1/2"
segments.

1 1/2"

2 1/2"

4 1/2"

Strip Set 21. Make 1.
Cut into 28 - 1 1/2"
segments.

1"

5"

4 1/2"

Strip Set 22. Make 1.
Cut into 28 - 1 1/2"
segments.

1 1/2"

1 1/2"

Strip Set 23. Make 4.
Cut into 96 - 1 1/2"
segments.

1"

1 1/2"

1"

Strip Set 24. Make 2.
Cut into 48 - 1 1/2"
segments.

1"

1 1/2"

2"

Strip Set 25. Make 1.
Cut into 24 - 1 1/2"
segments.

1"

1 1/2"

1"

Strip Set 18. Make 2.
Cut into 44 - 1 1/2"
segments.

1 1/2"

5 1/2"

Strip Set 19. Make 2.
Cut into 48 - 1 1/2"
segments.

1 1/2"

6 1/2"

Strip Set 20. Make 2.
Cut into 48 - 1 1/2"
segments.

3 1/2"

5"

1"

Strip Set 26. Make 1.
Cut into 24 - 1 1/2"
segments.

4 1/2"

5"

1"

Strip Set 27. Make 1.
Cut into 24 - 1 1/2"
segments.

1 1/2"

1 1/2"

Strip Set 14. Make 1.
Cut into 24 - 1 1/2"
segments.

1"

1 1/2"

1"

Strip Set 15. Make 2.
Cut into 48 - 1 1/2"
segments.

Block A Assembly

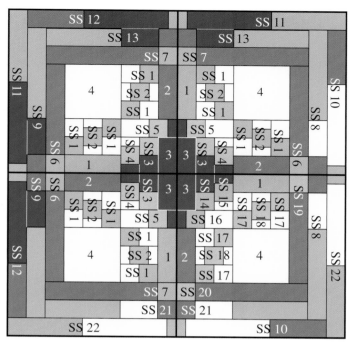

Block A. Make 4. When complete, block should measure 18 1/2" sq.

1. * *Please note that all strip sets in these instructions will be abbreviated (SS1 for Strip Set 1).* To assemble Block A, begin with the top left side. Join SS1, SS2, and SS1 in a vertical row. Refer to diagram above for correct placement of SS 1. Join Unit 4 to left side of these combined units, and Unit 2 to right side. For the mirror image on the right corner, refer to the diagram and join Unit 4 to the right side and Unit 1 to the left side of combined units. Join these two sections together.

2. For the center section, working toward the left, join Unit 3, SS3, and SS4 in a row; then add SS5 to top of row. Repeat this for the right side, checking for correct placement of units as they are a mirror image. Join SS1, SS2, and SS1 in a row as shown. Join Unit 1 to bottom of the row. Repeat for the right side, checking for correct placement of SS units. For the right side, join Unit 2 to the bottom. Join the combined Unit 3 sections together, joining the top section to the bottom section.

3. Again referring to diagram, join SS 6 to opposite sides of combined sections. Join two SS7's together and two SS13's as shown. Add them to top of combined units. Join SS9 to left side. Join SS8 and SS 10 together and add them to the right side of combined units. Join SS12 and SS11 together. Join them to top of combined units; then add SS11 to left side to complete the top section.

4. For bottom left section, beginning on the right side, join Unit 3, SS3, and SS4; then join SS 5 to bottom of these units. Join SS1, SS2, and SS 1 in a row. Add Unit 1 to right side and join these combined units to the bottom of SS 5 as shown. Once again join SS1, SS2, and SS1 in a row. Add Unit 4 to bottom and Unit 2 to top. Join this section to the Unit 3 section. Join SS6 to left side of combined units. Join SS7 and SS21 together and add them to bottom of combined units. Join SS9 and SS12 together. Add them to left side of combined units; then add SS22 to bottom.

5. To piece the bottom right section, begin by joining Unit 3, SS14, and SS15 together in a row; then add SS 16 to bottom of combined units. Join SS17, SS18, and SS17 in a row; then add Unit 1 to top of row. Join this section to the Unit 3 section. Again join SS17, SS18, and SS17 in a row, checking diagram for correct placement of SS units. Add Unit 4 to right side of combined units and Unit 2 to left side. Join these combined units to Unit 3 combined units. Join SS 19 to right side. Join SS 20 and

SS 21; then add them to the bottom of the combined units. Join SS8 to right side; then join SS10 to bottom. Join SS22 to right side to complete the bottom right section. Join the two sections together; then join the top and bottom together to complete the block. Make 4.

Block B Assembly

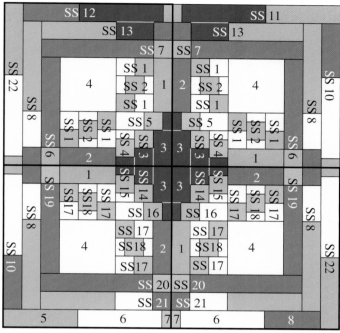

Block B. Make 10. When complete, block should measure 18 1/2" sq.

1. This section is a mirror image of the top of Block A, except for the positions of Unit 1 and Unit 2. Refer to the diagram above for correct placement of these units. Refer to Step 2 for Block A to piece the Unit 3 sections. Once again, the only difference is the position of units 1 and 2. Join the two top sections together. Strip sets 6 and 7 are the same. Join them to top section.

2. Join the two SS13 units together as shown and add them to the top of the block. Join SS 8 to left side as shown. Join SS8 and SS 10; then add them to right side of section. Join SS12 and SS11. Add them to top of combined unit section. Join SS22 to left side to complete the top section.

3. For the left bottom section, join Unit 3, SS14, and SS15; then add SS16 to bottom. Join SS17, SS18 and SS17 as shown. Add Unit 1 to top of combined strip set units. Join this section to the Unit 3 section. Join SS17, SS18, and SS17. Join Unit 4 to left side of combined strip sets, and Unit 2 to right side. Join this completed section to other joined units as shown. Join Unit 19 to left side of combined units. Join SS20 and SS21 as shown. Join them to bottom of section. Join SS8 and SS10. Add them to left side of section.

4. The bottom right section is the same as Block A. Refer to Block A, Step 5 for instructions. The only difference is the position of units 1 and 2. Refer to the diagram above for correct placement of these units. Complete the section through SS8. Join the right and left sections together; then join SS10 to left side. Join units 5, 6, 7, 7, 6, and 8 in a long horizontal row. Add to bottom of combined bottom sections; then add SS 22 to right side to complete the bottom section. Join the top and bottom sections together to complete the block. Make 10.

Block C Assembly

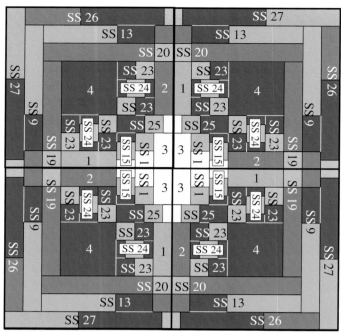

Block C. Make 6. When complete, block should measure 18 1/2" sq.

1. To assemble Block C, begin with the top left side. Join SS23, SS24, and SS23 in a vertical row. Refer to diagram above for correct placement of SS 23. Join Unit 4 to left side of these combined units, and Unit 2 to right side. For the mirror image on the right corner, refer to the diagram and join Unit 4 to the right side and Unit 1 to the left side of combined units. Join these two sections together.

2. For the center section, working toward the left, join Unit 3, SS1, and SS15 in a row; then add SS25 to top of row. Repeat this for the right side, checking for correct placement of units as they are a mirror image. Join SS23, SS2,4 and SS23 in a row as shown. Join Unit 1 to bottom of the row. Repeat for the right side, checking for correct placement of SS units. For the right side, join Unit 2 to the bottom. Join the combined Unit 3 sections together, joining the top section to the bottom section.

3. Again referring to diagram, join SS 19 to opposite sides of the combined sections. Join two SS20's together and two SS13's as shown. Add them to top of combined units. Join SS9 to opposite sides. Join SS26 to right side of combined units. Join SS26 and SS27 together and add them to top of combined top section; then join SS 27 to left side. Make twelve of these 1/2 blocks. To piece together, turn six of them 180° and piece the block together, matching seams. Make 6 blocks.

5. Join the top and bottom sections to complete the block. Make 6.

Quilt Assembly

1. The quilt will be assembled in five rows, beginning at the top. Join two Block B's together; then add Block A to opposite sides of the combined Block B's. Make two of these rows.

2. For row 2, join two Block C's together; then add Block B to opposite sides of the combined Block B's. Make three of these rows.

3. Refer to quilt diagram on page 71 and join the rows together as shown. Join pieced sashing 2 to top and bottom of quilt top; then add pieced sashing 1 to opposite sides. Join pieced border 3 to top and bottom of quilt top; then join pieced border 4 to opposite sides to complete the quilt top.

4. Mary quilted a feather design in the border, "ditched" the patchwork and quilted small feathery designs in the block centers and corners.

5. Use the nine 2 1/2" wide strips of Fabric II and make straight-grain binding. Refer to page 12 for instructions, and bind your quilt.

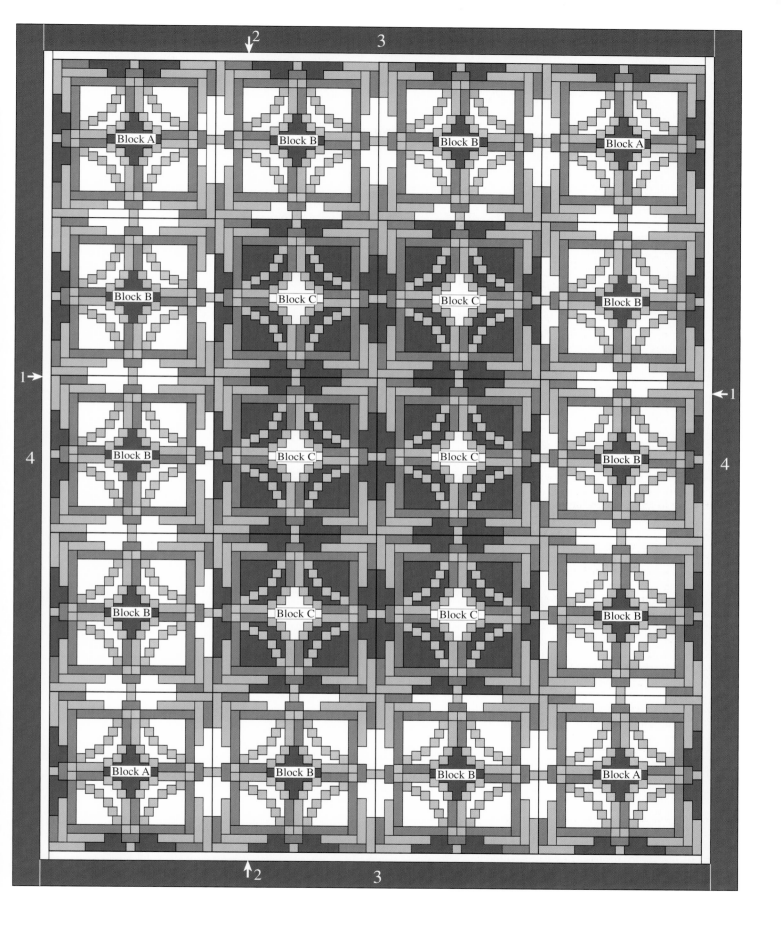

Pennsylvania Dutch Table Runner

Table Runner finishes to: 25" x 69".
Techniques used: diagonal corners, diagonal ends and triangle-squares.

Materials

	Fabric I (light tan print)	Need 42"	1 3/8 yards
	Fabric II (bright red print)	Need 7"	1/4 yard
	Fabric III (dark red print)	Need 14 1/2"	1/2 yard
	Fabric IV (dark green print)	Need 21 7/8"	3/4 yard
	Fabric V (medium green print)	Need 6 1/8"	1/4 yard
	Fabric VI (white print)	Need 6 1/2"	1/4 yard
	Fabric VI (bright yellow print)	Need 1 3/4"	1/8 yard
	Backing		2 1/8 yards

Cutting

From Fabric I, cut: (light tan print)
- Two 5 1/2" wide strips. From these, cut:
  * Eight - 5 1/2" squares (A21, A56)
  * Twelve - 1 1/2" x 5 1/2" (A9, A45, A59)
  * Four - 1 3/8" x 5 1/2" (A6)
- Stack the following cuts:
  * Four - 2" x 2 1/2" (A26)
  * Sixteen - 1 1/2" x 2 1/2" (A35, A36a, A42, B3)
- One 4 1/2" wide strip. From this, cut:
  * Four - 4 1/2" x 8 1/2" (B1)
  * Four - 3 5/8" x 4 1/2" (A37)
  * Four - 2 1/2" x 4 1/2" (A44)
  * Two - 1 1/4" x 4 1/2" (A11)
  * Two - 2" x 9 1/2" (B17) Stack this cut.
- One 4" wide strip. From this, cut:
  * Four - 4" x 5 5/8" (A32)
  * Two - 3 1/2" x 7 1/4" (A7)
- One 3" wide strip. From this, cut:
  * Sixteen - 2 1/2" x 3 1/2" (A17, A40, A48, B7)
- One 2 7/8" wide strip. From this, cut:
  * Four - 2 7/8" squares (B5, B14) Cut in half diagonally.
  * Four - 1 1/2" x 2 3/8" (A39a)
  * Four - 1 1/2" x 2" (A27)
  * Four - 1" x 8 1/2" (A22) Stack this cut.
- Four 2 1/2" wide strips. From this, cut:
  * Forty - 2 1/2" squares (A13a, A20, A38a, A54, A55a, B1b, B13)
  * Forty-eight - 1 1/8" squares (A3a, A4a)
- One 1 7/8" wide strip. From this, cut:
  * Four - 1 7/8" squares (B18a)
  * Four - 1 5/8" x 6" (A23)
  * Four - 1" x 1 1/2" (A24)

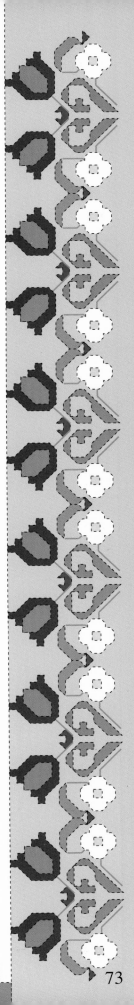

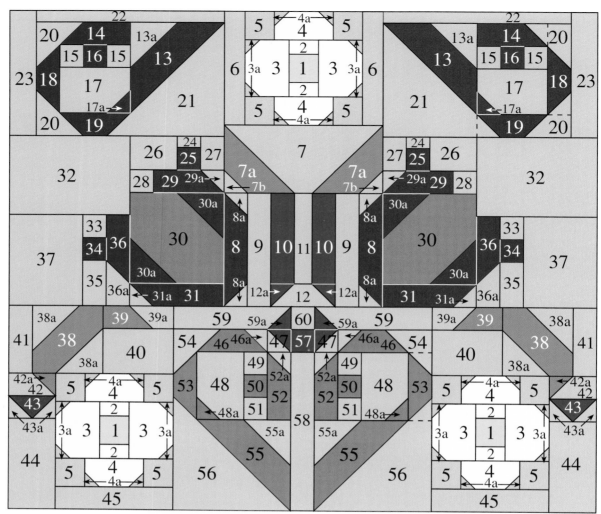

Block A. Make 2. When completed, block should measure 22 1/2" x 25 1/2"

- One 1 3/4" wide strip. From this, cut:
  - * Twenty-four - 1 3/4" squares (A5)
- Four 1 1/2" wide strips. From these, cut:
  - * Two - 1 1/2" x 8 1/2" (B16)
  - * Two - 1 1/2" x 7 1/2" (A58)
  - * Four - 1 1/2" x 3 1/2" (A41)
  - * Two - 1 1/2" x 3 1/4" (A12)
  - * Eighty-six - 1 1/2" squares (A7b, A8a, A15, A28, A29a, A31a, A33, A43a, A46a, A47, A49, A51, A52a, A60, B2a, B4a, B8, B10)

From Fabric II, cut: (bright red print)
- One 4 1/2" wide strip. From this, cut:
  - * Four - 4 1/2" x 5 1/2 (A55)
  - * Four - 4 1/2" squares (A30)
- Two 1 1/2" wide strips. From these, cut:
  - * Four - 1 1/2" x 4 1/2" (A46)
  - * Eight - 1 1/2" x 3 1/2" (A52, A53)
  - * Eight - 1 1/2" squares (A48a, A50)

From Fabric III, cut: (dark red print)
- Two 4 1/2" wide strips. From these, cut:
  - * Four - 4 1/2" x 5 1/2" (A13)
  - * Four - 4 1/2" squares (B1a)
  - * Twelve - 1 1/2" x 4 1/2" (A18, A19, A31)
  - * Eight - 1 1/2" x 5 1/2" (A8, B6) Stack this cut.
- From scrap, cut:
  - * Twenty - 1 1/2" squares (A16, A17a, A25, A34, B7a, B9)
- One 2 1/2" wide strip. From this, cut:
  - * Eight - 2 1/2" squares (A30a)

- * Four - 1 1/2" squares (add to 1 1/2" sq. above)
- Two 1 1/2" wide strips. From these, cut:
  - * Twenty - 1 1/2" x 3 1/2" (A14, A29, A36, B11, B12)

From Fabric IV, cut: (dark green print)
- 1/2 yard for bias binding.
- One 3 7/8" wide strip. From this, cut:
  - * Two - 3 7/8" squares (B18) Cut in half diagonally
- Stack the following cuts:
  - * Four - 1 1/2" x 4 1/2" (A10)
  - * Eight - 1 1/2" x 2 1/2" (A43, B4)
  - * Fourteen - 1 1/2" squares (A12a, A47, A57, A59a)

From Fabric V, cut: (medium green print)
- One 3 1/2" wide strip. From this, cut:
  - * Eight - 3 1/2" squares (A7a, A38)
  - * Eight - 1 1/2" x 3 1/2" (B2, B15)
- One 2 5/8" wide strip. From this, cut:
  - * Four - 1 1/2" x 2 5/8" (A39)
  - * Four - 2 1/8" squares (B1c)
  - * Eight - 1 1/2" squares (A42a, B12a)

From Fabric VI, cut: (white print)
- One 3" wide strip. From this, cut:
  - * Twelve - 2 3/8" x 3" (A3)
- Two 1 3/4" wide strips. From these, cut:
  - * Twelve - 1 3/4" x 3" (A4)
  - * Twelve - 1 1/8" x 1 3/4" (A2)

74

From Fabric VII, cut: (bright yellow print)
- One 1 3/4" wide strip. From this, cut:
  * Six - 1 3/4" squares (A1)

Block A Assembly

1. Use diagonal corner technique to make six of units 3 and 4. Use this technique to make two each of units 7, 8, 10, 13, 29, 30, 31, 38, 42, 43, 46,48, 52, 55, and 59. Make one of Unit 12.
2. Use diagonal end technique to make mirror image units 36 and 39 as shown below.

Making mirror image Unit 36

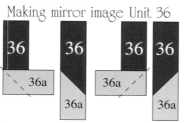

Making mirror image Unit 39

3. To make the Unit 47 triangle squares, refer to illustrations and instructions below. Refer to block diagram frequently as most of the diagonal corners are mirror images. Make sure that the corners are placed correctly for mirror image units.

4. For the flowers, join units 2-1-and 2 in a row. Join Unit 3 to opposite sides of the row. Join units 5-4-and 5. Make 2

for each flower. Join to top and bottom of flowers.

5. To make the combined units at the bottom of the page, refer to the diagrams and step-by-step instructions for making the combined units. As they are mirror images, refer to block diagram often for correct placement of mirror image units.

6. Combined units 46-56 are made in the same way as the combined units shown below. To make the mirror image red heart, begin by joining units 49, 50 and 51 in a row. Join Unit 52 to one side of combined units, and Unit 48 to the other side. Join Unit 53 to Unit 48. Unit 53 will be all red. Join units 46 and 47, being careful to turn Unit 47 in the right direction. Join these two combined units to the top of other heart combined units as shown; then join diagonal corner Unit 54. If you are using a lighter fabric for Unit 54, do not trim the seam as the darker fabric may show through.

7. Unit 55 should be ready to join with diagonal corner 55a in place. Join Unit 55 to bottom of other combined units. Join diagonal corner Unit 56 along side of heart as shown. Trim seam and press. Make a mirror image of the red heart.

8. To assemble the block, join Unit 6 to opposite sides of one flower; then join Unit 7 to bottom of flower. Join units 10, 11, and 10 in a row; then add Unit 12 to bottom of this row. Refer to block diagram for correct position of mirror image units. Join units 8 and 9 as shown. Add them to opposite sides of combined 10-12 units; then add these combined units to bottom of Unit 7.

9. Join units 24 and 25. Add Unit 27 to one side of the combined units, and Unit 26 to the other side. Join units 28 and 29. Add them to bottom of combined units 24-27. Join units 30 and 31. Add them to bottom of other combined units. Join units 33, 34 and 35 in a vertical row; then join Unit 36 to one side of row and Unit 37 to other side. Join Unit 32 to top. Add these combined units to the tulip as shown. Join combined units 13-23 (previously made) to top of tulip. Join the mirror image tulips to opposite sides of the flower section. Set aside.

10. For bottom of block, join units 39 and 40. Join units 41 and 38. Join these two combined unit sections together as shown. Join units 42, 43 and 44 in a vertical row. Join Unit 45 to bottom of remaining flowers. Add combined units 42-44 to side of flower; then join combined units 38-41 to the top. Join units 57 and 58. Join the two mirror image heart sections (previously made) to opposite sides of combined 57-58 units. Join units 59, 60, and 59 in a row as shown. Join to top of heart, matching seams. Add the flower combination to opposite sides of heart, making sure that mirror image units are placed correctly. Join the bottom heart section to the top tulip section to complete the block. Make 2.

Making Unit A47

Place 1 1/2" squares of Fabrics I and IV right sides together, raw edges matching, and stitch a diagonal as shown. Trim seam and press.

Making units A13-A23

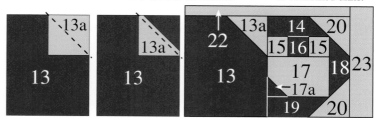

Join units 15-16 and 15 in a row and add them to Unit 14. Join diagonal corner 17a to Unit 17 as shown; then join Unit 17 to combined 14-16 units.

Join Unit 18 to right side of other combined units; then add Unit 19 to bottom.

Join Unit 20 to opposite sides of combined units.

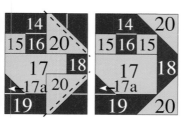

Trim Unit 20 seam and press.

Join Unit 13a to Unit 13. Trim seam and press. Join to left side of combined units 14-20 as shown. Add Unit 22 to top and Unit 23 to right side as shown.

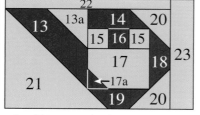

Join Unit 21 to left side of combined units. Trim seam and press in place.
Units A46-A56 are made in the same way, along with units B7-B13.

Block B Assembly

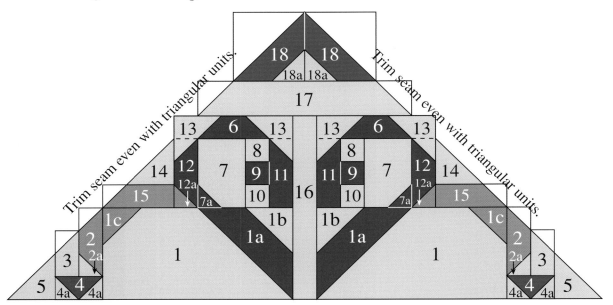

Block B. Make 2. When completed, bottom of triangle should be 25 1/2" long.
Triangle should be 13" deep

1. Use diagonal corner technique to make two each of mirror image units 1, 2, 4, 7 12, and 18.. To make Unit 1, join diagonal corner 1a. Trim seam and press. Join diagonal corner 1b. Do not trim seam as 1b is a lighter fabric and if seam is trimmed, the darker fabric may show through. Join Unit 1c. Trim seam and press.

2. To make combined units which comprise the top of the heart, refer to Block B diagram above frequently for correct placement of mirror image units. Begin by joining units 8, 9, and 10 in a vertical row. Join Unit 7 to one side of combined units, and Unit 11 to the other side. Please note that Unit 11 will be all dark red. Join Unit 12 to side of Unit 7; then join Unit 6 to top. Add diagonal corners Unit 13 as shown. Press.

3. Unit 18 will be a triangle. Add diagonal corner 18a to bottom of triangle as shown.

4. When joining the units, keep in mind that we are building a triangle from the base up. To begin, join units 2 and 3, matching them at the bottom raw edges. Add Unit 4 to bottom of the combined 2-3 units. Join triangle Unit 5 to side as shown so that it lines up on the bottom with Unit 4. Join Unit 1 to side of combined units 2-5. Join triangle Unit 14 to Unit 15, lining up the flat side of the triangle with one short side of Unit 15. Join the top part of the heart (previously made) to combined units 14-15 as shown. Bottom of heart section should line up with sides of combined 14-15 units. Join the two heart sections to opposite side of Unit 16.

5. Center Unit 17, and join it to the top of the heart section. Join the two mirror image Unit 18's together and center them on the top of Unit 17. Using the Unit 5 and Unit 14 triangles as a guide, lay your ruler down and trim the 45° angles on both sides of the block as shown.

3. Use the 1/2 yard piece of Fabric IV to cut 2 1/2" wide bias binding and bind the table runner.

Table Runner Assembly

1. Join the two Block A's together as shown in diagram at right; then add Block B to opposite ends.

2. Mary did some great things with the quilting on this piece. She used gold metallic thread and stitched a flower, inside the flower blocks. She also used the metallic on the tulips, stitching a floral shape inside of the tulips. The patchwork was "ditched", and she used her swirl design to stipple the background.

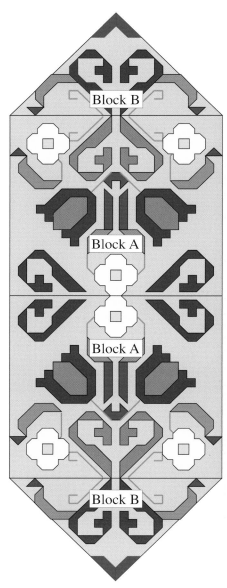

Pennsylvania Dutch Tablecloth

*Tablecloth finishes to: 65" square.
90" from tip to tip.
Techniques used: diagonal corners,
diagonal ends and triangle-squares.*

Materials

☐ Fabric I (ivory with metallic gold print) Need 99 1/4"
3 yards

■ Fabric II (dark green print) Need 76 3/8"
2 1/4 yards

▨ Fabric III (medium green print) Need 11 1/4"
1/2 yard

▨ Fabric IV (light green textured print) Need 16 3/4"
5/8 yard

■ Fabric V (burgundy print) Need 52 7/8"
1 5/8 yards

▨ Fabric VI (bright red print) Need 16 1/2"
5/8 yard

▨ Fabric VII (dark gold print) Need 10 3/4"
3/8 yard

▨ Fabric VIII (light gold print) Need 21 1/2"
3/4 yard

Backing 8 1/4 yards

Cutting

☐ **From Fabric I, cut: (ivory with metallic gold)**
- One 11 1/2" wide strip. From this, cut:
  * Four - 2 1/2" x 11 1/2" (A57)
  * Four - 1 1/2" x 10 3/4" (A19)
  * Four - 2 1/2" x 9 1/2" (A56)
  * Four - 2" x 9 1/2" (D17)
  * Eight - 1" x 8" (A16)
- Two 8 1/2" wide strips. From these, cut:
  * Eight - 4 1/2" x 8 1/2" (D11)
  * Eight - 4" x 8 1/2" (A20, A22)
  * Four - 1 1/2" x 8 1/2" (D16)
  * Four - 1 1/2" x 8" (A21)
- Two 5 1/2" wide strips. From these, cut:
  * Four - 5 1/2" squares (C12)
  * Eight - 1 3/4" x 5 1/2" (C15)
  * Eight - 1 1/2" x 5 1/2" (C6)
  * Four - 1" x 5 1/2" (C13)
  * Sixteen - 1 1/2" x 5 1/4" (A14)
  * Forty - 1" squares (A1b, C1b) Stack this cut
- Two 4 1/2" wide strips. From these, cut:
  * Eight - 4 1/2" squares (B16)
  * Eight - 2" x 4 1/2" (C2)
  * Four - 1 3/4" x 4 1/2" (A2)
  * Eight - 2 3/4" x 4 1/4" (A29, A52)
- Three 3 1/2" wide strips. From these, cut:
  * Twenty-four - 3 1/2" squares (A15, C7)
  * Eight - 2 1/2" x 3 1/2" (D1)
  * Two - 1 1/2" x 3 1/2" (C25)
  * Four - 3" squares (A35)
  * Eight - 1 3/4" squares (A18, C5) Stack this cut.
- One 3 1/4" wide strip. From this, cut:
  * Eight - 3 1/4" squares (A9, A48)
- One 2 7/8" wide strip. From this, cut:
  * Eight - 2 7/8" squares (D3, D13) Cut in half diagonally to = sixteen triangles.
  * Four - 2 3/4" squares (A49)
  * Sixteen - 1" squares (add to 1" squares above)
- One 2 1/2" wide strip. From this, cut:
  * Sixteen - 2 1/2" squares (D9, D11c)
- Four 2" wide strips. From these, cut:
  * Forty - 2" sq. (A6a, A6b, A8a, A8b, A10a, A23, A50)
  * Eight - 2" x 2 1/4" (A27, A34)
  * Sixteen - 1 3/4" x 2" (A37, A38, A43, A44)
  * Sixteen - 1 1/4" x 2" (A26, A33, A39, A45)
- One 1 7/8" wide strip. From this, cut:
  * Eight - 1 7/8" squares (D18a)
  * Eight - 1 3/4" squares (add to 1 3/4" squares above)
  * Eight - 1 1/2" x 1 3/4" (A36, A42)
- Two 1 3/4" wide strips. From these, cut:
  * Four - 1 3/4" x 5 3/4" (A3)
  * Eight - 1 3/4" x 4 3/4" (A5, A7)
  * Eight - 1 1/4" x 2 3/4" (A28, A51)
- Eight 1 1/2" wide strips. From these, cut:
  * Four - 1 1/2" x 7 1/2" (C3)
  * Four - 1 1/2" x 3 1/4" (A4)
  * Twenty-eight - 1 1/2" x 2 1/2" (B35, C8, C22, C24, D15)
  * 119 - 1 1/2" squares (A12b, A25b, B34, C10, C14a, C17a, C18a, C19, C23, D2a, D5, D7a, D10, D12a, D14a)
  * Eight - 1" squares (add to 1" squares above)
- Five 1 1/4" wide strips. From these, cut:
  * 148 - 1 1/4" squares (A1a, A11a, A12a, A24a, A25a, A32, A55, B1c, C1a)

■ **From Fabric II, cut: (dark green print)**
- Three 5 1/2" wide strips. From these, cut:
  * Eight - 5 1/2" x 6 1/4" (B12)
  * Eight - 3 1/2" x 5 1/2" (B24)
  * Eight - 1 3/4" x 5 1/2" (B15)
  * Four - 1" x 5 1/2" (B13)
  * Eight - 2 1/2" x 4 1/2" (B25)
  * Four - 2" squares (A25)
- Four 4 1/2" wide strips. From these, cut:
  * Eight - 4 1/2" x 6 1/4" (B46)
  * Eight - 4 1/2" squares (B48)
  * Eight - 4 1/4" x 4 1/2" (B6)
  * Eight - 2" x 4 1/2" (B3)
  * Eight - 1 3/4" x 4 1/2" (B28)
  * Four - 1 1/4" x 4 1/2" (B2)
  * Twenty-four - 1 1/2" squares (B4a, B9, B14a, B17a, B18a, B20, B26a, B27a, B29b, B35b, B40a, B42, B44, B45a, C20, C23, C24a, D2b)
- Two 3 3/4" wide strips. From these, cut:
  * Eight - 3 3/4" squares (B31)
  * Eight - 2 1/2" x 3 1/2" (B39)
  * Four - 1" x 1 1/2" (B5)
- Three 2 3/4" wide strips. From this, cut:
  * Eight - 2 3/4" x 6 3/4" (B32)
  * Eight - 2 1/2" x 2 3/4" (B30)
  * Eight - 1 1/2" x 2 3/4" (B36)
- Three 2 1/2" wide strips. From these, cut:
  * Sixteen - 2 1/2" squares (B23, B46b)
  * Eight - 2 1/2" x 2 1/2" (B37)
  * Twenty-four - 1 1/2" x 2 1/2" (B7, B11, B19)
  * Eighteen - 1 1/4" squares (B1a)
- One 2 1/8" wide strip. From this, cut:
  * Eight - 2 1/8" squares (D11a)
  * Eight - 1 1/4" x 2" (A24)
  * Thirty - 1" squares (B1b)
- Eight 1 1/2" wide strips. From these, cut:
  * Four - 1 1/2" x 7 1/2" (B47)
  * Eighteen - 1 1/2" x 3 1/2" (C21, D4, D12)
  * Twenty - 1 1/2" x 1 3/4" (B29a, B33, B35a)
  * 118 - 1 1/2" squares (add to 1 1/2" squares above)
- Two 1 1/4" wide strips. From these, cut:
  * Eight - 1 1/4" x 5 3/4" (B41)
  * Thirty - 1 1/4" squares (add to B1a above)
- Two 1" wide strips. From these, cut:
  * Sixty-six - 1" squares (add to 1" squares above)

▨ **From Fabric III, cut: (medium green print)**
- One 3 1/4" wide strip. From this, cut:
  * Eight - 3 1/4" squares (A17)
- One 2" wide strip. From this, cut:
  * Sixteen - 2" squares (A6b, A8b, A9a)

78

- Four 1 1/2" wide strips. From these, cut:
  * Sixteen - 1 1/2" x 5 1/2" (B14, C14)
  * Sixteen - 1 1/2" x 2 1/2" (B29, D14)

From Fabric IV, cut: (light green print)
- One 4 1/2" wide strip. From this, cut:
  * Eight - 4 1/2" squares (B46a)
  * Twelve - 1 1/2" squares (B36a, B43)
- One 3 3/4" wide strip. From this, cut:
  * Eight - 3 3/4" squares (C4)
  * Eight - 1 1/2" x 3 3/4" (B4)
- Two 2" wide strips. From these, cut:
  * Eight - 2" x 4 3/4" (A6, A8)
  * Eight - 2" x 2 3/4" (B3a)
  * Eight - 1 3/4" squares (B39a)
  * Four - 1 1/2" squares (add to 1 1/2" squares above)
- Three 1 1/2" wide strips. From these, cut:
  * Eight - 1 1/2" x 5 3/4" (B40)
  * Eight - 1 1/2" x 3 1/2" (B45)
  * Eight - 1 1/2" x 2 1/2" (B38)

From Fabric V, cut: (burgundy print)
- One twenty-seven x 42" strip for 2 1/2" wide bias binding.
- One 3 7/8" wide strip. From this, cut:
  * Four - 3 7/8" squares (D18) Cut in half diagonally.
  * Eight - 2 1/2" squares (C16a)
  * Twelve - 1 1/4" squares (A1c, C1c) Stack this cut.
- Two 2 3/4" wide strips. From these, cut:
  * Sixteen - 2 3/4" squares (A10b, A10c)
  * Eight - 1 1/2" x 2 1/2" (C11)
  * Sixteen - 1 1/4" x 2 1/4" (A11)
- Two 2" wide strips. From these, cut:
  * Sixteen - 2" x 2 1/4" (A12)
  * Sixteen - 2" squares (A10a)
  * Twelve - 1 1/4" squares (add to 1 1/4" squares above)
- Two 1 3/4" wide strips. From these, cut:
  * Sixteen - 1 3/4" x 5 1/4" (A13)
- Six 1 1/2" wide strips. From these, cut:
  * Four - 1 1/2" x 20 1/2" (A59)
  * Four - 1 1/2" x 19 1/2" (A58)
  * Four - 1 1/2" x 5 1/2" (C18)
  * Four - 1 1/2" x 4 1/2" (C17)
  * Sixteen - 1 1/2" squares (C6a, C9)
  * Eight - 1 1/4" squares (add to 1 1/4" squares above)

From Fabric VI, cut: (bright red print)
- One 4 1/2" wide strip. From this, cut:
  * Four - 4 1/2" squares (C16)
  * Eight - 1 1/2" x 4 1/2" (B17)
  * Six - 1 1/2" squares (B7a, B8, B21, B23a) Stack this cut.
- Three 2 1/2" wide strips. From these, cut:
  * Forty-eight - 2 1/2" squares (B1, B16a)
- Three 1 1/2" wide strips. From these, cut:
  * Eight - 1 1/2" x 5 1/2" (B18)
  * Sixteen - 1 1/2" x 2 1/2" (B10, B22)
  * Twenty-six - 1 1/2" squares (add to 1 1/2" sq. above)

From Fabric VII, cut: (dark gold print)
- Two 2 3/4" wide strips. From these, cut:
  * Sixteen - 2 3/4" squares (A31, A54)
  * Eight - 1 1/4" x 2 3/4" (A30, A53)
  * Eight - 2 1/4" squares (A35a)
  * Eight - 1 1/4" x 2" (A40, A46)
- Two 2" wide strips. From these, cut:
  * Eight - 2" x 3" (A41, A47)
  * Sixteen - 2" squares (A27b, A34b, A48a)
  * Eight - 1 3/4" squares (A27a, A34a)
  * Eleven - 1 1/4" squares (A36a, A37a, A38a, A39a, A42a, A43a, A44a, A45a)

- One 1 1/4" wide strip. From this, cut:
  * Twenty-nine - 1 1/4" squares (add to 1 1/4" sq. above)

From Fabric VIII, cut: (light gold print)
- One 4 1/2" wide strip. From this, cut:
  * Eight - 4 1/2" squares (D11b)
  * Twenty-four - 1 1/2" x 4 1/2" (B26, B27, D8)
  * Sixteen - 1 1/2" squares (D1a, D6) Stack this cut.
- Two 3 1/2" wide strips. From these, cut:
  * Eight - 3 1/2" x 7" (A10)
  * Sixteen - 1 1/2" x 3 1/2" (D2, D7)
- Four 2 1/2" wide strips. From these, cut:
  * Fifty-six - 2 1/2" squares (A1, B1, B25a, C1)

Block A Assembly

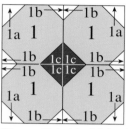

Flower Unit A1. Make 4
When completed, unit
should measure 4 1/2" sq.

Step 1

Place 2"
squares
of Fabrics I
and V right
sides together
and stitch
diagonally
down the
center.
Trim seam
and press.
Make 2.

Step 2

Use triangle-square Unit A10a
as a diagonal corner and place
as shown, raw edges matching.
Stitch a diagonal seam. Trim
seam and press. Place A10b
as shown. Stitch diagonal
and trim seam.

1. Refer to the diagram at left and make the flower as show, using diagonal corners 1a, 1b, and 1c. Refer to block diagram on page 80, and join Unit 2 to top of flower; then add Unit 3 to left side.

2. Refer to diagram of Unit 10a below left and Units A6 and A8. Place 2" squares of Fabric I and III right sides together as shown in diagram, and stitch a diagonal down the center as shown. Open, trim seam and press. Use this as diagonal corners for units A6 and A8.

3. Use diagonal corner technique to make the following units that are not illustrated: 9, 11, 12, 24, 25, 27, 31, 32, 34, 35, 36, 37, 38, 39, 42, 43, 44, 45, 48, 54, and 55.

4. Join units 5 and 6; then add Unit 4 to left side. Join units 7 and 8; then add Unit 9 to bottom of these combined units. Join these units to right side of flower. Refer to the Step 2 diagram on bottom left and the other illustrations on page 80. These are step-by-step illustrations and instructions for making the tulip. Follow the drawings closely. You may learn a few, new quick piecing techniques. There are two tulips, one of which is mirror imaged. Refer frequently to Block A diagram for correct placement of the tulip units.

5. Join the mirror imaged tulip to Unit 22; then join this tulip section to bottom of flower section as shown. Join the other tulip to Unit 20 and set aside.

6. To make combined units 29-32, join units 29 and 30 together; then add diagonal corner unit 31 to the top sides of both units. Trim seam and press. Join Unit 32 as shown and press. Refer to combined units 52-55. This combined unit is made the same way.

7. Join units 50 and 24 as shown. Make a vertical row of units 49, combined 50/24, 51 and combined units 52-55. Set this section aside.

8. Please note that units 27 and 34 are made the same way. Diagonal corners are added in alphabetical order. To make Section 2, begin by making a vertical

Units A6 and A8

Units A6 and A8
are made the same
as A10a.

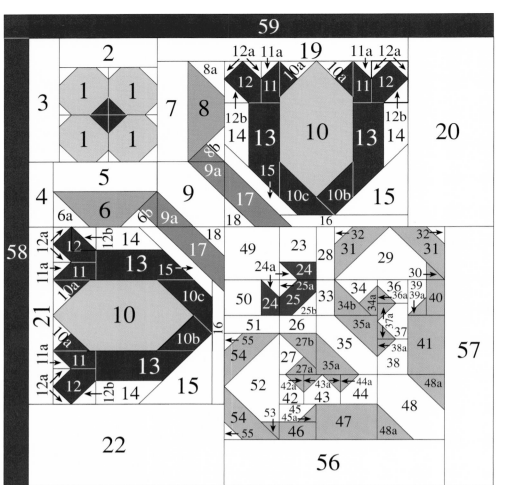
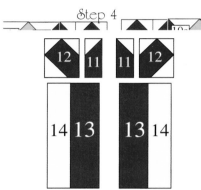

Use remaining triangle-square Unit A10a as diagonal corner and place as shown. Stitch a diagonal seam. Trim seam and press.
Place diagonal corner A10c as shown, raw edges matching. Stitch a diagonal seam, trim and press.

Step 4

Join units A13 and A14 as shown. Join units A11 and A12, making certain that mirror image units are placed correctly.

Block A. Make 4. When complete, block should measure 20 1/2" square.

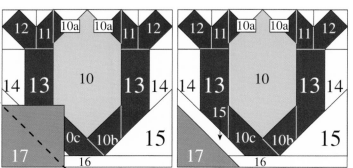

Step 5

Join mirror image combined units 11-14 to opposite sides of Unit A10.

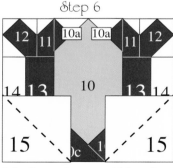

Step 6

Join diagonal corners A15 as shown. Stitch diagonal, and press.

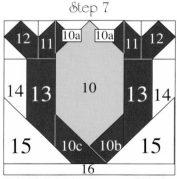

Step 7

Join Unit A16 to bottom of block as shown.

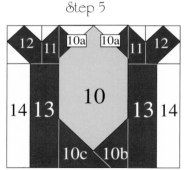

Step 8

Join diagonal corner Unit 17. Trim seam and press.

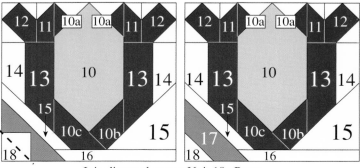

Step 9

Join diagonal corner Unit 18. Press.

Block B Assembly Continued

row. Join units 23, 24, 25, 26, and 27. Join units 28 and combined units 29-32. Join units 33 and 34; then add Unit 35 to bottom of these combined units. Join units 36, 37, and 38 in a vertical row; then add them to the right side of combined units 33-35. Join units 39 and 40; then add Unit 41 to bottom. Join this row to right side of combined units 33-38; then add combined units 28-32 to the top. Join the vertical row of units 23-27 to left side of other joined units to complete Section 2.

9. For Section 3 of heart, begin by joining units 42, 43, and 44 in a horizontal row. Join units 45 and 46; then add Unit 47 to right side. Join these combined units to the 42-44 horizontal row. Add Unit 48 to right side, matching seams to complete Section 3.

10. Join Sections 2 and 3 together as shown; then add Section 1 to left side to complete the heart. Join Unit 56 to bottom; then add Unit 57 to right side. Join Unit 58 to left side of block; then add Unit 59 to top to complete the block. Make 4.

Block B Assembly

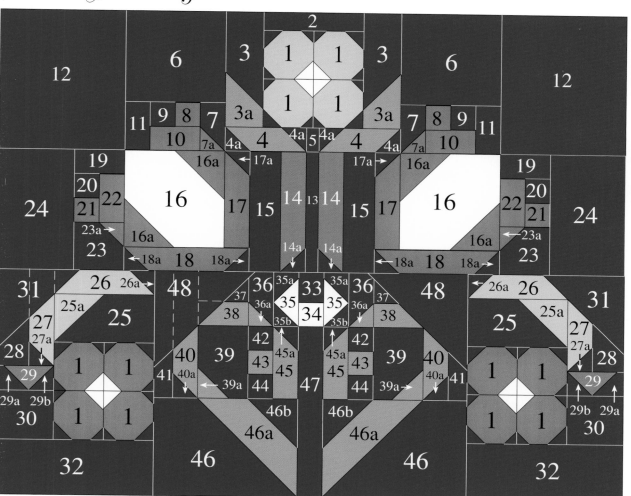

Making Unit B35

Block B. Make 4. When complete, block should measure 20 1/2" x 25 1/2".

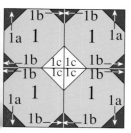

Flower Unit B1 for gold and red flower. Make 4 gold and 8 red. When completed, unit should measure 4 1/2" square.

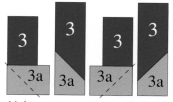

Making mirror image Unit B3

1. To make Block B, begin by making the flowers, shown on the left. Use diagonal corner technique to make the number and colors shown. For Block B, use diagonal corner technique to make two each of mirror image units 4, 7, 14, 16, 17, 18, 23, 25, 26, 27, 29, 36, 39, 40, 45, and 46. Use diagonal end technique to make mirror image units 3 and 35 as shown in illustrations.

2. Please note that assembly instructions and diagrams are shown on page 82 for making the top of the heart. This is a mirror image combined unit, so refer frequently to Block B diagram above for correct placement of mirror image units.

3. To assemble the block, begin by joining Unit 2 to top of one completed gold flower; then add mirror image Unit 3 to opposite sides as shown. Join mirror image Unit 4 to opposite sides of Unit 5; then add to bottom of flower. Join units 8 and 9; then add Unit 10 to bottom of these combined units. Join Unit 11 to one side and Unit 7 to the other, referring to the block diagram for correct placement of mirror image units. Join Unit 6 to the top of combined units 7-11; then add Unit 12 to side as shown. Join these combine units to opposite sides of the flower to complete the top section of the block.

4. For the tulip section, join units 20 and 21; then add Unit 22 to side of these combined units. Join Unit 19

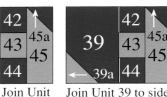

Join units 42, 43 and 44 in a row.

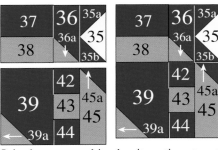

Join Unit 45 to side.

Join Unit 39 to side.

Join units 37 and 38.

Join units 35 and 36.

Join the two combined unit sections together.

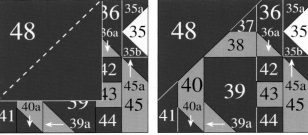

Join the two combined unit sections together.

Join units 40 and 41.

Join units 40 and 41 to side of other combined units.

Join diagonal corner Unit 48 over the combined units as shown. Trim seam and press..

to the top, and Unit 23 to the bottom, matching seams. Join Unit 24 to sides of the combined 19-23 units. Join Unit 17 to side of Unit 16; then add Unit 18 to bottom as shown. Join the 19-24 units to sides of tulips. For the center of the section, join units 15, 14, 13, 14, and 15 in a row. Join mirror image tulips to opposite sides of the 13-15 combined units to complete the tulip section.

5. For the heart section, refer to the diagrams at left to complete the top of the heart. As this is mirror imaged, refer frequently to Block B diagram for correct placement of mirror image units. When both top parts of the heart are complete, join mirror image Unit 46 to bottom of heart tops, carefully matching seams. Join units 33, 34, and 47 in a vertical row. Join the two mirror image heart sections to opposite sides of this vertical row. Join units 27 and 28. Join units 29 and 30. Join the 27/28 combined units to the top of the 29/30 units. Join mirror image units 26, and 25. Join a red flower to bottom of the 25/26 combined units. Add this flower section to side of combined 27-30 units; then add Unit 32 to bottom of combined units. Join diagonal corner Unit 31 to top corner of the combined flower units as shown. Join the mirror image flower sections to opposite sides of the heart to complete the heart section.

6. Join the top section of the block to the top of the tulip section, matching seams. Add the heart section to the bottom to complete Block B. Make 4.

Block C Assembly

1. To make Block C, begin by making the flower unit shown below Use diagonal corner technique to make 4 flowers.. Refer to the diagrams on page 83 for making the combined units for the flower. Follow the diagrams and instructions to complete those combined units.

2. Refer to the diagram of Unit 23 on page 83 and complete that unit.

3. Use diagonal corner technique to make four mirror image units of units 6, 14, 16, 17, 18, and 24.

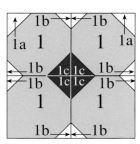

Flower Unit C1. Make 4. When completed, unit should measure 4 1/2" sq.

4. To assemble the center section of the block, begin by joining units 20, 19, and 20; then add Unit 21 to opposite sides of these combined units. Join units 22 and 23. Join these units to opposite sides of combined unit center section. Join units 24 and 25. Join these combined units to top and bottom of center section. Join units 15, 14, 13, 14, and 15 in a row as shown. Make 4. Join two of these rows to top and bottom of center section. To make the tulip center, join Unit 17 to sides of tulip Unit 16 as shown; then add Unit 18. Make four, and join the

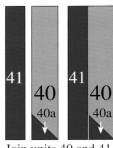

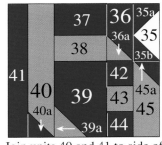
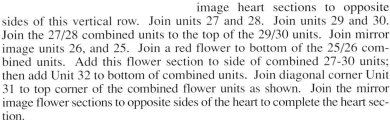

Block C. Make 1. When complete, block should measure 25 1/2" square.

Making combined units C1-C5

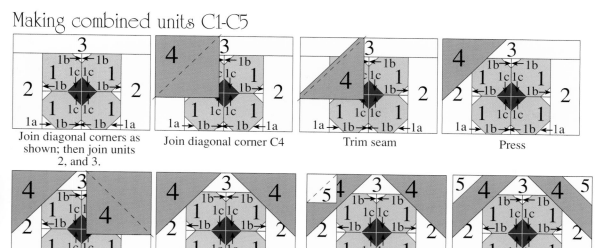

Join diagonal corners as shown; then join units 2, and 3.

Join diagonal corner C4

Trim seam

Press

Repeat for opposite side.

Add diagonal corner C5. Do not trim seam. Press.

Place 1 1/2" squares of Fabrics I and II right sides together and stitch diagonally down the center. Trim seam and press. Make 2.

tulip center to opposite sides of remaining 13-15 rows. Join to opposite sides of center section.

5. For the side sections, begin by joining units 10 and 11. Join units 8 and 9; then add Unit 7 to side of 8/9 combined units. Join the 7-9 combined units to the 10/11 combined units as shown. Join mirror image Unit 6 as shown. Join the combined 6-11 units to opposite sides of flower section, shown above. Make 4 Join these mirror image sections to opposite sides of center section. Add Unit 12 to opposite sides of the remaining flower combined units, and add to top and bottom to complete the block.. Make 1.

Block D Assembly

Block D. Make 4. When complete, base of block should measure 25 1/2" long. Triangle should measure 13" deep.

1. To assemble Block D, use diagonal corner technique and make two mirror image units of units 1, 2, 7, 11, 12, 14, and 18. For Unit 10, cut the squares in half diagonally for small triangles.

2. Join units 14 and 15. Join units 12 and 13, lining up triangle Unit 13 at bottom of Unit 12 as shown. Join these combined units to combined 14/15 units, lining them up on the Unit 14 side as shown. Join these combined mirror image units to opposite sides of Unit 11.

3. Join units 3 and 4, lining Unit 3 triangle up along Unit 4 long side as shown. Join units 1 and 2; then add them to combined 3/4 units as shown. Join units 5, 6, and 5 in a row. Join Unit 8 to side of these combined units. Join units 7 and 10 as shown. Join the combined 7/10 units to top of other combined units; then add diagonal corner, Unit 9 to top corner of heart, referring to block diagram for correct placement of mirror image units. Join the heart top combined units to the heart bottom combined units; then join them to opposite sides of Unit 16. Center Unit 17 on top of the combined units. Diagonal corners for Unit 18 are added to the triangles as shown. Join two Unit 18's together; then center them on Unit 17. Using your ruler, line it up along the triangles and trim the sides on a 45° angle to complete the block.

Tablecloth Assembly

1. To assemble the tablecloth, beginning at top left, join Block A, Block B, and Block A in a row. Make two of these rows. For center row, join Block B, Block C and Block B in a row. Refer to diagram at left and join the rows together.

2. Center long raw edge of triangular Block D on Block B edge as shown. Stitch together.

3. Mary quilted the smaller flowers and tulips as she did for the table runner using gold metallic thread. She "ditched" the patchwork and quilted holly between the block.

4. Use the large strip of Fabric V to cut 2 1/2" wide bias binding to bind the tablecloth.

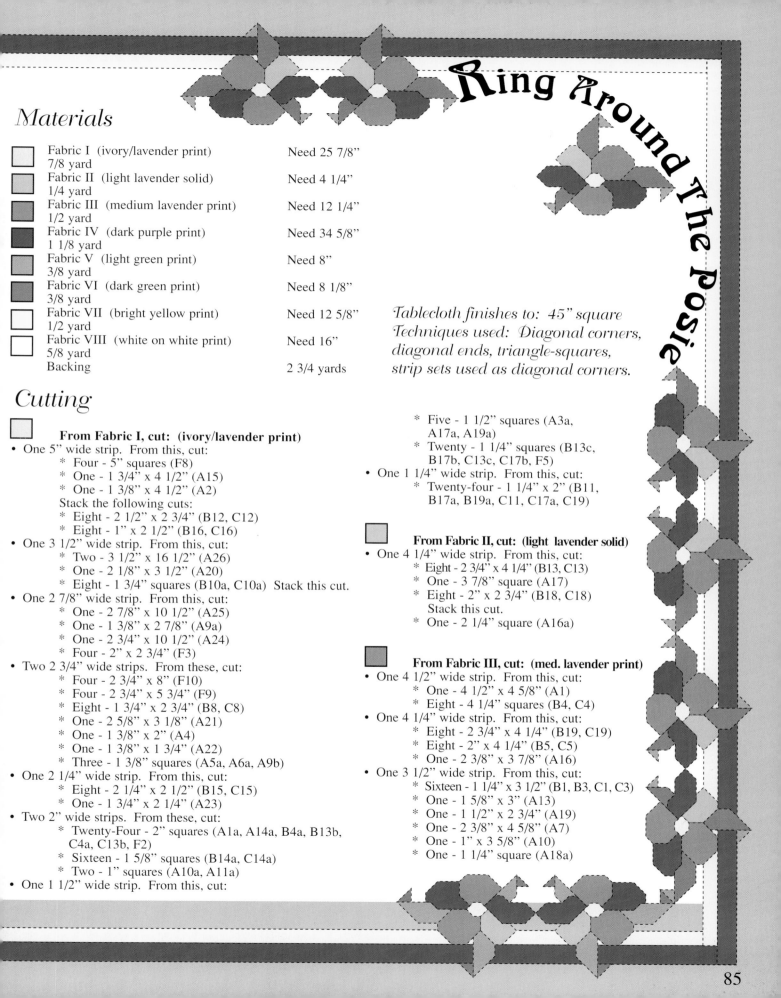

Materials

☐	Fabric I (ivory/lavender print) 7/8 yard	Need 25 7/8"
☐	Fabric II (light lavender solid) 1/4 yard	Need 4 1/4"
☐	Fabric III (medium lavender print) 1/2 yard	Need 12 1/4"
☐	Fabric IV (dark purple print) 1 1/8 yard	Need 34 5/8"
☐	Fabric V (light green print) 3/8 yard	Need 8"
☐	Fabric VI (dark green print) 3/8 yard	Need 8 1/8"
☐	Fabric VII (bright yellow print) 1/2 yard	Need 12 5/8"
☐	Fabric VIII (white on white print) 5/8 yard	Need 16"
	Backing	2 3/4 yards

Tablecloth finishes to: 45" square
Techniques used: Diagonal corners, diagonal ends, triangle-squares, strip sets used as diagonal corners.

Cutting

☐ **From Fabric I, cut: (ivory/lavender print)**
- One 5" wide strip. From this, cut:
  * Four - 5" squares (F8)
  * One - 1 3/4" x 4 1/2" (A15)
  * One - 1 3/8" x 4 1/2" (A2)
  Stack the following cuts:
  * Eight - 2 1/2" x 2 3/4" (B12, C12)
  * Eight - 1" x 2 1/2" (B16, C16)
- One 3 1/2" wide strip. From this, cut:
  * Two - 3 1/2" x 16 1/2" (A26)
  * One - 2 1/8" x 3 1/2" (A20)
  * Eight - 1 3/4" squares (B10a, C10a) Stack this cut.
- One 2 7/8" wide strip. From this, cut:
  * One - 2 7/8" x 10 1/2" (A25)
  * One - 1 3/8" x 2 7/8" (A9a)
  * One - 2 3/4" x 10 1/2" (A24)
  * Four - 2" x 2 3/4" (F3)
- Two 2 3/4" wide strips. From these, cut:
  * Four - 2 3/4" x 8" (F10)
  * Four - 2 3/4" x 5 3/4" (F9)
  * Eight - 1 3/4" x 2 3/4" (B8, C8)
  * One - 2 5/8" x 3 1/8" (A21)
  * One - 1 3/8" x 2" (A4)
  * One - 1 3/8" x 1 3/4" (A22)
  * Three - 1 3/8" squares (A5a, A6a, A9b)
- One 2 1/4" wide strip. From this, cut:
  * Eight - 2 1/4" x 2 1/2" (B15, C15)
  * One - 1 3/4" x 2 1/4" (A23)
- Two 2" wide strips. From these, cut:
  * Twenty-Four - 2" squares (A1a, A14a, B4a, B13b, C4a, C13b, F2)
  * Sixteen - 1 5/8" squares (B14a, C14a)
  * Two - 1" squares (A10a, A11a)
- One 1 1/2" wide strip. From this, cut:
  * Five - 1 1/2" squares (A3a, A17a, A19a)
  * Twenty - 1 1/4" squares (B13c, B17b, C13c, C17b, F5)
- One 1 1/4" wide strip. From this, cut:
  * Twenty-four - 1 1/4" x 2" (B11, B17a, B19a, C11, C17a, C19)

☐ **From Fabric II, cut: (light lavender solid)**
- One 4 1/4" wide strip. From this, cut:
  * Eight - 2 3/4" x 4 1/4" (B13, C13)
  * One - 3 7/8" square (A17)
  * Eight - 2" x 2 3/4" (B18, C18)
  Stack this cut.
  * One - 2 1/4" square (A16a)

☐ **From Fabric III, cut: (med. lavender print)**
- One 4 1/2" wide strip. From this, cut:
  * One - 4 1/2" x 4 5/8" (A1)
  * Eight - 4 1/4" squares (B4, C4)
- One 4 1/4" wide strip. From this, cut:
  * Eight - 2 3/4" x 4 1/4" (B19, C19)
  * Eight - 2" x 4 1/4" (B5, C5)
  * One - 2 3/8" x 3 7/8" (A16)
- One 3 1/2" wide strip. From this, cut:
  * Sixteen - 1 1/4" x 3 1/2" (B1, B3, C1, C3)
  * One - 1 5/8" x 3" (A13)
  * One - 1 1/2" x 2 3/4" (A19)
  * One - 2 3/8" x 4 5/8" (A7)
  * One - 1" x 3 5/8" (A10)
  * One - 1 1/4" square (A18a)

From Fabric IV, cut: (dark purple print)
- One 4 1/2" wide strip. From this, cut:
  * One - 4 1/2" square (A14)
  * Eight - 2 3/4" x 4" (B14, C14)
  * One - 3 5/8 x 3 7/8" (A3)
  * One - 1 1/8" x 3 5/8" (A11)
  * Sixteen - 1 1/4" squares (B9a, B17c, C9a, C17c)
    Stack this cut.
- Two 2 3/4" wide strips. From these, cut:
  * Eight - 2 3/4" x 3 1/2" (B6, C6)
  * Eight - 1 3/4" x 2 3/4" (B10, C10)
  * Eight - 2" x 2 3/4" (B19b, C19b)
  * One - 2 1/4" square (A7a)
  * Sixteen - 2" squares (B5a, B18a, C5a, C18a)
- Five 2 1/2" strips for straight-grain binding.
- Three 1 7/8" wide strips. From these, cut:
  * Two - 1 7/8"" x 23 1/2" (Q6)
  * Two - 1 7/8" x 20 3/4" (Q5)
  * Four - 1 3/4" x 9" (Q9)
- Three 1 3/4" wide strips. From these, cut:
  * Four - 1 3/4" x 13 3/4" (Q11)
  * Four - 1 3/4" x 13" (Q8)
  * Four - 1 3/4" x 2 1/2" (Q12)
- One 1 1/4" wide strip. From this, cut:
  * Eight - 1 1/4" squares (Q7a, Q10a)

From Fabric V, cut: (light green print)
- One 2 3/4" wide strip. From this, cut:
  * Four - 2 3/4" x 5 3/4" (F7)
  * Four - 2 1/2" x 2 3/4" (Q7)
  * One - 2 5/8" square (A21)
  * One - 1 1/2" x 2 3/8" (A8)
  * One - 2 1/8" x 2 1/4" (A6)
- Two 2" wide strips. From these, cut:
  * Eight - 2" x 3 1/2" (B17, C17)
  * Twenty - 2" squares (B4b, C4b, F1, Q13a, Q16a)
  * Four - 1 3/4" x 2 3/4" (B9, C9)
- One 1 1/4" wide strip. From this, cut:
  * Eight - 1 1/4" x 2 3/4" (B19b, C19b)
  * One - 1 1/4" x 1 1/2" (A18)
  * Two - 1 1/4" squares (A7c, A20)

From Fabric VI, cut: (dark green print)
- One 2 3/4" wide strip. From this, cut:
  * Four - 2 3/4" x 3 1/2" (F6)
  * Four - 2 1/2" x 2 3/4" (Q10)
  * Four - 1 3/4" x 2 3/4" (B9, C9)
- Two 2" wide strips. From these, cut:
  * Twenty-four - 2" squares (B4b, B13a, C4b, C13a, F1, Q14a, Q15a)
  * Nine - 1 3/4" squares (A23a, B16a, C16a)
- One 1 3/8" wide strip. From this, cut:
  * One - 1 3/8" x 4" (A9)
  * One - 1 3/8" x 2" (A5)
  * One - 1 3/8" square (A6b)
  * Eight - 1 1/4" x 2" (B11, C11)

From Fabric VII, cut: (bright yellow print)
- One 1 5/8" wide strip. From this, cut:
  * One - 1 5/8" x 2 1/4" (A12)
  * Four - 1 3/8" squares (A1b, A7b, A14b, A16b)
  * Twenty-seven - 1 1/4" squares (B4c, B5b, B5c, B18a, B19c, C4c, C5b, C5c, C18a, C19c, F4)
- Seven 1 1/4" wide strips. From these and scrap, cut:
  * Four - 1 1/4" x 13 3/4" (Q11)
  * Four - 1 1/4" x 13" (Q8)
  * Four - 1 1/4" x 9" (Q9)
  * Eight - 1 1/4" x 2 3/4" (B7, C7)

* Eight - 1 1/4" x 2 1/2" (B16, C16)
* Twenty-four - 1 1/4" x 2" (B2, B17a, B19a, C2, C17a, C19a)
* Eight - 1 1/4" x 1 3/4" (B10b, C10b)
* Seventeen - 1 1/4" squares (add to 1 1/4" sq. above)
- Two 1 1/8" wide strips. From these, cut:
  * Two - 1 1/8" x 20 3/4" (Q4)
  * Two - 1 1/8" x 19 1/2" (Q3)

From Fabric VIII, cut: (white on white print)
- Eight 2" wide strips. From these, cut:
  * Two - 2" x 19 1/2" (Q2)
  * Six - 2" x 16 1/2" (Q1, Q16)
  * Four - 2" x 15" (Q14)
  * Four - 2" x 13 1/2" (Q13, Q15)

Block A Assembly

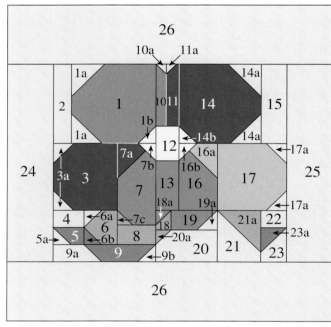

Block A. Make 1. When block is completed, it should measure 16 1/2" square

1. Use diagonal corner technique to make one each of units 1, 3, 5, 6, 7, 10, 11, 14, 16, 17, 18, 19, 20, 21 and 23.
2. Use diagonal end technique to make one of Unit 9 as shown
3. To assemble the block, begin by joining units 1 and 2. Join units 4 and 5; then add Unit 6 to right side of these combined units;

Making Unit A9

then join Unit 3 to top. Join units 7 and 8; then add them to right side of combined units 3-6. Join combined units 1/2 to top of other combined units, matching seams; then join Unit 9 to the bottom of combined units.
4. Join units 10 and 11. Join units 12 and 13. Join these two combined unit combinations together in a vertical row as shown. Join units 14 and 15. Join units 16 and 17. Matching flower center seams, join the 14/15 and 16/17 combinations together; then add them to units 10-13 vertical row as shown. Join units 18 and 19; then add Unit 20 to bottom of 18/19 units. Join Unit 21 to side of these combined units. Join units 22 and 23 and add them to right side of 18-21 combined units. Join these combined units to bottom of flower as shown. Join the two flower sections together.
5. Join Unit 24 to left side of flower; then join Unit 25 to right side. Join Unit 26 to top and bottom to complete Block A.

Blocks B, C, D, and E Assembly

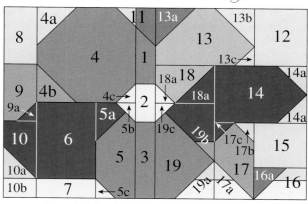

Block B. Make 2. When block is completed, it should measure 8" x 12"

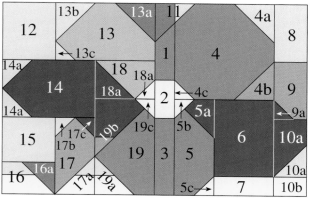

Block C. Make 2. When block is completed, it should measure 8" x 12"

1. As these blocks are mirror images, refer to block diagrams frequently for correct position of mirror image units. Blocks D and E have one color change on the leaves, (units 9 and 4b). Otherwise they are the same as B and C blocks. Instructions are for one block. Use diagonal corner technique to make one each of units 4, 5, 9, 10, 13, 14, 16, 17, 18, and 19. Refer to illustrations below for making diagonal corner mirror image units 17 and 19. Refer to block diagrams for correct placement of mirror image units.

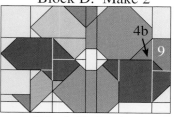

Block D. Make 2

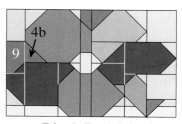

Block E. Make 2

2. To begin, join units 1, 2, and 3 in a horizontal row. Join units 6 and 7; then add Unit 5 to side of these combined units as shown. Join Unit 4 to top of combined units. Join units 8, 9, 10, and 10b in a vertical row; then join to other combined units, matching seams. Refer to diagram on lower left which is illustrated for Blocks C and E. Join 1 1/4" x 2" strips of fabrics I and VI to make the small Unit 11 strip set. Use it as a diagonal corner across units 1 and 4 as shown. Refer to Block B diagram for mirror image position. Join 1" x 2 1/2" strip of Fabric I and 1 1/4" x 2 1/2" strip of Fabric VII to make small strip set for Unit 16. Join diagonal corner 16a to this strip set to complete Unit 16.

3. Join units 15 and 16; then add Unit 17 to side of these combined units. Join Unit 14 to the top. Join units 18 and 19. Join these combined units to combined units 14-17, matching seams. Join units 12 and 13; then add to the top of other combined units.. Join the two sections of the flower together to complete the blocks. Make 2 of each block.

Block F Assembly

1. To assemble mirror image Block F, refer to diagram below, to make Unit 1. Join 2" squares of fabrics V and VI, right sides together. Stitch a diagonal line. Trim and press. Join units 1 and 2. Join units 4 and 5; then add Unit 3 to top of these combined units. Join the 1/2 and 3-5 combined units together. Join Unit 6 to side as shown. Join Unit 7 to top of combined units; then join diagonal corner, Unit 8 to top corner, stitching the diagonal, and pressing. Join Unit 9 to top of combined units; then add Unit 10 to side to complete the block.

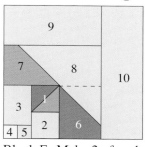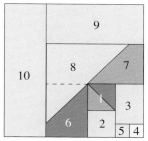

Block F. Make 2 of each. When block is completed, it should measure 8" square.

Strip set diagonal corner for combined units B, C, D, and E 1-10

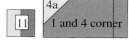

Making Mirror Image Unit 19 for Blocks B, C, D, and E.

Join 2" x 2 3/4" strip of Fabric IV and 1 1/4" x 2 3/4" strip of Fabric V.

Use 19b strip set as a diagonal corner and place as shown above. Stitch diagonal, trim seam and press.

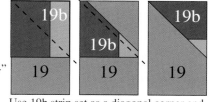

Join 1 1/4" x 2" strips of Fabrics I and VII.

Use 19a strip set as a diagonal corner and place as shown above. Stitch diagonal, trim seam and press.

Making Unit F1

Making Mirror Image Unit 17 for Blocks B, C, D, and E.

Join 1 1/4" x 2" strips of Fabrics I and VII.

Use 17a strip set as a diagonal corner and place as shown above. Stitch diagonal, trim seam and press.

Join 17c diagonal corner. Trim seam and press. Join 17c diagonal corner. Trim seam and press.

Tablecloth Assembly

1. To assemble the tablecloth, begin by joining Unit Q1 to top and bottom of Block A. Join Unit Q2 to opposite sides. Join Unit Q3 to top and bottom; then add Unit Q4 to opposite sides as shown. Join Unit Q5 to top and bottom; then add Unit Q6 to opposite sides. Refer to diagram below and begin with top flower blocks. Join blocks B and C as shown. Make two. Join one to center section top, and one to bottom For sides, join Block F, Block E, Block D and Block F in a vertical row as shown on left of diagram. Make two, and join them to opposite sides of tablecloth.

2. Use diagonal corner technique to make four each of units Q7, Q10, Q14, and Q16.. Use this technique to make two each of units Q13, and Q15. Join 1 1/4" x 13" strip of Fabric VII with 1 3/4" x 13" strip of Fabric IV for Unit Q8. Make 4. For Unit Q9, join 1 1/4" x 9" strip of Fabric IV with 1 3/4" x 9" strip of Fabric VII. Make 4. Join completed units Q8, Q7, Q9, Q7, and Q8 in a horizontal row. Make 2 and join them to top and bottom of tablecloth as shown.

3. Join 1 1/4" x 13 3/4" strip of Fabric VII with 1 3/4" x 13 3/4" strip of Fabric IV for Unit Q11. Make 4. Join units Q12, Q11, Q10, Q9, Q10, Q11, and Q12 in a long vertical row. Make 2 and join them to opposite sides of tablecloth. Join units Q14, Q13 and Q14 in a row as shown. Make two and join them to top and bottom of tablecloth. Join units Q16, Q15, and Q16 in a row. Make two and join them to opposite sides of tablecloth to complete the top.

4. Mary stippled the Fabric I background. She quilted a small feather border on the white, and quilted leaves inside the leaves. For a finishing touch, she quilted veins in the flowers.

5. Use the five 2 1/2" wide strips of Fabric IV and make straight-grain binding. Bind your tablecloth.

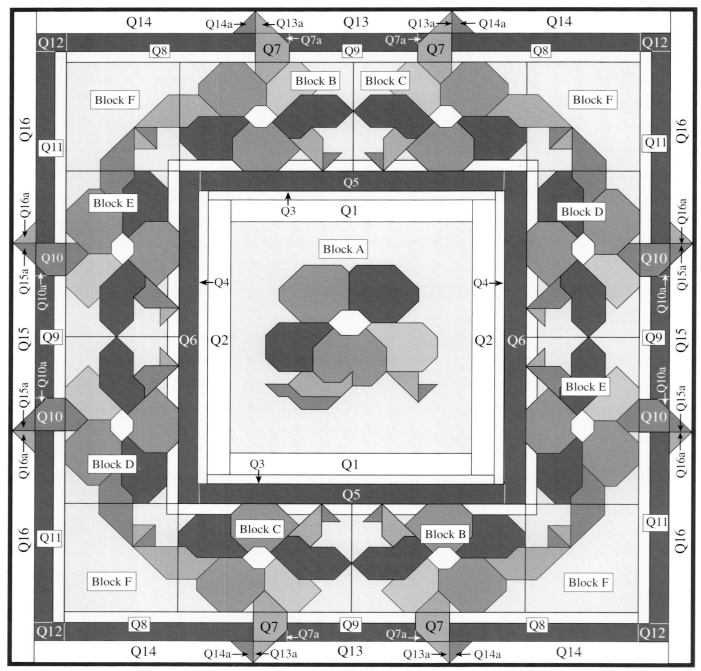

Materials For Four Place Mats

	Fabric		Need
☐	Fabric I (ivory/lavender print) 1/2 yard		Need 11 1/2"
☐	Fabric II (light lavender solid) 1/4 yard		Need 4 1/4"
☐	Fabric III (medium lavender print) 3/8 yard		Need 9 1/4"
☐	Fabric IV (dark purple print) 7/8 yard		Need 26 3/4"
☐	Fabric V (light green print) 1/4 yard		Need 6 3/4"
☐	Fabric VI (dark green print) 1/8 yard		Need 2"
☐	Fabric VII (bright yellow print) 3/8 yard		Need 4 1/4"
☐	Fabric VIII (white on white print) 1/4 yard		Need 6"
	Backing		1 yard

Cutting For Four Place Mats

☐ **From Fabric I, cut: (ivory/lavender print)**
- One 3 1/4" wide strip. From this, cut:
  * Four - 3 1/4" x 3 1/2" (20)
  * Four - 2 3/4" x 4 1/2" (14)
  * Four - 2 1/2" x 2 3/4" (16)
- One 2" wide strip. From this, cut:
  * Sixteen - 2" squares (4a, 12b, 13a, 17a)
- One 1 3/4" wide strip. From this, cut:
  * Four - 1 3/4" x 2 3/4" (8)
  * Four - 1 3/4" x 2 1/2" (10a)
  * Four - 1 3/4" x 2 1/4" (18)
  * Four - 1 3/4" squares (19)
- Two 1 5/8" wide strips. From these, cut:
  * Four - 1 5/8" x 14" (21)
  * Eight - 1 5/8" squares (15a)
- One 1 1/4" wide strip. From this, cut:
  * Four - 1 1/4" x 2 3/4" (7)
  * Sixteen - 1 1/4" squares (13b, 4c, 5c, 17c)

☐ **From Fabric II, cut: (light lavender solid)**
- One 2 3/4" wide strip. From this, cut:
  * Four - 2 3/4" x 4 1/4" (11)
  * Eight - 2" x 2 3/4" (13, 23)
  * Four - 1 1/2" squares (26)
  * Four - 1 1/4" squares (24a)
- One 1 1/2" wide strip. From this, cut:
  * Four - 1 1/2" x 5 1/8" (25)

☐ **From Fabric III, cut: (medium lavender print)**
- One 4 1/4" wide strip. From this, cut:
  * Four - 4 1/4" squares (4)
  * Four - 2 3/4" x 4 1/4" (12)
  * Four - 2" x 4 1/4" (5)
  * Four - 1 1/4" x 2 3/4" (1)
- Two 2 1/2" wide strips. From these, cut:
  * Four - 2 1/2" x 7" (28)
  * Four - 2 1/2" x 6 3/4" (30)
  * Four - 1 1/4" x 3 1/2" (3) Stack this cut.
  * Four - 1 1/4" squares (29a)

☐ **From Fabric IV, cut: (dk. purple print)**
- One 2 3/4" wide strip. From this, cut:
  * Four - 2 3/4" x 4" (15)
  * Four - 2 3/4" x 3 1/2" (6)
  * Four - 2" x 2 3/4" (12a)
- Seven 2 1/2" wide strips for straight-grain binding.

Place mats finish to: 13 5/8" x 18"
Techniques used: Diagonal corners, diagonal ends, triangle-squares, strip sets used as diagonal corners.

- One 2" wide strip. From this, cut:
  * Eight - 2" squares (5a, 11c)
  * Four - 1 1/2" x 2 (34)
  * Four - 1 3/4" x 2 3/4" (10)
  * Four - 1 1/4" squares (17b)
- Three 1 1/2" wide strips. From these, cut:
  * Four - 1 1/2" x 14 1/2" (27)
  * Four - 1 1/2" x 13 1/8" (33)
  * Four 1 1/4" squares (9a)

☐ **From Fabric V, cut: (light green print)**
- One 2 3/4" wide strip. From this, cut:
  * Four - 2 1/2" x 2 3/4" (29)
  * Four - 2" x 2 3/4" (24)
  * Four - 1 3/4" x 2 3/4" (9)
  * Four - 1 1/4" x 2 3/4" (12a)
  * Four - 1 1/4" x 2" (1a)
- Two 2" wide strips. From these, cut:
  * Four - 2" x 3 1/2" (17)
  * Sixteen - 2" squares (4b, 11a, 32a, 35a)

☐ **From Fabric VI, cut: (medium green print)**
- One 2" wide strip. From this, cut:
  * Eight - 2" squares (31a, 36a)
  * Four - 1 3/4" squares (19)

☐ **From Fabric VII, cut: (bright yellow print)**
- One 1 1/4" wide strip. From this, cut:
  * Sixteen - 1 1/4" squares (4d, 5b, 11b, 12c)
  * Four - 1 1/4" x 2" (2)
  * One - 1" x 5 1/8" (25)
- Three 1" wide strips. From these, cut:
  * Four - 1" x 14" (22)
  * Four - 1" x 13 1/8" (33)
  * Three - 1" x 5 1/8" (add to 25)

☐ **From Fabric VIII, cut: (white on white print)**
- Three 2" wide strips. From these, cut:
  * Four - 2" x 9" (32)
  * Four - 2" x 8 1/2" (35)
  * Four - 2" x 7" (31)
  * Four - 2" x 6 1/8" (36)

Place Mat Assembly

1. Use diagonal corner technique to make one each of units 4, 5, 9, 11, 12, 13, 15, 17, 24, 29, 31, 32, 35, and 36.. Use diagonal end technique to make one each of units 1 and 10 shown at right. Refer to the diagram below right of triangle-square, Unit 19. Follow instructions and drawing. To make Unit 12, refer to illustration below and begin by joining 2" x 2 3/4" piece of Fabric IV with 1 1/4" x 2 3/4" piece of Fabric V, forming Unit 12a. Use this small strip set as a diagonal corner as shown.

2. To assemble the place mat, join units 1, 2, and 3 in a vertical row. Join units 6 and 7; then add Unit 5 to right side of these combined units. Join Unit 4 to top; then add the 1-3 vertical row to the right

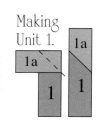

Making Unit 1.

Making Unit 10

Place 1 3/4" squares of fabrics I and VI right sides together with raw edges matching. Stitch a diagonal down the center. Trim and press

side. Join units 8, 9, and 10 in a vertical row. Join this row to left side of flower, matching seams. Join Units 11 and 12 and add them to the other combined units as shown.

3. Join units 13 and 14. Join units 15 and 16. Join units 18 and 19; then add Unit 17 to left side of these combined units, and Unit 20 to right side. Join combined units 13/14 to combined units 15/16 and add them to the top of combined units 17-20. Join the right side of the flower to the left side, matching seams. Join units 21 and 22 and add them to the bottom of the flower. Refer to the diagram below for making Unit 25. Join units 23, 24, and 25 in a vertical row and add them to the left side of the flower. Join units 26 and 27. Add these combined units to bottom of place mat. Join units 28, 29, and 30 in a horizontal row and add these combined units to top of

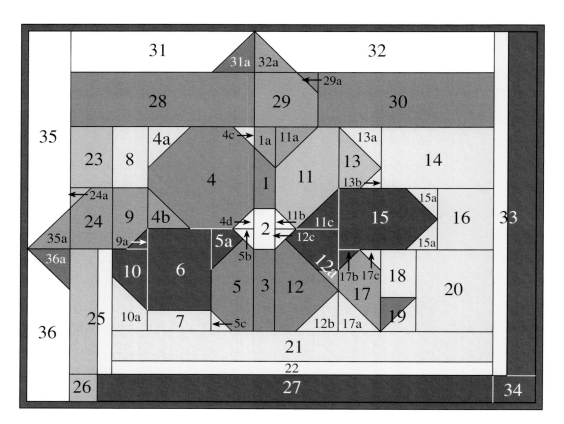

flower.

4. Join units 31 and 32; then add them to the top of the place mat. Refer to the diagram below for making Unit 33. Join units 33 and 34; then add them to the right side of the place mat. Join units 35 and 36, and add them to the left side of the place mat, matching leaf seams.

5. Quilt the place mat, "ditching" the patchwork. Use the seven 2 1/2" wide strips of Fabric IV to make straight-grain binding, and bind your place mats.

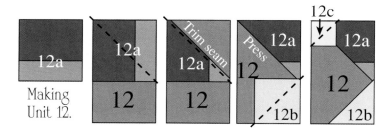

Making Unit 12.

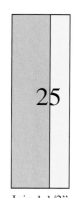

Join 1 1/2" x 5 1/8" strip of Fabric II with 1" x 5 1/8" Fabric VII for Unit 25.

Join 1 1/2" x 13 1/8" strip of Fabric IV with 1" x 13 1/8" Fabric VII for Unit 33.

Butterflies

Small quilt finishes to: 41 5/8" x 55 1/8"
Large quilt finishes to: 83 1/4" x 110 1/4"
Techniques used: strip sets as diagonal corners and triangle-squares.

There is an interesting story about this quilt which will hopefully show you our very human side, and the fact that we do make mistakes, and when we do, sometimes they are pretty good ones! This is a story that must be shared with quilters.

In March of this year we bought our dream home in Pagosa Springs, Colorado which served our business and personal needs perfectly. We were thrilled and excited about our move. During this time, we had to change personnel and find new people to work with us on our samples as we were on work overload!

Robert and I have always drawn our quilts full size on the computer. For some strange reason or other, this one was drawn half size, which meant doubling the size of the units and adding seam allowance when putting together the cutting instructions. After the completion of the cutting instructions and the graphics, the fabric was chosen and the quilt was given to one of our new sewers who had just completed the "Whirly Gig" wall quilt. As she was familiar with the techniques used in that quilt, I decided to give her the Butterflies quilt as the techniques are basically the same.

As it seemed to be taking her a long time to get back to us, I called her one evening and she appeared with the blocks that she had completed and joined. She spread them out on our dining room table. The thing that makes this even worse, is that I looked at them and had to contemplate what was wrong. I said "Is this it?" She replied "Well, I have a few more rows to add, but that shouldn't take too long." I said "Now wait a minute! What's wrong with this picture?"

It would seem by this interaction that sometimes I have to be hit over the head with a baseball bat to recognize something that is right in front of my face. It finally dawned! I said to our very confused sewer, "Oh My God! The computer drawing was half size, and we forgot to double it! Well........It could make a nice baby quilt!"

Chris Marona, our photographer, has a great sense of humor. I was trying to think of anything to keep this poor lady from making the quilt over again full size, as she was already close to tears. I called Chris at home. I explained the situation. To this day, I can not believe what I asked of him. I said "Chris, is there anything we can do to make this quilt look full size in a room, as computers do such wonderful things these days?" Chris said "Go out and buy some doll furniture!"

Having finally come to my senses, and looking at the beautiful little quilt spread in front of me, I decided to let our sewer complete it, as I fell in love with it. The colors were beautiful together and the design exceeded my expectations. I knew it would look stunning on a wall, or draped over a sofa.

Therefore, we are giving you a choice. The instructions that follow are for the little quilt and the big quilt. If any one of you make the big quilt, please, please send me a picture, as I sure would love to see it full size!

Materials For Small Quilt

- ■ Fabric I (dark teal print)   Need 59 1/2"
  1 3/4 yards
- □ Fabric II (pale yellow print)   Need 46"
  1 1/2 yards
- ■ Fabric III (medium teal print)   Need 27 7/8"
  7/8 yard
- ■ Fabric IV (bright turquoise print)   Need 28 1/4"
  1 yard
- ■ Fabric V (medium green print)   Need 46"
  1 3/8 yards
  Backing   2 3/4 yards

Cutting For Small Quilt

From Fabric I, cut: (dark teal print)
- Five 2 1/2" wide strips for straight-grain binding.
- Twenty-four 1 5/8" wide strips. From these, cut:
  * Ten - 1 5/8" x 6 1/8" (Q1)
  * 126 - 1 5/8" x 2 3/4" (A1, B1, C1, D1, F1, G1, H1, L1)
  * 348 - 1 5/8" squares (A2a, A5, B2a, B5, D2a, D4, E2a, E5, H2a, H5, J2a, J5, K1, K2a, M1, M2a)
- Eight 1" wide strips for Strip Set 1.

From Fabric II, cut: (pale yellow print)
- Thirteen 2 3/4" wide strips. From these, cut:
  * Eighty - 2 3/4" squares (F2, G2)
  * 168 - 1 5/8" x 2 3/4" (A2, A3, B2, B3, E2, E3, H2, H3, J2, J3)
- Two 1 5/8" wide strips. From these, cut:
  * Forty-eight - 1 5/8" squares (C3, E1, E6, L3)
- Seven 1" wide strips for Strip Set 2.

From Fabric III, cut: (medium teal print)
- Eleven 1 5/8" wide strips. From these, cut:
  * 252 - 1 5/8" squares (A3a, A6, B3a, B6, C3, D3, E3a, H3a, H6, J3a, J6, K3, L3, M3)
- Seven 1 1/8" wide strips for Strip Set 2.

From Fabric IV, cut: (bright turquoise print)
- Seven 2 3/4" wide strips. From these, cut:
  * 104 - 2 3/4" squares (C2, F2a, G2a, L2)
- Eight 1 1/8" wide strips for Strip Set 1.

From Fabric V, cut: (medium green print)
- Twelve 2 3/4" wide strips. From these, cut:
  * Eighty - 2 3/4" squares (F2, G2)
  * 144 - 1 5/8" x 2 3/4" (D2, K2, M2)
- Eight 1 5/8" wide strips. From these, cut:
  * 183 - 1 5/8" squares (A4, B4, C4, E4, F3, H4, J4, L1a, L4, M4)

Strip Sets For Small Quilt

Strip Set 1. Make 8. Cut into
192 - 1 5/8" segments

Strip Set 2. Make 7. Cut into
160 - 1 5/8 inch segments

1. For both quilt sizes, refer to page 7 for strip piecing, and piece the strip sets. Cut the number of segments required for the quilt.

Materials For Large Quilt

- ■ Fabric I (dark teal print)   Need 162 3/4""
  4 3/4 yards
- □ Fabric II (pale yellow print)   Need 137 1/2"
  4 1/4 yards
- ■ Fabric III (medium teal print)   Need 66"
  1 7/8 yard
- ■ Fabric IV (bright turquoise print)   Need 87 3/4"
  2 3/4 yard
- ■ Fabric V (medium green print)   Need 135 3/4"
  4 yards
  Backing   7 1/2 yards

Cutting For Large Quilt

From Fabric I, cut: (dark teal print)
- Ten 2 1/2" wide strips for straight-grain binding.
- Forty-three 2 3/4" wide strips. From these, cut:
  * Ten - 2 3/4" x 11 3/4" (Q1)
  * 126 - 2 3/4" x 5" (A1, B1, C1, D1, F1, G1, H1, L1)
  * 348 - 2 3/4" squares (A2a, A5, B2a, B5, D2a, D4, E2a, E5, H2a, H5, J2a, J5, K1, K2a, M1, M2a)
- Thirteen 1 1/2" wide strips for Strip Set 1.

From Fabric II, cut: (pale yellow print)
- Twenty-two- 5" wide strips. From these, cut:
  * Eighty - 5" squares (F2, G2)
  * 168 - 2 3/4" x 5" (A2, A3, B2, B3, E2, E3, H2, H3, J2, J3)
- Four 2 3/4" wide strips. From these, cut:
  * Forty-eight - 2 3/4" squares (C3, E1, E6, L3)
- Eleven 1 1/2" wide strips for Strip Set 2.

From Fabric III, cut: (medium teal print)
- Seventeen 2 3/4" wide strips. From these, cut:
  * 252 - 2 3/4" squares (A3a, A6, B3a, B6, C3, D3, E3a, H3a, H6, J3a, J6, K3, L3, M3)
- Eleven 1 3/4" wide strips for Strip Set 2.

From Fabric IV, cut: (bright turquoise print)
- Thirteen 5" wide strips. From these, cut:
  * 104 - 5" squares (C2, F2a, G2a, L2)
- Thirteen 1 3/4" wide strips for Strip Set 1.

From Fabric V, cut: (medium green print)
- Twenty 5" wide strips. From these, cut:
  * Eighty - 5" squares (F2, G2)
  * 144 - 2 3/4" x 5" (D2, K2, M2)
- Thirteen 2 3/4" wide strips. From these, cut:
  * 183 - 2 3/4" squares (A4, B4, C4, E4, F3, H4, J4, L1a, L4, M4)

Strip Sets For Large Quilt

Strip Set 1. Make 13. Cut into
192 - 2 3/4" segments

Strip Set 2. Make 11. Cut into
160 - 2 3/4" segments.

To make a strip set diagonal corner, the most important thing to become accustomed to is: If you want your stripes to end up vertically, the strip set is placed on the unit it is to be sewn to horizontally. If you want your stripes toend up horizontally, the strip set must be placed on the unit vertically. Practice this and it will become second nature. In the unit above, place your strip set horizontally, stitch the diagonalseam as you would for any diagonal corner, trim the center seam and press. **This technique is used throughout the project. All strips set segments are used as diagonal corners.**

1. Both size quilts are assembled exactly the same way. The diagrams on the left show how to use the strip set segments for diagonal corners, how to make easy triangle-squares and how to make tri-squares. These techniques are used throughout this project and are simple to do. Accuracy is the key. If you are not familiar with these techniques, practice before you begin this project.

The first two diagrams above show how to make a triangle square. In this case, place the two 2 3/4" squares of fabrics II and V right sides together with raw edges matching. Stitch a diagonal down the center. Trim the center seam. To make the complete F and G Tri-squares (Unit 2's), place the third 2 3/4" square from Fabric IV right sides together on top of the triangle-square and stitch the diagonal seam.

Please note that you must refer to the block diagrams to see which way the seam line should be stitched for mirror image units. Trim your seam as shown and press.

The triangle-squares are used for Unit C3 and L3. The Tri-squares are also used for units E1, E6 and M4. Refer to the diagram above for assembly of these units.

2. Assembly instructions are given for each block. Make the number of blocks designated under the block diagram, and check the size of your block when it is complete. Cut your strip set segments and put them in a zip top labeled bag. Have them ready to use for diagonal corners as each block utilizes them.

BLOCK A.
1. Use diagonal corner technique to make two of units 2 and 3. To assemble Block A, begin by joining units 1 and 2 at the top left corner of the block. Join units 1 and 3. Join the two combined unit sections together for the top of the block. Join units 4 and 5; then add Unit 2 to top of these combined units. Join units 4 and 6; then join Unit 3 to left of these combined units. Join the two bottom sections together as shown to complete the block. Make 4.

BLOCK B
1. Use diagonal corner technique to make four of units 2 and 3. To assemble Block B, the top section will be made first, beginning in the top left corner. Join units 4 and 5; then add Unit 2 to right side of 4/5 combined units. Join units 1 and 2 and add them to the 4-5-2 combined units. Join units 1 and 3; then add Unit 2 to left side of the 1/3 combined units. Join these units to other combined units to complete the top of the block.
2. For the block bottom, join units 6 and 4 as shown in the bottom left corner; then add Unit 3 to top of these combined units. Join another Unit 3 to right side of combined units as shown. Join units 4 and 5; then add Unit 2 to top of these combined units. Add to other combined units. Join units 4 and 6; then add Unit 3 to left side of the 4/6 combined units. Join to other bottom combined units. Join the top and bottom section together, matching seams to complete the block. Make 2.

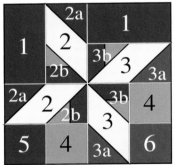

Block A. Make 4. For small quilt, when completed, block should measure 5" square. For large quilt it should measure 9 1/2" square.

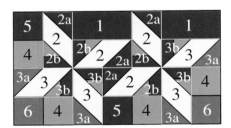

Block B. Make 2. For small quilt, when completed, block should measure 5" x 8 3/8".For large quilt it should measure 9 1/2" x 16 1/4".

BLOCK C
1. Refer to diagram above for making triangle-squares. Use this technique to make Unit 3. Join units 3 and 4. Join units 1 and 2; then join the combined units together to make the block. Make 8.

BLOCK D
1. Use diagonal corner technique to make eight of Unit 2. For top half of block, refer to Block D diagram and join three unit 1-2 combinations as shown. From the top left of the block, join the first two 1/2 combinations together. Add another Unit 2 to right side of the combined units; then join the final 1/2 combination to right side of other combined units as shown.
2. For bottom of block, begin in bottom left corner and join units 3 and 4. Add Unit 2 to top of the 3/4 combined units. Join another Unit 2 to right side as shown. Make another 3/4/2 combination and add to right side of other combined units. Join another Unit 2 to right side. Join units 3 and 4 and add them to right side of bottom units. Join the top and bottom sections together to complete Block D. Make 4.

Block C. Make 8. For small quilt, when completed, block should measure 2 3/4" x 5". For large quilt, it should measure 5" x 9 1/2".

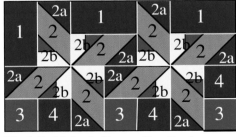

Block D. Make 4. For small quilt,when completed,block should measure 5" x 8 3/8". For large quiltit should measure 9 1/2" x 16 1/4"

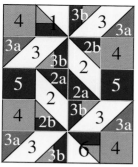

Block E. Make 12. For small quilt, when completed, block should measure 5" x 6 1/8". For large quilt it should measure 9 1/2" x 11 3/4"

BLOCK E

1. Use diagonal corner technique to make two of Unit 2, and four of Unit 3. Refer to diagram on page 94 for making tri-squares and use this technique to make one each of units 1 and 6.

2. To assemble the block, begin at top left and join units 1 and 4; then add Unit 3 to bottom of these combined units. Join units 4 and 5; then add Unit 2 to right side of 4/5 units. Join Unit 3 to bottom as shown. Join the top and bottom units together to complete the left side of the block.

3. For right side, join units 4 and 5 together; then add Unit 2 to left side of 4/5 combined units. Join Unit 3 to the top. Join tri-square Unit 6 and Unit 4; then add Unit 3 to top. Join the two combined unit sections together. Join the right and left sides of the block, matching seams. Make 12.

BLOCK F

1. Refer to instructions for making tri-squares on page 94, and make four mirror image Unit 2's as shown. Join them together with Unit 1 between them, checking Block F diagram for correct position of Unit 2. Make two. For center row, join Unit 1, Unit 3 and Unit 1 in a horizontal row. Join the two tri-square sections to top and bottom of center section to complete the block. Make 15.

BLOCK G

1. Once again refer to instructions for making tri-squares on page 94. Use this technique to make two of Unit 2. Refer to block diagram for correct position of Unit 2's and join them to top and bottom of Unit 1 as shown. Make 10 of this block.

BLOCK H

1. Use diagonal corner technique to make one of Unit 2, and three of Unit 3. To assemble block, join units 1 and 3 together. Add Unit 2 to bottom of these combined units. Join units 4 and 5; then add them to bottom of other combined units.

2. Join units 4 and 6; then add Unit 3 to bottom of these combined units. Join another Unit 4 and Unit 6; then add Unit 3 to left side as shown. Join the top and bottom joined units together. Join the left and right side of the block together, matching seams. Make 8.

of Unit 3. To assemble the block, begin at top left corner and join units 6 and 4; then add Unit 3 to right side of these combined units. Join units 4 and 5; then join Unit 2 to bottom of the 4/5 units. Join Unit 3 to right side of the 4/5/2 combined units. Join units 4 and 6 ; then join Unit 3 to bottom. Join all of the combined units together to complete the top of the block.

2. For the bottom of the block, begin in the bottom

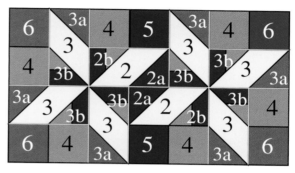

Block J. Make 4. For small quilt, when completed, block should measure 5" x 8 3/8". For large quilt it should measure 9 1/2" x 16 1/4".

left corner and join units 6 and 4; then add Unit 3 to top. Join another Unit 3 to right side. Join units 4 and 5; then add Unit 2 to top. Join Unit 3 to right side. Join the two combined unit sections together. Join units 4 and 6 and add them to the bottom combined units. Join the top and bottom section together, matching seams. Make 4.

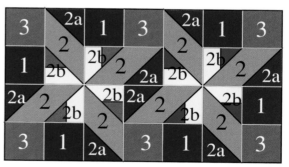

Block K. Make 8. For small quilt, when completed, block should measure 5" x 8 3/8". For large quilt, it should measure 9 1/2" x 16 1/4".

BLOCK K

1. Use diagonal corner technique to make 8 of Unit 2. To assemble the block, begin at top left corner and join units 3 and 1; then add Unit 2 to right side of 3/1 combined units. Join Unit 1 and 3; then add another Unit 2 to bottom of these combined units. Join the two combined unit sections together; then add another Unit 2 to right side. Join another unit 1/3 combination; then add another Unit 2 to bottom. Join these combined units to other combined units to complete the top of the block.

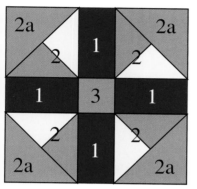

Block F. Make 15. For small quilt, when completed, block should measure 6 1/8" square. For large quilt it should measure 11 3/4" square.

Block G. Make 10. For small quilt, when completed, block should measure 2 3/4" x 6 1/8". For large quilt it should measure 5" x 11 3/4"

BLOCK J

1. Use diagonal corner technique to make two of Unit 2, and six

2. For bottom of Block K, begin in lower left corner and join units 3 and 1; then add Unit 2 to top of these combined units. Join another Unit 2 to right side. Join another unit 3/1 combination; then add Unit 2 to top of combined units. Join one more 1/3 unit combination; then add Unit 2 to left side of the 1/3 combined units. Join this unit section to right side of other combined units to complete the bottom of the block. Join the top and bottom, matching seams. Make 8.

BLOCK L

1. Refer to page 94 for making Unit 3 triangle-square. Join units 4 and 3. Join units 1 and 2 as shown. Join the two combined unit sections together to complete Block L. Make 16.

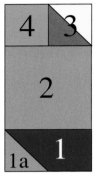

Block L. Make 16. For small quilt, when completed, block should measure 2 3/4" x 5". For large quilt, it should measure 5" x 9 1/2".

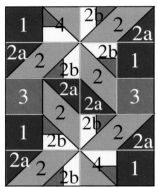

Block M. Make 8. For small quilt, when completed, block should measure 5" x 6 1/8" For large quilt it should measure 9 1/2" x 11 3/4".

BLOCK M

1. Use diagonal corner technique to make six of Unit 2. Refer to page 94 for making tri-squares, and use this technique to make two of Unit 4.

2. To assemble the block, join units 1, and 4.. Join units 3 and 1; then add Unit 2 to right side of the 3/1 combined units and another Unit 2 to top. Join a third Unit 2 to bottom. Join the 1/4 combined units to the top of the other combined units to complete the left side of the block.

3. For the right side, join units 1 and 3; then add Unit 2 to left side of the 1/3 combined units. Join Unit 2 to top and bottom of these combined units. Join units 4 and 1 and add them to the bottom of the other combined units to complete the right side of the block. Join the right and left sides of the block together, matching seams. Make 8.

Quilt Assembly

The complete quilt is shown on page 97 and is broken down into rows, comprised of the blocks. Begin with the top row and follow the diagram and instructions.

1. For Row 1, join the following blocks in a horizontal row: Block A, Block C, Block D, Block C, Block B, Block C, Block D, BLock C, and Block 1. Match seams carefully. Make two of these rows. One for Row 1 and one for Row 11.

2. For Row 2, join Unit Q1, Block G, Block E, Block F, BLock E, BLock F, Block E, BLock F, BLock E, Block G, and Unit Q1. Make two of these rows. One for Row 2, and one for Row 10.

3. For Row 3, join Block H, Block L, Block K, Block L, Block J, Block L, Block K, Block L, and Block H. Make two of these rows. One for Row 3, and one for Row 9.

4. For Row 4, join Unit Q1, Block G, Block M, Block F, Block M, Block F, Block M, Block F, Block M, Block G, and Unit Q1. Make two of these rows. One for Row 4, and one for Row 8.

5. For Row 5, join Block H, Block L, Block K, Block L, Block J, Block L, Block K, Block L, and Block H. Make two of these rows. One for Row 5, and one for Row 7.

6. For Row 6, join Unit Q1, Block G, Block E, Block F, Block E, Block F, Block E, Block F, Block E, Block G, and Unit Q1.

Beginning at the top of the quilt, join the rows together, carefully matching seams.

For quilting, Mary "ditched" all of the patchwork.

For small quilt, use the five 2 1/2" wide strips of Fabric I for binding.
For large quilt, use the ten 2 1/2" wide strips of Fabric I for straight-grain binding and bind your quilt.

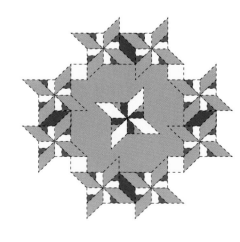

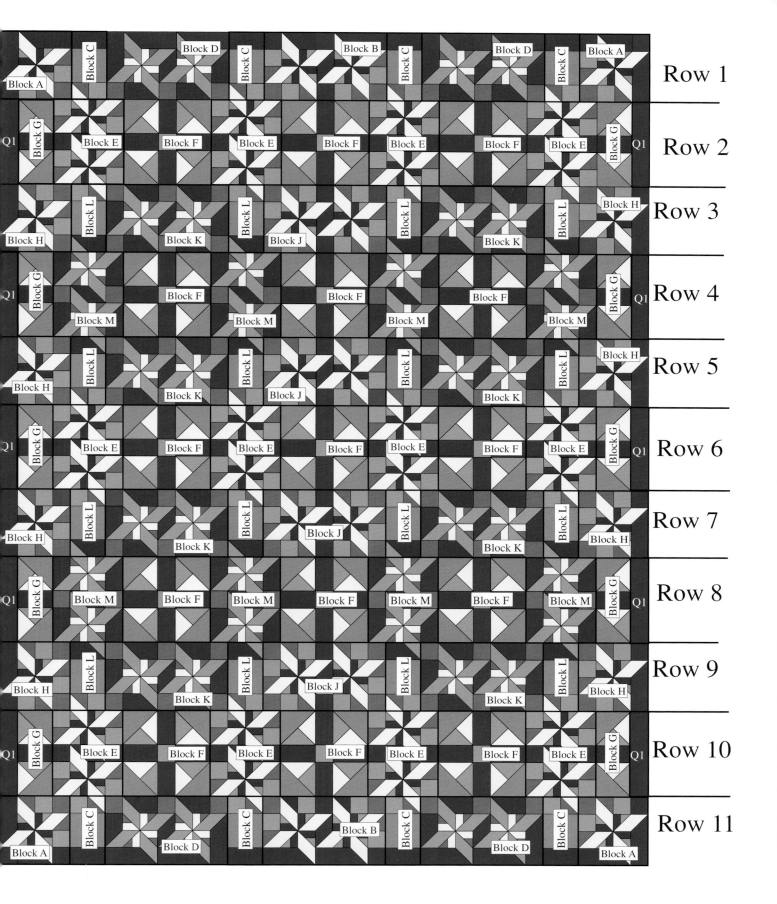

Row 1

Row 2

Row 3

Row 4

Row 5

Row 6

Row 7

Row 8

Row 9

Row 10

Row 11

97

Grandmother's Magnolias

Quilt finishes to: 86" square. From point to point, finished size is 112".

Techniques used: Diagonal corners, diagonal ends, triangle-squares used as diagonal corners.

Materials

⬜	Fabric I (light blue print) 4 3/8 yards	Need 149 1/4"
⬜	Fabric II (white on white print) 3 1/8 yards	Need 106 1/2"
⬜	Fabric III (light pink print) 3/4 yard	Need 22 3/4"
⬜	Fabric IV (dark pink print) 1 1/8 yards	Need 36"
⬜	Fabric V (light green textured print) 3/4 yard	Need 24"
⬜	Fabric VI (dark green textured print) 1/2 yard	Need 13 3/4"
⬜	Fabric VII (light yellow print) 1 yard	Need 31 3/8"
⬜	Fabric VIII (medium yellow print) 3/8 yard	Need 10 1/2"
⬜	Fabric IX (medium blue textured print) 3/4 yard	Need 22 1/2"
	Backing	9 yards

Cutting

⬜ **From Fabric I, cut: (light blue print)**
- Two 15 1/2" wide strips. From these, cut:
  - * Four - 15 1/2" x 17" (Q1)
  - * Eight - 1 1/4" x 12" (A28)
- Three 7" wide strips. From these, cut:
  - * Sixteen - 7" squares (B24, B33)
  - * Eight - 2 1/2" x 3 1/4" (A21, C13)
- Two 5" wide strips. From these, cut:
  - * Sixteen - 5" squares (A37, A48)
- Four 3 3/4" wide strips. From these, cut:
  - * Thirty-two - 3" x 3 3/4" (A34, A45, B21, B30)
  - * Sixteen - 2 1/4" x 3 3/4" (A39, A50)
  - * Sixteen - 2 1/4" x 3" (C17, C19)
- Two 3 1/4" wide strips. From these, cut:
  - * Eight - 2 1/2" x 3 1/4" (add to A21, C13)
  - * Sixteen - 1 1/2" x 3 1/4" (A25, C12)
  - * Twenty-four - 1 1/2" x 3" (A35, A46, B22, B32)
- One 3" wide strip. From this, cut:
  - * Eight - 1 1/2" x 3" (add to 1 1/2" x 3" above)
  - * Forty - 1 1/2" squares (A7a, A9a, A24a, A29a, A40a, B7a, B9a, B16a, B25a, C10a)
- Two 2 1/2" wide strips. From these, cut:
  - * Sixteen - 2 1/2" squares (A27, C15)
  - * Sixteen - 1 1/4" x 2 1/2' (A26, C14)
  - * Thirty-six - 1 1/4" squares (A2a, A3a, A14b, A15b, A22a, A36a, A47a, B2a, B3a, B23a, B31a, C2a, C3a, C11a) Stack this cut.
- Five 2 1/4" wide strips. From these, cut:

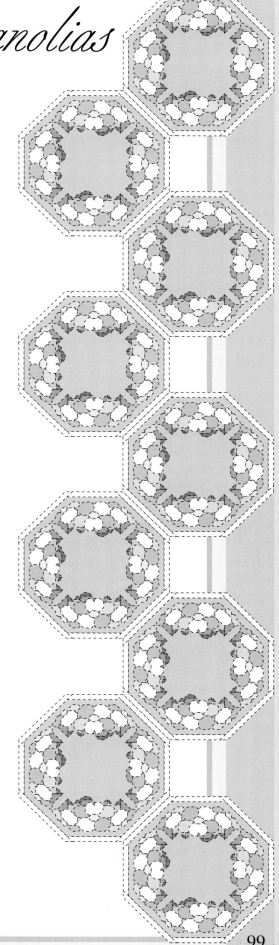

* Sixteen - 2 1/4" squares (A19, C6)
* Forty-eight - 2" x 2 1/4" (A20, A30, A41, B17, B26, C8)
* Thirty-two - 1 3/4" x 2 1/4" (A38, A49, C16, C18)
* Twelve - 1 3/4" squares (A4b, A5b, B4b, B5b)
• Twenty-one 2" wide strips. From these, cut:
* Eight - 2" x 40 1/2" (Q3)
* Eight - 2" x 37 1/2" (Q2)
* Ninety-six - 2" squares (A4a, A5a, A31a, A33c, A42a, A44c, B4a, B5a, B18a, B20c, B27a, B29c)
* Sixteen - 1 1/4" x 2" (A23, C9)
* Sixteen - 1 3/4" squares (add to 1 3/4" sq. above)
• One 1 3/4" wide strip. From this, cut:
* Four - 1 3/4" squares (add to 1 3/4" sq. above)
* Twenty-three - 1 1/2" squares (add to 1 1/2" sq. above)
• One 1 1/2" wide strip. From this, cut:
* Seventeen - 1 1/2" squares (add to 1 1/2" sq. above)
• Three 1 1/4" wide strips. From these, cut:
* Seventy-six - 1 1/4" squares (add to 1 1/4" sq. above)

◻ **From Fabric II, cut: (white on white print)**
• One 22 1/2" x 42" for bias binding.
• Two 5 3/4" wide strips. From these, cut:
* Twelve - 3" x 5 3/4" (A13, D11)
* Eight - 2" x 5 3/4" (B13)
* Eight - 1 1/2" x 5 3/4" (C1)
* Thirty-nine - 1 1/2" squares (A1a, A10a, A10b, A14a, A15a, A21b, B1a, B10a, B10b, B14a, B15a, C13a, D1a, D8a, D8b, D16c, D23b)
• Two 4 1/2" wide strips. From these, cut:
* Twenty - 3 1/2" x 4 1/2" (A4, B4, D4)
• Three 4 1/4" wide strips. From these, cut:
* Thirty-two - 3 3/4" x 4 1/4" (A33, A44, B20, B29)
• Two 2 1/4" wide strips. From these, cut:
* Twenty - 2 1/4" x 3 1/2" (A2, B2, D2)
• Eighteen 2" wide strips. From these, cut:
* Sixteen - 2" x 23 1/2" (Q5)
* Sixteen - 2" x 16" (Q4)
* Thirty-two - 2" x 2 1/2" (A32, A43, B19, B28)
* Twenty - 1 1/2" x 2" (A17, C7, D21)
• Six 1 1/2" wide strips. From these and scrap, cut:
* Sixteen - 1 1/2" x 3 1/4" (A16, C4)
* Thirty-two - 1 1/2" x 2 3/4" (A7, A9, B7, B9)
* Four - 1 1/2" x 2 1/4" (D17)
* Seventy-seven - 1 1/2" squares (add to 1 1/2" sq. above)
• One 1 1/4" wide strip. From this, cut:
* Thirty-two - 1 1/4" squares (A29b, A40b, B16b, B25b)

◻ **From Fabric III, cut: (light pink print)**
• Three 3 1/2" wide strips. From these, cut:
* Twelve - 3 1/2" x 4" (A15, D13)
* Eight - 3" x 3 1/2" (B15)
* Eight - 1 1/2" x 3 1/2" (C3)
* Forty-eight - 1 1/2" squares (A10b, A12, A13b, A33a, B10b, B12, B13b, B20a, D8b, D10, D11b)
• Three 2 1/4" wide strips. From these, cut:
* Sixteen - 2 1/4" x 2 1/2" (A42, B27)
* Sixteen - 2 1/4" squares (A5a, B5a)
* Thirty-two - 1 1/2" x 2 1/4" (A8, A35a, B8, B22a)
• Two 2" wide strips. From these, cut:
* Sixteen - 2" x 3 3/4" (A36, B23)
* Sixteen - 1 1/4" squares (A43a, B28a)
• One 1 1/2" wide strip. From this, cut:
* Twenty-eight - 1 1/2" squares (add to 1 1/2" sq. above)

◻ **From Fabric IV, cut: (dark pink print)**
• Two 4 1/2" wide strips. From these, cut:
* Twenty - 3 1/2" x 4 1/2" (A5, B5, D6)
• Three 3 3/4" wide strips. From these, cut:
* Twelve - 3 3/4" x 4" (A14, D12)

* Eight - 3" x 3 3/4" (B14)
* Sixteen - 2" x 3 3/4" (A47, B31)
* Eight - 1 1/2" x 3 3/4" (C2)
* Twenty-four - 1 1/4" squares (A13a, A32a, B13a, B19a, D11a)
• Five 2 1/4" wide strips. From these, cut:
* Twenty - 2 1/4" x 3 1/2" (A3, B3, D3)
* Sixteen - 2 1/4" x 2 1/2" (A31, B18)
* Sixteen - 2 1/4" squares (A4a, B4a)
* Thirty-two - 1 1/2" x 2 1/4" (A6, A46a, B6, B32a)
* Twelve - 1 1/4" squares (add to 1 1/4" squares above)
• Three 1 1/2" wide strips. From these, cut:
* Fifty-six - 1 1/2" squares (A1b, A10a, A44a, B1b, B10a, B29a, D1b, D8a)
* Twenty - 1 1/4" x 1 1/2" (A11, B11, D9)

◻ **From Fabric V, cut: (light green textured print)**
• Three 3 1/2" wide strips. From these, cut:
* Thirty-two - 3 1/2" squares (A37a, A48a)
* Four - 2 1/2" x 3 1/4" (D16)
• One 3 1/4" wide strip. From this, cut:
* Sixteen - 1 1/4" x 3 1/4" (A18, C5)
* Four - 1 1/2" x 2 1/4" (D18)
* Twenty - 1 1/2" squares (A16a, A33b, A36b, A44b, A47b, B20b, B23b, B29b, B31b, C4a, D17a)
• Two 2 1/2" wide strips. From these, cut:
* Twenty - 2 1/2" squares (A21a, C13b, D23a)
* Fourteen - 2 1/4" squares (A22, C11)
• One 2 1/4" wide strip. From this, cut:
* Two - 2 1/4" squares (add to A22, C11 above)
* Twenty-five - 1 1/2" squares (add to 1 1/2" sq. above)
• Two 1 1/2" wide strips. From these, cut:
* Fifty-five - 1 1/2" squares (add to 1 1/2" sq. above)

◻ **From Fabric VI, cut: (dark green textured print)**
• Two 2 1/4" wide strips. From these, cut:
* Thirty-two - 2 1/4" squares (A39a, A50a, C17a, C19a)
• One 1 3/4" wide strip. From this, cut:
* Twenty - 1 3/4" squares (A27a, C15a, D25a)
• Five 1 1/2" wide strips. From these, cut:
* Four - 1 1/2" x 4 3/4" (D19a)
* Sixteen - 1 1/2" x 3 1/4" (A18, C5)
* Thirty-six - 1 1/2" x 2" (A24, A25a, C10, C12a, D15)
* Twenty - 1 1/2" squares (A22b, C11b, D16b)

◻ **From Fabric VII, cut: (light yellow print)**
• One 14 1/8" wide strip. From this, cut:
* One - 14 1/8" square (E1) cut in half diagonally. Stack the following cuts:
* Eight - 1 1/2" x 4 1/2" (D5, D7)
* Four - 2 1/2" x 3 1/2" (D23)
* Four - 1 1/2" x 3 1/4" (D19)
* Four - 2 1/2" squares (D20)
* Four - 2 1/2" x 2 3/4" (D25)
* Four - 2" x 2 1/2" (D22)
* Four - 1 1/4" x 2 1/2" (D24)
* Eight - 2 1/4" squares (D4a, D6a)
* Eight - 1 3/4" squares (D4b, D6b)
* Twenty-four - 1 1/2" squares (D12a, D13a, D15a, D16a)
* Eight - 1 1/4" squares (D1a, D2a)
• One 8 7/8" wide strip. From this, cut:
* Four - 8 7/8" squares (D27) cut in half diagonally.
* Four - 1 1/2" x 2" (D14)
• One 8 3/8" wide strip. From this, cut:
* Four - 8 3/8" squares (D26) cut in half diagonally.

◻ **From Fabric VIII, cut: (medium yellow print)**
• Two 2 1/4" wide strips. From these, cut:
* Thirty-two - 2 1/4" squares (A29, A40, B16, B25)

100

- Four 1 1/2" wide strips. From these, cut:
  * Forty - 1 1/2" x 4" (A1, A10, B1, B10, D1, D8)

From Fabric IX, cut: (medium blue textured print)
- Ten 2 1/4" wide strips. From these, cut:
  * One - 2 1/8" x 27" (E4)
  * Eight - 2 1/8" x 19 1/4" (D29)
  * One - 2 1/8" x 17 3/4" (E3) Trim if necessary.
  * Eight - 2 1/8" x 16" (D28)
  * One - 2 1/8" x 15 1/2" (E2) Trim if necessary.

Block A Assembly

1. Use diagonal corner technique to make one each of units 1, 2,

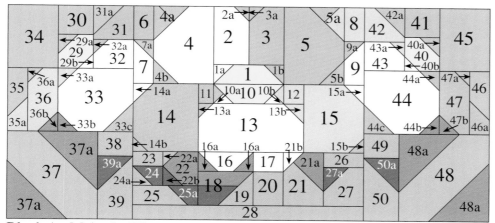

Block A. Make 8. When completed, block should measure 11 1/2" x 24 1/2"

3, 4, 5, 7, 9, 10, 13, 14, 15, 16, 18, 21, 22, 24, 27, 29, 31, 32, 33, 36, 37, 39, 40, 42, 43, 44, 47, 48, and 50.

2. Use diagonal end technique to make one each of units 25, 35, and 46.

3. To make diagonal corners 4 and 5, use diagonal corner technique to make units 4a and 5a, illustrated below. Use the diagonal corners as diagonal corners as shown. Stitch them in place. Trim seam and press.

4. Unit 10, shown below is made in the same way as units 4 and

Making Units 4 and 5 for blocks A and B.

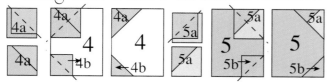

5 above, except that the diagonal corner is a triangle-square. To make the triangle-square for 10a diagonal corners, place 1 1/2" squares of fabrics II and IV right sides together with raw edges matching. Stitch a diagonal down the center as shown. Press. For 10b, place 1 1/2" squares of fabrics II and III right sides together. Stitch the diagonal and press. Refer to the illustration below, and use the triangle-squares as diagonal corners as shown. Stitch the diagonal, trim seam and press.

5. Refer to diagram at bottom of page for making combined units 18 and 19. Follow

Making combined units A18/19

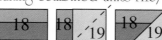

Join 1 1/4" x 3 1/4" strip of Fabric V with 1 1/2" x 3 1/4" strip of Fabric VI. Add diagonal corner A19.

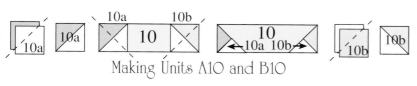

Making Units A10 and B10

Making Unit A25

Making Unit A35

Making Unit A46

illustration and instructions.

6. Diagrams at left show how to make all of the diagonal end units. Refer to these drawings for correct positioning of the units.

7. To assemble the block, begin by joining units 2 and 3, matching diagonal seams. Join Unit 1 to bottom of combined units. Join Unit 4 to left side and Unit 5 to right side of combined units. Join units 6 and 7. Join units 8 and 9. Add the 6/7 combined units to left side of other combined units and units 8/9 to right side.

8. Join units 11, 10, and 12 in a horizontal row; then add Unit 13 to bottom of these combined units. Join Unit 14 to left side and Unit 15 to right side. Add these combined units to the 1-9 combined units, matching seams.

9. Join units 23 and 24 as shown; then add Unit 22 to right side. Join Unit 25 to bottom of these combined units. Join units 16 and 18/19. Join units 17 and 20; then add Unit 21 to right side of 17/20 combined units. Join the two unit combinations together as shown. Join units 26 and 27 and add them to right side of combined units; then join Unit 28 to bottom. Join this leaf section to bottom of center flower to complete the center section.

10. For left side section, join units 29 and 30; then add Unit 34 to left side of the 29/30 combined units. Join units 31 and 32. Join them to the right side of other combined units. Join units 35, 36, and 33 in a row as shown, matching diagonal seams. Add this row to bottom of other combined units. Join units 38 and 39; then add Unit 37 to left side of 38/39 combination. Join these combined units to bottom of left flower units, matching seams to complete the left section of the block.

11. For the right side section, join units 42 and 43. Join units 40 and 41 as shown; then join Unit 45 to right side of 40/41 combined units. Join these combined units to 42/43 units. Join units 44, 47, and 46 in a row and add this row to other combined units. Join units 49 and 50; then add Unit 48 to right side of the 49/50 combined units. Join these units to bottom of flower to complete the right section of the block.

12. Join the left section to left side of center flower, matching seams; then join the right section to the right side of center flower to complete Block A. Make 8.

Block B Assembly

1. Refer to Block B diagram on page 102, and use diagonal corner technique to make one each of units 1, 2, 3, 4, 5, 7, 9, 10, 13, 14, 15, 16, 18, 19, 20, 23, 25, 27, 28, 29, and 31.

2. Use diagonal end technique to make one each of units 22 and 32. Refer to the diagram on the left for making units B4 and B5. Illustration for making Unit B10 is on left.

3. Drawings above for units A35 and A46 are the same as for units B22, and B32.

4. To assemble the block, refer to steps 7 and 8 for Block A. For left side of block, join units 16 and 17; then add Unit 21 to left side of these combined units. Join units 18 and 19. Join these combined units to right side of other combined units. Join units 22, 23, and 20 in a row and

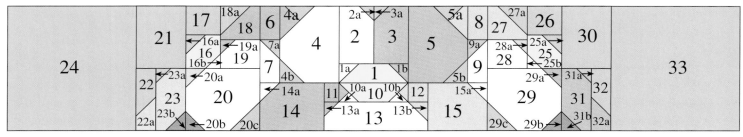

Block B. Make 8. When completed, block should measure 7" x 37 1/2"

add them to bottom of other combined units. Join Unit 24 to left side of combined units to complete left side of block.

5. For right side of block, join units 27 and 28. Join units 25 and 26; then add Unit 30 to right side of 25/26 combined units. Join combined units 27/28 to left side of combined units. Join units 29, 31, and 32 in a row, and add the row to the bottom of other combined units. Join Unit 33 to right side to complete the right section.

6. Join the three sections together to complete Block B. Make 8.

to diagram at top of page 101 for making Unit A25. Unit D19 is made the same way. For Unit 23, be sure to add diagonal corners in alphabetical order.

2. To assemble the block, begin by joining units 2 and 3; then add Unit 1 to bottom of the 2/3 combined units. Join units 4 and 5 as shown. Join units 6 and 7. Join the 4/5 unit combination to left side of center units, and combined units 6/7 to right side to complete the top row.

Block C. Make 8. When completed, block should measure 4 1/4" x 15 1/2"

Block C Assembly

1. Use diagonal corner technique to make one each of units 2, 3, 4, 5, 10, 11, 13, 15, 17, and 19. Refer to diagram below for assembling combined units 5 and 6. Follow the instructions below the illustration. Use diagonal end technique to make one of Unit 12. See diagram below for assembly. For Unit 13, be sure to add diagonal corners in alphabetical order.

2. To assemble the block, begin by joining units 2, 1, and 3 in a horizontal row. Join units 9 and 10; then add Unit 11 to right side of combined 9/10 units. Join Unit 12 to the bottom of these combined units. Join units 4 and combined 5/6 units. Join units 7 and 8; then add Unit 13 to right side of these combined units. Join units 14 and 15. Add these units to right side of Unit 13, matching seams. Join the 4-13 units to the 9-12 combined units, matching seams. Join the top and botom sections together.

Making combined units C5/C6

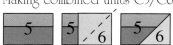

Join 1 1/4" x 3 1/4" strip of Fabric V with 1 1/2" x 3 1/4" strip of Fabric VI. Add diagonal corner C6.

Making Unit C12

3. Join units 18 and 19. Join units 16 and 17. Add the 18/19 combined units to the left side of the block, and the 16/17 units to the right side of the block. Make 8 of Block C

Block D Assembly

1. Use diagonal corner technique to make one each of units 1, 2, 3, 4, 6, 8, 11, 12, 13, 15, 16, 17, 23, and 25. Refer to diagram on page 101 for making units A10 and B10. Unit D8 is made the same way.
   Use diagonal end technique to make one of Unit 19. Refer

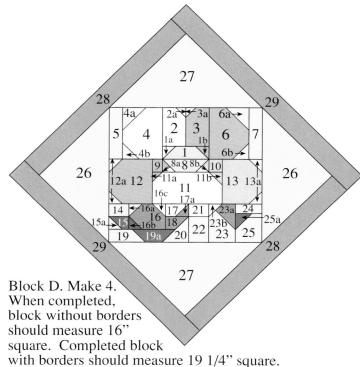

Block D. Make 4. When completed, block without borders should measure 16" square. Completed block with borders should measure 19 1/4" square.

3. For center section, join units 9, 8, and 10 in a horizontal row as shown. Add Unit 11 to bottom, matching seams. Join Unit 12 to left side of combined units; then add Unit 13 to right side to complete the center section. Join the two sections together, matching flower center seams.

4. For bottom section, join units 14 and 15; then add Unit 16 to right side of combined units. Join units 17 and 18. Join them to right side of Unit 16; then add Unit 19 to bottom of the combined units. Join diagonal corner, Unit 20 to right side of the leaf units. Join units 21 and 22; then add Unit 23 to right side of these combined units. Join units 24 and 25. Join the 24/25 combined units to right side of Unit 23. Join this bottom section to top section of flower.

5. Join triangle units 26 to opposite sides of flower block as shown; then join triangle Unit 27 to top and bottom. Add Unit 28 to opposite sides; then join Unit 29 to opposite sides as shown to complete Block D. Make 4.

This block, when completed should measure 40 1/2" square.

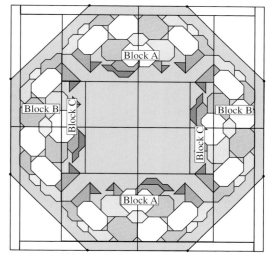

Mark the center. Mark
7 3/4" on each side of center.

Making the Octagon block.

1. Refer to large diagram at left to make the Octagon block. Join Block C to opposite short sides of Unit Q1. Join Block A to top and bottom of center section. Join Block B to opposite sides of block; then add Unit Q2 to top and bottom, and Unit Q3 to opposite sides. The block should measure 40 1/2" square when completed.

2. Find the center of the block and mark the center along the outside edges. Refer to the diagram at left, and mark 7 3/4" from each center point. This measurement will be 15 1/2" on all four sides of the block. Mark the points clearly; then cut diagonally between the points as shown. The diagonal should measure 17 1/2" between the marks.

3. Join Unit Q4 along each untrimmed edge as shown below. Join Unit Q5 along the diagonal edge. Trim off even with Unit Q4 as indicated by dashed lines.

4. Refer to the diagrams on page 104 for joining the quilt top, and follow the pictures and written instructions for each.

5. After completion of Step 5 on page 104, join the fourth Octagon block and stitch it in place as you did for Step 5, thus closing the Block D seams. Open out. Refer to the diagram below of the completed quilt. The three remaining D blocks will be sewn on two sides exactly as the center was. Begin and end stitching 1/4" from edge, reinforcing stitching at those points. Block E is sewn into the top in the same manner.

6. To make Block E, join unit E2 to one short side of triangle; then add Unit E3 as shown. Trim these strips even with diagonal. Join Unit E4 on the long bias edge and trim to form the triangle.

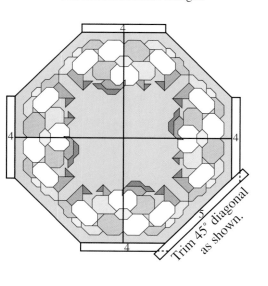

Block trimmed into octagon

Block E. Make 1.

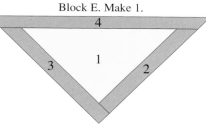

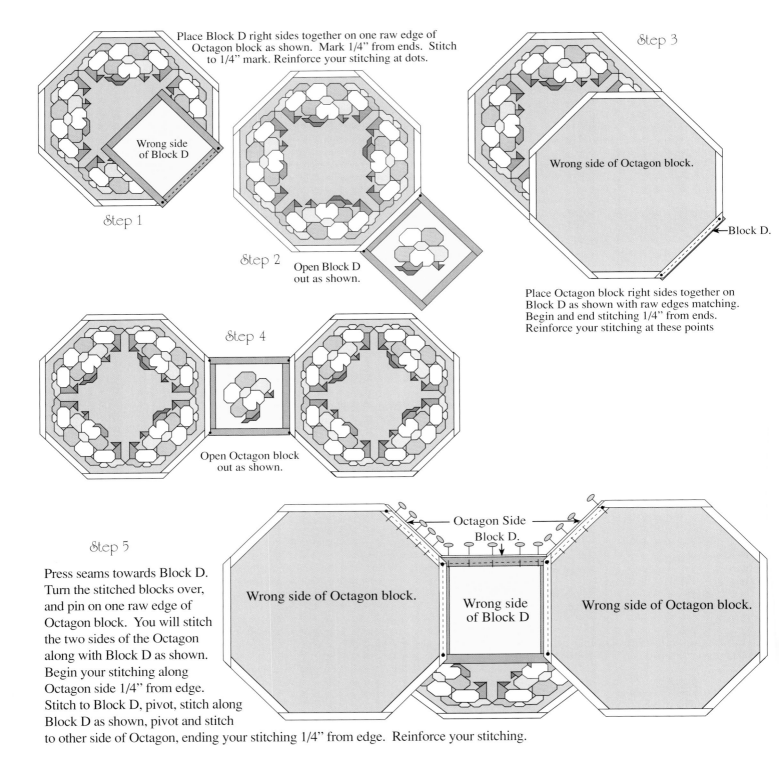

Step 1 Place Block D right sides together on one raw edge of Octagon block as shown. Mark 1/4" from ends. Stitch to 1/4" mark. Reinforce your stitching at dots.

Wrong side of Block D

Step 2 Open Block D out as shown.

Step 3 Wrong side of Octagon block.

←Block D.

Place Octagon block right sides together on Block D as shown with raw edges matching. Begin and end stitching 1/4" from ends. Reinforce your stitching at these points

Step 4 Open Octagon block out as shown.

Octagon Side
Block D.

Step 5

Press seams towards Block D. Turn the stitched blocks over, and pin on one raw edge of Octagon block. You will stitch the two sides of the Octagon along with Block D as shown. Begin your stitching along Octagon side 1/4" from edge. Stitch to Block D, pivot, stitch along Block D as shown, pivot and stitch to other side of Octagon, ending your stitching 1/4" from edge. Reinforce your stitching.

Wrong side of Octagon block.

Wrong side of Block D

Wrong side of Octagon block.

Quilting and Finishing

Mary did some beautiful things with this quilt. She quilted a circular feather design in the center of the large blocks with different butterflies in the center. She quilted a feathery design in blue thread on the white sashing, and stippled the background on the D Blocks. The patchwork was "ditched".

Use the 22 1/2" wide strip of Fabric II, and cut 2 1/2" wide bias for the binding, and bind your quilt.

Quilt finishes to: 89 1/2" x 105 3/4"
Wall Quilt finishes to: 31" x 57 3/4"
Techniques used: diagonal corners, diagonal ends, strip sets used as diagonal corners, diagonal corners used as diagonal corners.

Materials

☐	Fabric I (white with tan print) 3 1/4 yards	Need 108 1/4"
◻	Fabric II (dark salmon textured print) 2 1/2 yards	Need 74 5/8"
◻	Fabric III (pale green textured print) 1 5/8 yards	Need 54"
◻	Fabric IV (leafy medium peach print) 1/2 yard	Need 13 1/2"
◻	Fabric V (light peach textured print) 1 yard	Need 31 3/4"
◻	Fabric VI (medium peach print) 5/8 yard	Need 18 3/4"
◻	Fabric VII (white on white print) 1 1/8 yards	Need 36 1/4"
◻	Fabric VIII (light green print) 7/8 yard	Need 24 3/4"
◻	Fabric IX (medium green print) 3/4 yard	Need 23 7/8"
◻	Fabric X (dark green print) 2 1/8 yards	Need 69"
◻	Fabric XI (light yellow print) 1/8 yard	Need 1 3/4"
◻	Fabric XII (rust print) 3/8 yard	Need 10"
	Backing	8 1/4 yards

Cutting

☐ **From Fabric I, cut: (white with tan print**

• One 11 5/8" wide strip. From this, cut:
  * Four - 9 7/8" x 11 5/8" (Q26)
• Six 7 1/8" wide strips. From these, cut:
  * Two - 7 1/8" x 13 (Q2)
  * Two - 7 1/8" x 11 5/8" (Q27)
  * Two - 7 1/8" x 8 7/8" (Q41)
  * Two - 7 1/8" x 7 7/8" (Q22)
  * Four - 7 1/8" x 7 1/4" (Q33)
  * Four - 6 7/8" x 7 1/8" (Q24)
  * Two - 5 7/8" x 7 1/8" (Q37)
  * Four - 5 1/2" x 7 1/8" (Q36)
  * Four - 5 1/4" x 7 1/8" (Q23)
  * Two - 4 1/4" x 7 1/8" (Q21)
  * Four - 3 7/8" x 7 1/8" (Q35)
  * Two - 3 1/2" x 7 1/8" (Q38)
  * Four - 2 1/8" x 7 1/8" (Q34)
  * One - 6 7/8" x 14 1/4" (Q3)
• One 6 7/8" wide strip. From this, cut:
  * One - 6 7/8" x 18" (Q5)
  * One - 4 1/4" x 6 7/8" (Q4)
  * Four - 3 1/4" x 6 7/8" (Q25)
  * Two - 2 3/4" x 3 1/4" (Q39)
• Two 6 3/4" wide strips. From these, cut:
  * Four - 6 3/4" x 15 1/4" (Q32)
  * Fifteen - 2" squares (A4a, A46a, A57a, B4a, B46a, B57a)

Dogwoods

* Twenty-four - 1 1/8" x 1 5/8" (N3c, O3c)
* Two 4 3/8" wide strips. From these, cut:
  * Twenty-four - 3 1/2" x 4 3/8" (N5, O5)
* Two 3 1/4" wide strips. From these and scrap, cut:
  * Twenty-four - 3 1/4" squares (N6a, O6a)
  * Five - 1 1/4" x 2" (A15a, B15a)
* Two 3" wide strips. From these, cut:
  * Twenty-four - 3" squares (N3b, O3b)
  * Three - 1 1/4" x 1 1/2" (Q1b)
  * Five - 1 3/8" squares (Q3b, Q22b, Q40b)
* One 2 3/4" wide strip. From this, cut:
  * Two - 2 3/4" x 14 1/4" (Q40)
* One 1 1/2" wide strip. From this, cut:
  * Three - 1 1/2" x 12 1/4" (Q1)
* Four 1 3/8" wide strips. From these, cut:
  * Twenty-four - 1 3/8" x 4 7/8" (N1, O1)
  * Twenty-four - 1 1/4" x 1 3/8" (N2, O2)
* One 1 1/4" wide strip. From this, cut:
  * Twenty-four - 1 1/4" squares (N4b, O4b)
* One 1 1/8" wide strip. From this, cut:
  * Twenty-four - 1 1/8" squares (N6b, O6b)

From Fabric II, cut: (dark salmon textured print)
All units listed below are for blocks A, B, C, D, E, F, G and H unless otherwise indicated. Unit numbers only will be given.

* Four 5 3/4" wide strips. From these, cut:
  * Seventeen - 4 5/8" x 5 3/4" (57)
  * Seventeen - 4" x 5 3/4" (46)
  * Seventeen - 1 1/4" x 2 1/2" (43) Stack this cut.
* One 4 3/8" wide strip. From this, cut:
  * Four - 3 1/2" x 4 3/8" (J5, K5)
  * Four - 3 1/4" squares (J6a, K6a)
  * Four - 3" squares (J3b, K3b)
* Three 4" wide strips. From these, cut:
  * Seventeen - 4" x 6 1/4" (4)
* Three 2" wide strips. From these, cut:
  * Fifty-one - 2" squares (9a, 14b, 56a)
  * Seventeen - 1 1/8" x 2" (47)
* Four 1 7/8" wide strips. From these, cut:
  * Sixty-eight - 1 7/8" squares (1a, 18a, 37a, 49b)
  * Seventeen - 1 3/4" squares (37b)
* Three 1 3/8" wide strips. From these, cut:
  * Four - 1 3/8" x 4 7/8" (J1, K1)
  * Seventeen - 1 3/8" x 3 7/8" (12)
  * Twenty-one - 1 1/4" x 1 3/8" (13, J2, K2)
* Six 1 1/4" wide strips. From these, cut:
  * Seventeen - 1 1/4" x 3 3/8" (15)
  * Seventeen - 1 1/4" x 2 5/8" (45)
  * 106 - 1 1/4" squares (11a, 17b, 24a, 39a, 52a, J4b, K4b)
  * Four - 1 1/8" squares (1b, 26a, 44a, 49a, J6b, K6b)
* Nine 1 1/8" wide strips. From these, cut:
  * Seventeen - 1 1/8" x 3 1/4" (25)
  * Thirty-four - 1 1/8" x 2 1/2" (5, 55)
  * Seventeen - 1 1/8" x 2 1/4" (20)
  * Seventeen - 1 1/8" x 1 7/8" (18b)
  * Thirty-eight - 1 1/8" x 1 5/8" (2, 14c, J3c, K3c)
  * Sixty-eight - 1 1/8" squares (add to 1 1/8" squares above)

From Fabric III, cut: (pale green textured print)
* One 10 3/4" wide strip. From this, cut:
  * Four - 10 1/4" x 10 3/4" (Q16)
* One 7 1/8" wide strip. From this, cut:
  * Four - 7 1/8" x 7 3/8" (Q13)
  * Four - 3 1/2" x 4 5/8" (Q15) Stack this cut
* One 4 3/8" wide strip. From this, cut:
  * Four - 3 1/2" x 4 3/8" (L5, M5)
  * Four - 2 3/4" x 4 1/4" (Q30)
  * Four - 2 1/8" x 4 1/4" (Q12)

* Twelve - 1 1/4" x 2" (C15a, D15a, E15a, F15a, G15a, H15a)
* One 3 1/2" wide strip. From this, cut:
  * Four - 3 1/2" x 6 1/8" (Q14)
  Stack the following cuts:
  * Eight - 1 1/4" x 1 1/2" (Q9, Q29)
  * Four - 1 1/4" x 1 3/8" (L2, M2)
  * Four - 1 1/4" squares (L4b, M4b)
  * Four - 1 1/8" x 1 5/8" (L3c, M3c)
  * Four - 1 1/8" squares (L6b, M6b)
* One 3 1/4" wide strip. From this, cut:
  * Four - 3 1/4" squares (L6a, M6a)
  * Four - 3" squares (L3b, M3b)
  * Four - 1 3/8" x 4 7/8" (L1, M1)
* Six 2 3/4" wide strips. From these, cut:
  * Two - 2 3/4" x 28" (Q20)
  * Four - 2 3/4" x 14 1/4" (Q31)
  * Four - 2 3/4" x 3 1/4" (Q19)
  * Four - 2 1/8" x 12" (Q11)
  * Twelve - 1 3/8" squares (Q11b, Q20b, Q31b)
* Two 2" wide strips. From these, cut:
  * Twenty-four - 2" squares (Q7a, C4a, C46a, C57a, D4a, D46a, D57a, E57a, F57a, G4a, H4a)
* Three 1 1/2" wide strips. From these, cut:
  * Two - 1 1/2" x 24" (Q8)
  * Four - 1 1/2" x 12 1/4" (Q28)

From Fabric IV, cut: (leafy medium peach print)
All units listed below are for blocks A, B, C, D, E, F, G and H. Unit numbers only will be given.

* Three 3 1/4" wide strips. From these, cut:
  * Seventeen - 3 1/4" x 3 3/8" (23)
  * Seventeen - 3 1/4" squares (38)
* Three 1 1/4" wide strips. From these, cut:
  * Seventeen - 1 1/4" x 2 1/2" (33)
  * Seventeen - 1 1/4" x 1 3/4" (29)
  * Seventeen - 1 1/4" squares (28a)

From Fabric V, cut: (light peach textured print)
All units listed below are for blocks A, B, C, D, E, F, G and H. Unit numbers only will be given.

* One 2 5/8" wide strip. From this, cut:
  * Seventeen - 1 1/4" x 2 5/8" (40)
  * Seventeen - 1 1/8" x 2 5/8" (44)
* One 2 1/2" wide strip. From this, cut:
  * Seventeen - 1 1/8" x 2 1/2" (41)
  * Seventeen - 1" x 2 1/4" (22)
* One 2 1/8" wide strip. From this, cut:
  * Seventeen - 2 1/8" squares (23a)
* Nine 1 7/8" wide strips. From these, cut:
  * Thirty-four - 1 7/8" x 5 3/8" (18, 37)
  * Seventeen - 1 7/8" x 3 1/4" (39)
  * Fifty-one - 1 7/8" squares (26, 38a)
  * Seventeen - 1 5/8" squares (23b)
  * One - 1 1/2" x 2 1/2" (19)
* One 1 1/2" wide strip. From this, cut:
  * Sixteen - 1 1/2" x 2 1/2" (add to 19 above)
* Four 1 1/4" wide strips. From these, cut:
  * Seventeen - 1 1/4" x 3 1/4" (24)
  * Sixty-eight - 1 1/4" squares (34, 38b, 42a)
* One 1 1/8" wide strip. From this, cut:
  * Thirty-four - 1 1/8" squares (21a)

From Fabric VI, cut: (medium peach print)
All units listed below are for blocks A, B, C, D, E, F, G and H. Unit number only will be given.

* Two 3 1/4" wide strips. From these, cut:
  * Seventeen - 2" x 3 1/4" (50)
  * Seventeen - 1 7/8" x 3 1/4" (51)

- Four 2 1/2" wide strips. From these, cut:
  * Seventeen - 2 1/2" x 3 7/8" (8)
  * Seventeen - 2 1/2" x 2 5/8" (28)
  * Seventeen - 1 7/8" x 2 1/2" (35)
  * Seventeen - 1 1/4" x 2 1/2" (31)
- One 2 1/4" wide strip. From this and scrap, cut:
  * Seventeen - 1 1/4" x 2 1/4" (10)
  * Seventeen - 1 1/4" squares (9b)

From Fabric VII, cut: (white on white print)
All units listed below are for blocks A, B, C, D, E, F, G and H. Unit numbers only will be given.

- Four 2" wide strips. From these, cut:
  * Seventeen - 2" x 4 1/2" (9)
  * Seventeen - 2" x 2 7/8" (56)
  * Seventeen - 1 1/4" x 2" (48)
  * Eighteen - 1 1/8" squares (54a)
- Eight 1 7/8" wide strips. From these, cut:
  * Seventeen - 1 7/8" x 5 1/8" (1)
  * Seventeen - 1 7/8" x 4 1/4" (49)
  * Thirty-four - 1 7/8" squares (51a)
  * Sixty-eight - 1 1/4" x 1 7/8" (18b, 27, 32, 36)
  * Seventeen - 1 5/8" squares (8a)
  * Fourteen- 1 1/4" x 1 5/8" (3)
- Three 1 1/2" wide strips. From these, cut:
  * Thirty-four - 1 1/2" x 2 1/2" (7, 53)
  * Seventeen - 1 3/8" squares (8b)
  * Three - 1 1/4" x 1 5/8" (add to 3)
- Seven 1 1/4" wide strips. From these, cut:
  * Seventeen - 1 1/4" x 3 3/8" (52)
  * Seventeen - 1 1/4" x 2 1/4" (11)
  * 136 - 1 1/4" squares (6a, 10a, 23c, 31a, 33a, 34, 50a)
  * Sixteen - 1 1/8" squares (add to 54a)

From Fabric VIII, cut: (light green print)
All (6, 4, and 3c) units listed below are for blocks J, K, L, M, N, and O. All other units are for blocks A, B, C, D, E, F, G and H. Unit numbers only will be given.

- Three 3 1/4" wide strips. From these, cut:
  * Thirty-two - 3 1/4" x 3 1/2" (6)
- Five 3" wide strips. From these, cut:
  * Seventeen - 3" x 4 5/8" (14)
  * Thirty-two - 2 1/8" x 3" (4)
  * Seventeen - 1 3/8" x 3" (12a)
  * Thirty-two - 1" x 1 5/8" (3c)
  * Seventeen - 1 3/8" squares (17a)

From Fabric IX, cut: (medium green print)
All (1a, 3, and 4a) units listed below are for blocks J, K, L, M, N, and O. All other units are for blocks A, B, C, D, E, F, G and H unless otherwise indicated. Unit numbers only will be given except for "Q" units.

- Three 4 1/2" wide strips. From these, cut:
  * Thirty-two - 3" x 4 1/2" (3)
  * Thirty - 1 3/8" x 2 7/8" (1a)
- Two 2 3/4" wide strips. From these, cut:
  * Thirteen - 2 3/4" squares (Q3a, Q20a, Q22a, Q31a, Q40a)
  * Four - 2 1/8" x 2 3/4" (Q11a)
  * Nine - 2 1/8" x 3 3/4" (17)
- One 2 1/8" wide strip. From this, cut:
  * Eight - 2 1/8" x 3 3/4" (add to 17)
  * Seventeen - 1" x 1 1/4" (16)
- Two 1 3/8" wide strips. From these, cut:
  * Thirty-two - 1 3/8" squares (4a)
  * Two - 1 3/8" x 2 7/8" (add to 1a above)
  * Four - 1 1/8" squares (Q14a)
  * Seventeen - 1" x 1 5/8" (14c)

From Fabric X, cut: (dark green print)
- Five 3" wide strips. From these, cut:
  * Thirty-two - 3" x 4" (J3a, K3a, L3a, M3a, N3a, O3a)
  * Seventeen - 3" squares (A14a, B14a, C14a, D14a, E14a, F14a, G14a, H14a)
  * Seventeen - 1 1/2" squares (Q1a, Q8a, Q16a, Q27a, Q37a)
- Ten 2 1/2" wide strips for straight-grain binding.
- Seven 2" wide strips. From these and scrap, cut:
  * Two - 2" x 34 1/4" (Q7)
  * Two - 2" x 25 3/4" (Q6)
  * Four - 2" x 18 3/8" (Q18)
  * Four - 2" x 13 3/4" (Q17)
  * Four - 2" x 2 1/8" (Q10)
  * Sixteen - 2" squares (E4a, E46a, F4a, F46a, G46a, G57a, H46a, H57a)
- Ten 1 1/2" wide strips. From these, cut:
  * Six - 1 1/2" x 42" (Q42, Q43) Piece two together for two sets of Q42.
  * Four - 1 1/2" x 23 3/8" (Q42) Piece two to opposite ends of a 42" long strip to = two 87 3/4" lengths.
  * Four - 1 1/2" x 11 7/8" (Q43) Piece two to opposite ends of the joined Q42 strips to = two 106 1/4" lengths.

From Fabric XI, cut: (light yellow print)
All (30) units listed below are for blocks A, B, C, D, E, F, G and H.

- One 1 3/4" wide strip. From this, cut:
  * Seventeen - 1 3/4" squares (30)

From Fabric XII, cut: (rust print)
All units listed below are for blocks A, B, C, D, E, F, G and H. Unit numbers only will be given.

- Two 2 1/2" wide strips. From these, cut:
  * Fifty-one - 1 1/4" x 2 1/2" (6, 42, 54)
  * Thirty-four - 1 1/8" squares (5a, 20a, 55a)
- One 1 3/8" wide strip. From this, cut:
  * Seventeen - 1 3/8" x 2 1/4" (21)
- Two 1 1/4" wide strips. From these, cut:
  * Thirty-four - 1 1/4" squares (43a)
  * Thirty-six - 1 1/8" squares (add to 1 1/8" sq. above)
- One 1 1/8" wide strip. From this, cut:
  * Thirty-two - 1 1/8" squares (add to 1 1/8" sq. above)

Assembly Of Flower Blocks

All of the flower blocks are assembled in exactly the same way. All unit numbers are the same. The only difference in the blocks are color changes in the corners, and some of the blocks are mirror images.

When referring to the quilt diagram, it shows the block letter and you can also see which way the block is to be turned when assembling the quilt.

The instructions and illustrations shown on the following pages are for one block. We are using Block A for the written directions. Refer to the mirror image blocks for correct placement of mirror image units. Refer to the smaller block diagrams for the corner color changes and the mirror images. You will make a total of 17 blocks. Each block, when completed should measure 13" x 17". Because the units are the same (except for the corners), the main part of the blocks can be chain pieced to speed things along. Units that require unusual piecing techniques or diagonal ends are illustrated.

1. Use diagonal corner technique to make one each of units 1, 4, 5, 6, 8, 9, 10, 11, 14, 17, 18, 20, 21, 23, 24, 26, 28, 31, 33, 37, 38, 39, 42, 43, 44, 46, 49, 50, 51, 52, 54, 55, 56, and 57.

2. Use diagonal end technique to make one each of units 12 and 15

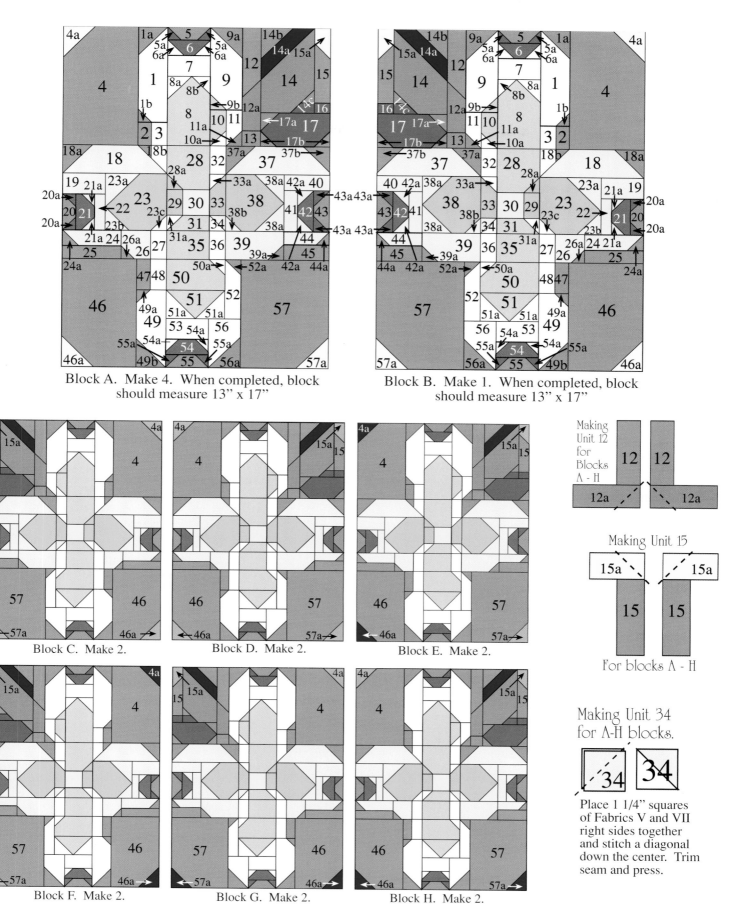

Block A. Make 4. When completed, block should measure 13" x 17"

Block B. Make 1. When completed, block should measure 13" x 17"

Block C. Make 2.

Block D. Make 2.

Block E. Make 2.

Block F. Make 2.

Block G. Make 2.

Block H. Make 2.

Making Unit 12 for Blocks A - H

Making Unit 15

For blocks A - H

Making Unit 34 for A-H blocks.

Place 1 1/4" squares of Fabrics V and VII right sides together and stitch a diagonal down the center. Trim seam and press.

3. Unit 34 is a small triangle-square. Follow the picture and instructions below it on page 109 for correct assembly.

28/30 units; then add to other combined units, matching seams. Join units 32, 33, 34, and 36. Join this row to right side of other

Making Unit 14 for blocks A-H

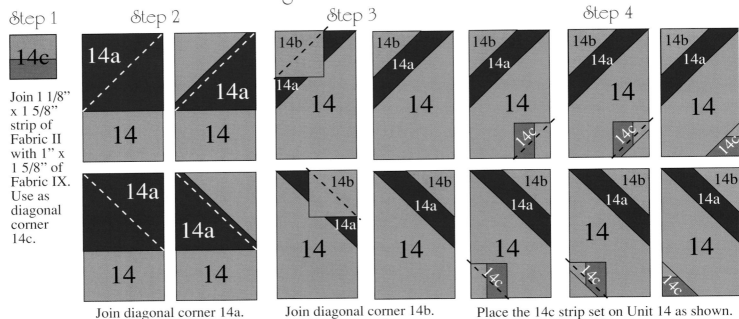

Step 1

14c

Join 1 1/8" x 1 5/8" strip of Fabric II with 1" x 1 5/8" of Fabric IX. Use as diagonal corner 14c.

Step 2

Join diagonal corner 14a. Trim seam and press.

Step 3

Join diagonal corner 14b. Trim seam, and press.

Step 4

Place the 14c strip set on Unit 14 as shown. Stitch diagonal, trim seam and press.

4. Unit 14, shown above has multiple diagonal corner, and a small strip set used as a diagonal corner. Refer to the illustration and instructions for the mirror image units. Unit 18, shown below also

Making Unit 18, Blocks A - H

18b

Join 1 1/8" x 1 7/8" strip of Fabric II with 1 1/4" x 1 7/8" strip of Fabric VII for diagonal corner 18b

uses a small strip set as a diagonal corner. Refer to the diagram and instructions for the strip set to assemble Unit 18.

5. To assemble the flower block, begin by joining units 2 and 3; then add Unit 1 to top of the 2/3 combined units, matching seams. Join Unit 4 to left side. Join units 5, 6, 7, and 8 in a vertical row and add them to combined units 1-4. Join units 10 and 11; then add Unit 9 to top of the 10/11 combined units. Join these combined units to right side of other combined units, matching seams. Join units 12 and 13; then join them to right side of other combined units, matching seams. Join units 15 and 16 as shown; then add Unit 14 to left side of these combined units, matching seams. Join Unit 17 to bottom of combined 14-16 units. Join these combined units to right side of combined 12/13 units to complete the flower top.

6. For flower center section, beginining on left side, join units 20, 21 and 22; then add Unit 19 to top of these combined units. Join Unit 23 to right side of combined units; then add Unit 18 to top. Join units 24 and 25. Join units 26 and 27. Join these two combined unit sections together and add them to the bottom of the other combined units. Join units 29, and 30; then add Unit 28 to top of these combined units. Join units 31 and 35. Join to bottom of combined

combined units. Join units 41, 42, and 43 in a row. Add Unit 40 to top of the 41-43 units. Join units 44 and 45. Join these combined units to bottom of combined units 40-43. Join units 38 and 39; then add them to left side of combined 40-45 units. Add Unit 37 to top. Join these combined units to other combined units to complete flower center.

7. For flower bottom, begin by joining units 47 and 48; then add Unit 49 to bottom of the 47/48 units. Join Unit 46 to left side. Join units 50 and 51; then add Unit 52 to right side. Join units 53, 54 and 55 in a row. Add Unit 56 to right side. Join these combined units to 50-52 combined units; then add Unit 57 to right side. Join the two combined unit sections together to complete the bottom of the flower.

8. Join the three flower sections together, carefully matching seams. Make 17 according to instructions beginning on page 108 for Making The Flower Blocks.

Assembly Of Leaf Blocks

All of the leaf blocks are assembled in exactly the same way. All units numbers are the same. The only difference in the blocks are color changes in the background, and half of the blocks are mirror images. When referring to the quilt diagram, it shows the block letter and you can also see which way the block is to be turned when assembling the quilt.

The instructions and illustrations shown on the following pages are for one block. We are using Block J for the written directions. Refer to the mirror image blocks for correct placement of mirror image units. Refer to the other block diagrams for the background color changes and the mirror images. You will make a total of 32 blocks. Each block, when completed should measure 6 7/8" x 7 1/8".

Units that require unusual piecing techniques or diagonal ends are illustrated.

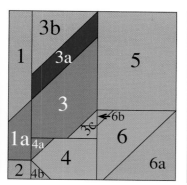

Block J. Make 2. When completed, block should measure 6 7/8" x 7 1/8"

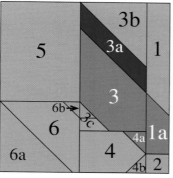

Block K. Make 2. When completed, block should measure 6 7/8" x 7 1/8"

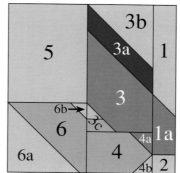

Block L. Make 2.

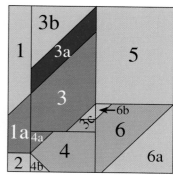

Block M. Make 2.

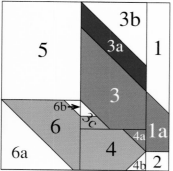

Block N. Make 12.

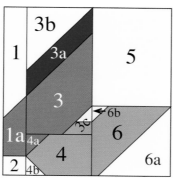

Block O. Make 12.

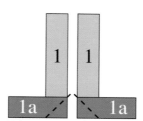

Making Unit 1, Blocks J - O

Making mirror image Unit 3, Blocks J - O

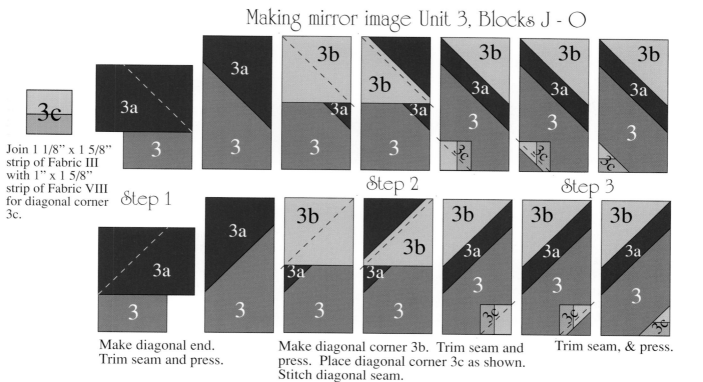

Join 1 1/8" x 1 5/8" strip of Fabric III with 1" x 1 5/8" strip of Fabric VIII for diagonal corner 3c.

Step 1

Make diagonal end. Trim seam and press.

Step 2

Make diagonal corner 3b. Trim seam and press. Place diagonal corner 3c as shown. Stitch diagonal seam.

Step 3

Trim seam, & press.

1. Use diagonal corner technique to make one each of units 3, 4, and 6. Use diagonal end technique to make one each of units 1 and 3.. Refer to the diagram above for assembly of Unit 3.

2. To assemble the block, begin by joining units 1 and 2. Join units 3 and 4; then add them to the 1/2 combined units, matching seams. Join units 5 and 6 and add them to the other combined units, again matching seams.

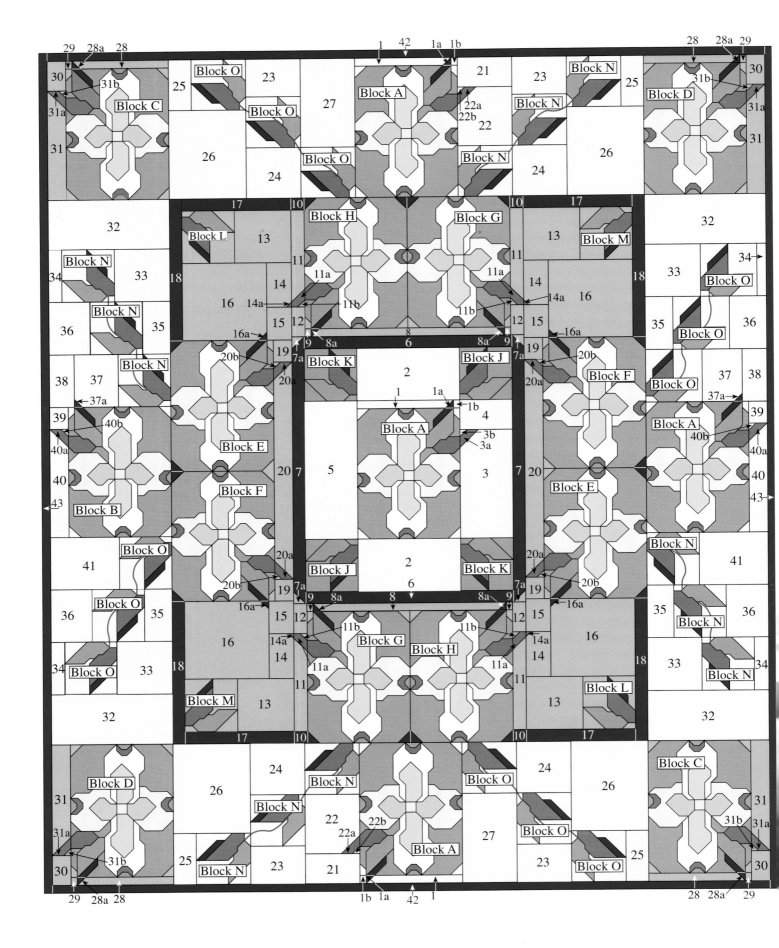

112

Quilt Assembly

1. Use diagonal corner technique to make four of mirror image, Unit Q11, shown on right. Make diagonal end first; then add diagonal corner 11b. Use this technique to make three of Unit Q1, one of Unit Q3, two of units Q7, Q8, Q20, Q22, Q37, and Q40. Make four each of units Q14, Q16, Q28, and Q31.

2. To assemble the quilt top, refer to quilt diagram at left, and begin in the center. Join Unit Q1 and Unit Q1b. Join these combined units to the top of Block A. Join units Q3 and Q4. Join these combined units to right side of Block A combination. Join Unit Q5 to left side. Referring to diagram, Join Block K to left side of one Unit Q2, and Block J to right side. Make two. Join one to the top of Block A combined units. Turn the second one 180° and join to bottom of other combined blocks and units, matching corner seams. Join Unit Q6 to top and bottom of center section; then join Unit Q7 to opposite sides.

3. Referring to top of center section, join blocks H and G as shown. Join Unit Q9 to opposite sides of Unit Q8 and add this horizontal row to botom of the combined H/G blocks, matching the leaf tips. Join units Q10, Q11 and Q12, keeping in mind that they are mirror images. Refer to quilt diagram for correct placement. Join the combined 10-12 units to opposite sides of the blocks H and G combination. Make two of these combinations. Again referring to quilt diagram, turn the second combination around 180°. Join to top and bottom of center section as shown.

4. For side sections, beginning in top left corner, join Block L and Unit Q13; then add Unit Q17 to top of the Block L/Q13 combination. Join units Q14 and Q15; then add Unit Q16 to left side of these combined units. Join the 14-16 units to bottom of Block L combination; then add Unit Q18 to left side. Make two.

5. For top right corner, join Unit Q13 and Block M; then add Unit Q17 to top of combined 13/Block M combination. Join units Q14 and Q15; then join Unit Q16 to right side of these combined units. Join these units to bottom of leaf combination; then join Unit Q18 to right side. Make 2. Join the leaf Block L combination to left side of the combined blocks H and G section; then join Block M combination to right side of the block H and G section. Make two.

5. Join units Q19, Q20, and Q19 in a row. These are mirror images, so check quilt diagram for correct placement of Unit Q20. For left side, join blocks E and F together; then add the combined Q19/Q20 units to right side of the block E and F combination, matching leaf tip seams. Make two. For the left side section, join combined leaf Block L section to top of the Block E and F combination; then add the leaf Block M combination to the bottom. Make two of these side sections. Turn one around 180°. Join these sections to opposite sides of the center section, matching seams.

6. To complete the large ivory side borders, begin on top left side of diagram and join Unit Q34, Block N, and Q33. Add Unti Q32 to top. Join Unit Q36, Block N, and Q35. Join to other Block N row. Dark green leaf tip should match with right side of Block N above it. Join Unit Q38, Q37 and Block N. Add to other rows, again matching the leaf tip. Join units 39 and 40 as shown. Add them to left side of Block B. Join Block B to bottom of the leaf Block N rows. Join unit Q41 and Block O. Join Unit Q36, Block O and Unit Q35. Join this row to other Block O row. Join Unit Q34, Block O, and Q33; then add Unit Q32 to bottom of this row. Join the last row with Unit Q32 to bottom of other rows to complete the left side border. Join this border to left side of quilt. To do so, find the center of the border and the quilt left side. Pin centers with right sides together. Pin the ends together; then contin-

Making Unit Q11

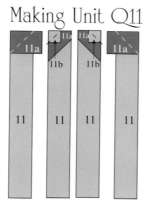

ue pinning to insure that border will fit properly.

7. For right side border, join units Q33, Block O, and Q34; then add Unit Q32 to top of row. Join Unit Q35, Block O, and Unit Q36. Join to bottom of other Block O row. Join Block O, Unit Q37, and Unit Q38 in a row. Add to bottom of other Block O rows. Join units Q39 and Q40. Add these combined units to right side of Block A. Join this combination to bottom of the leaf Block O rows. Join Block N and Unit Q41. Join Unit Q35, Block N, and Q36 in a row and add to Block N row above. Join Unit Q33, Block N, and Unit Q34; then add Unit Q32 to bottom of this row. Join these combined units and Block N to bottom of other rows to complete the right side border. Join this border to right side of quilt.

8. For top row, join units Q1 and Q1b together. Add to top of Block A, matching leaf tip. Working outwards to the left, join Block O and Unit Q27. Join Unit Q24, Block O, and Q23. Join to the Q27/Block O row as shown. Join Unit Q25 and Block O; then add Unit Q26 to bottom of the Q25/Block O combination. Join the three leaf rows together; then add them to the left side of Block A. For leaf row on the right of Block A, join Unit Q21, Q22, and Block N. Join Unit Q23, Block N, and Q24. Join Block N and Unit Q25; then add Unit Q26 to bottom of this combination. Join the three leaf rows together and add them to the right side of Block A. For the left corner, join units Q28 and Q29. Join these combined units to the top of Block C, matching leaf tips. Join Unit Q30 and Q31. Join to left side of Block C, matching leaf tip. Join this combination to left side of top row. For right corner, again join Unit Q28 and Q29. Join to top of Block D, matching leaf tip. Join Unit Q30 and Q31; then add this combination to right side of Block D, matching leaf tip. Join this combination to the right side of top row to complete the row. Make two of this row.

9. Join one row to top of quilt, pinning as you did for side rows. Turn the other row around 180° and add to quilt bottom. Join previously pieced border Q42 to top and bottom of quilt, trimming if necessary. Join previously pieced border Q43 to opposite sides of quilt.

Quilting and Finishing

Before quilting, run a triple stitch or narrow satin stitch in dark green between the leaf blocks. Put a tear-away stabilizer under your stitching, and tear it away when stitching is completed.

This quilt offers a world of opportunities to show off your quilting in the large open spaces. Mary quilted beautiful leaves with vines in the ivory borders using a medium brown thread. She stippled the background behind the flowers and added leaves to the border.

Join the ten 2 1/2" wide strips of Fabric X together to make straight-grain binding and bind your quilt. Refer to page 12 for binding instructions.

Materials for Wall Quilt

Fabric I (white with tan print) Need 12 5/8"
1/2 yard

Fabric II (dark salmon textured print) Need 12 7/8"
1/2 yard

Fabric III (pale green textured print) Need 8 3/4"
3/8 yard

Fabric IV (leafy medium peach print) Need 3 1/4"
1/4 yard

Fabric V (light peach textured print) Need 7 1/4"
3/8 yard

Fabric VI (medium peach print) Need 3 7/8"
1/4 yard

Fabric VII (white on white print) Need 8 1/4"
3/8 yard

Fabric VIII (light green print) Need 5 5/8"
1/4 yard

Fabric IX (medium green print) Need 5 7/8"
1/4 yard

Fabric X (dark green print) Need 21 1/2"
3/4 yard

Fabric XI (light yellow print) Need 4" square
Scrap

Fabric XII (rust print) Need 14 1/4"
1/2 yard

Fabric XIII (leafy dark salmon print) Need 8 3/4"
3/8 yard

Backing 1 3/4 yards

Cutting

From Fabric I, cut: (white with tan print)
- One 7 1/8" wide strip. From this, cut:
  * One - 7 1/8" x 8 7/8" (Q9)
  * One - 5 7/8" x 7 1/8" (Q5)
  * One - 3 1/2" x 7 1/8" (Q6)
  * Two - 3 1/4" x 5 5/8" ((Q4) Stack this cut
  * Two 3 1/4" x 3 3/4" ((Q2) Stack this cut
  * Two - 2 3/4" x 4 3/8" (Q12) Stack this cut
  * One - 2 3/4" x 3 1/4" (Q7)
  * Five - 2" squares (A57a B57a, C57a, B4a, C4a) Stack this cut
  * Three - 1 1/4" x 2" (A15a, B15a, C15a) Stack this cut from scrap.
- Two 2 3/4" wide strips. From these, cut:
  * One - 2 3/4" x 28 " (Q13)
  * One - 2 3/4" x 14 1/4" (Q8)
  * Two 1 1/4" x 1 5/8" (Q11) Stack this cut.
  * Two - 1 5/8" x 12 1/4" (Q10)
  * Three - 1 3/8" squares (Q8b, Q13b)

From Fabric II, cut: (dark salmon textured print)
All units listed below are for blocks A, B, and C. Unit numbers only will be given.
- One 5 3/4" wide strip. From this, cut:
  * Three - 4 5/8" x 5 3/4" (57)
  * Three - 4" x 5 3/4" (46)
  * Two - 4" x 6 1/4" (4)
  * Three - 1 1/4" x 3 3/8" (15) Stack this cut.
- One 4" wide strip. From this, cut:
  * One - 4" x 6 1/4" (add to 4)
  * Three 1 3/8" x 3 7/8" (12)
  * Three - 1 1/8" x 3 1/4" (25)
  Stack the following cuts:
  * Nine - 2" squares (9a, 14b, 56a)
  * Three - 1 1/4" x 2 5/8" (45)
  * Three - Three 1 1/4" x 2 1/2" (43)
  * Six - 1 1/8" x 2 1/2" (5, 55)

  * Three - 1 1/8" x 2 1/4" (20)
  * Three - 1 1/8" x 2" (47)
  * Three - 1 1/8" x 1 7/8" (18b)
  * Three - 1 1/8" x 1 5/8" (2)
- One 1 7/8" wide strip. From this, cut:
  * Twelve - 1 7/8" squares (1a,18a, 37a, 49b)
  * Three - 1 3/4" squares (37b)
  * Three - 1 1/4" x 1 3/8" (13)
- One 1 1/4" wide strip. From this, cut:
  * Eighteen - 1 1/4" squares (11a, 17b, 24a, 39a, 52a)
  * Three - 1 1/8" x 1 5/8" (14c)
  * Twelve - 1 1/8" squares (1b, 26a, 44a, 49a)

From Fabric III, cut: (pale green textured print)
All units listed below are for blocks L, and M. Unit numbers only will be given.
- One 4 3/8" wide strip. From this, cut:
  * Six - 3 1/2" x 4 3/8" (5)
  * Six - 3 1/4" squares (6a)
- One 3" wide strip. From this, cut:
  * Six - 3" squares (3b)
  * Six - 1 3/8" x 4 7/8" (1) Stack this cut
  * Twelve - 1 1/8" squares (4b, 6b) Stack this cut
- One 1 3/8" wide strip. From this, cut:
  * Six - 1 1/4" x 1 3/8" (2)
  * Six - 1 1/8" x 1 5/8" (3c)

From Fabric IV, cut: (leafy medium peach print)
All units listed below are for blocks A, B, and C. Unit numbers only will be given.
- One 3 1/4" wide strip. From this, cut:
  * Three - 3 1/4" x 3 3/8" (23)
  * Three - 3 1/4" squares (38)
  * Three - 1 1/4" x 2 1/2" (33)
  * Three - 1 1/4" x 1 3/4" (29)
  * Three - 1 1/4" squares (28a)

From Fabric V, cut: (light peach textured print)
All units listed below are for blocks A, B and C. Unit numbers only will be given.
- One 2 5/8" wide strip. From this, cut:
  * Three - 1 1/4" x 2 5/8" (40)
  * Three - 1 1/8" x 2 5/8" (44)
  * Three - 1 1/8" x 2 1/2" (41)
  * Three - 1" x 2 1/4" (22)
  * Three - 2 1/8" squares (23a)
  * Four - 1 7/8" x 5 3/8" (18, 37)
- One 1 7/8" wide strip. From this, cut:
  * Two - 1 7/8" x 5 3/8" (18, 37)
  * Three - 1 7/8" x 3 1/4" (39)
  * Nine - 1 7/8" squares (26, 38a)
- One 1 5/8" wide strip. From this, cut:
  * Three - 1 5/8" squares (23b)
  * Three - 1 1/2" x 2 1/2" (19)
  * Three- 1 1/4" x 3 1/4" (24)
  * Twelve- 1 1/4" squares (34, 38c, 42a)
- One 1 1/8" wide strip. From this, cut:
  * Six - 1 1/8" squares (21a)

From Fabric VI, cut: (medium peach print)
All units listed below are for blocks A, B, and C. Unit number only will be given.
- One 3 7/8" wide strip. From this, cut:
  * Three - 2 1/2" x 3 7/8" (8)
  * Three - 2" x 3 1/4" (50)
  * Three- 1 7/8" x 3 1/4" (51)
  * Three - 2 1/2" x 2 5/8" (28)
  * Three - 1 7/8" x 2 1/2" (35)
  * Three- 1 1/4" x 2 1/2" (31)
  * Three - 1 1/4" x 2 1/4" (10)

* Three - 1 1/4" squares (9b) Stack this cut.

From Fabric VII, cut: (white on white print)
*All units listed below are for blocks A, B and C.
Unit numbers only will be given.*
- One 5 1/8" wide strip. From this, cut:
  * Three - 1 7/8" x 5 1/8" (1)
  * Three - 2" x 4 1/2" (9)
  * Three - 1 7/8" x 4 1/4" (49)
  * Three- 1 1/4" x 3 3/8" (52) Stack this cut
  * Three - 2" x 2 7/8" (56)
  * Six - 1 1/2" x 2 1/2" (7, 53) Stack this cut
  * Three - 1 1/4" x 2 1/4" (11) Stack this cut.
  * Three - 1 1/4" x 2" (48) Stack this cut.
  * Six - 1 7/8" squares (51a) Stack this cut
- One 1 7/8" wide strip. From this, cut:
  * Twelve- 1 1/4" x 1 7/8" (18b, 27, 32, 36)
  * Three - 1 5/8' squares (8a)
  * Three - 1 1/4" x 1 5/8" (3)
  * Three - 1 3/8" squares (8b)
- One 1 1/4" wide strip. From this, cut:
  * Twenty-four - 1 1/4" squares (6a, 10a, 23c, 31a, 33a, 34, 50a)
  * Six - 1 1/8" squares (54a)

From Fabric VIII, cut: (light green print)
*All (6, 4, and 3c) units listed below are for blocks L, and M.
Units (12a, 14, and 17a) are for blocks A, B, and C.
Unit numbers only will be given.*
- One 3 1/2" wide strip. From this, cut:
  * Six - 3 1/4" x 3 1/2" (6)
  * Three - 3" x 4 5/8" (14)
  * Three - 1 3/8" x 3" (12a)
  * Six - 1" x 1 5/8" (3c)
- One 2 1/8" wide strip. From this, cut:
  * Six - 2 1/8" x 3" (4)
  * Three - 1 3/8" squares (17a)

From Fabric IX, cut: (medium green print)
All (1a, 3, and 4a) units listed below are for blocks L, and M. All other units are for blocks A, B, and C, unless otherwise indicated. Unit numbers only will be given except for "Q" units.
- One 4 1/2" wide strip. From this, cut:
  * Six - 3" x 4 1/2" (3)
  * Three - 2 1/8" x 3 3/4" (17)
  * Six - 1 3/8" x 2 7/8" (1a)
  * Three - 2 3/4" squares (Q8a, Q13a)
- One 1 3/8" wide strip. From this, cut:
  * Six - 1 3/8" squares (4a)
  * Three - 1" x 1 5/8" (14c)
  * Three - 1" x 1 1/4" (16)

From Fabric X, cut: (dark green print)
- One 3" wide strip. From this, cut:
  * Six - 3" x 4" (L3a, M3a)
  * Three - 3" squares (A14a, B14a, C14a)
  * Three - 1 1/2" squares (Q5a, Q10a)
- Five 2 1/2" wide strips for straight-grain binding.
- Three 2" wide strips. From these, cut:
  * One - 2" x 31 1/2" (Q18)
  * Two - 2" x 28 5/8" (Q17) Piece together to = two 56 3/4" lengths.

From Fabric XI, cut: (light yellow print)
- Three - 1 3/4" squares (A30, B30, C30)

From Fabric XII, cut: (rust print)
- Two 7 1/8" wide strips. From these, cut:

* Two - 7 1/8" x 21 7/8" (Q15)
* Two - 2 1/4" x 7 1/8" (Q16)
- From scrap, cut:
  * Nine - 1 1/4" x 2 1/2" (A6, A42, A54, B6, B42, B54, C6, C42, C54)
  * Three - 1 3/8" x 2 1/4" (A21, B21, C21)
  * Six- 1 1/4" squares (A43a, B43a, C43a)
  * Eighteen - 1 1/8" squares (A5a, A20a, A55a, B5a, B20a, B55a, C5a, C20a, C55a)

From Fabric XIII, cut: (leafy dark salmon print)
- Two 4 3/8" wide strips. From these, cut:
  * Two - 4 3/8" x 15 1/4" (Q14)
  * Two - 4 3/8" x 5 5/8" (Q3)
  * Two 3 3/4" x 4 3/8" (Q1)

Block Assembly

All of the flower blocks are assembled as they are for the quilt. All units numbers are the same except for diagonal corner A4a, which has been eliminated, and A, B, and C 46a, which has also been eliminated . The only difference in the blocks are the diagonal corner changes in the corners, and Block B is a mirror image. All flower blocks finish to 13" x 17".
When referring to the wall quilt diagram, it shows the block letter and you can also see which way the block is to be turned when assembling the wall quilt.
Block A is used for the written directions. Refer to the mirror image Block B for correct placement of mirror image units.
Refer to pages 109-111 for assembly of the flower and leaf blocks. Illustrations and instructions are the same for these blocks, except for the two diagonal corners mentioned above.

Quilt Assembly

1. Refer to wall quilt diagram on page 116. To assemble the quilt, begin by joining blocks B and C as shown. Please note that Block C is turned upside down Join units Q10 and Q11. Make two and join them to top and bottom of combined blocks B and C, matching Unit Q10a leaf tips. Join units Q12, Q13, and Q12 as shown. Add this row to left side of block row, matching leaf tips. Join Unit Q14 to top and bottom of combined block row.

2. Join units Q1 and Q2. Join units Q3 and Q4. Referring to diagram, join the Q1/Q2 combined units to left side of Block M; then add combined Q3/Q4 units to right side. Join Block M and units Q5 and Q6. Add them to the bottom of the first leaf row, matching the dark leaf tip to the left corner of Block M as shown. Join units Q7 and Q8; then add them to right side of Block A, matching the leaf tip. Join this row to bottom of combined Block M leaf rows. Join Block L and Unit Q9. Once again join units Q1 and Q2. Join units Q4 and Q3. Add these rows to right and left side of Block L as shown; then join this row to bottom of combined Block L/Unit Q9 row. Join these two combined rows to bottom of Block A row.

3. Join the left and right sides of the quilt top together, matching seams. Referring to top of wall quilt diagram, join Unit Q15, Block M and Q16. Join this row to top of wall quilt, matching seams. Join Unit Q15, Block L, and Unit Q16. Join this row to bottom of wall quilt. Join Unit Q17 to left side of quilt top; then add Unit Q18 to bottom to complete the quilt top.

Mary repeated the leaf motif and background stippling in the wall quilt. A beautiful leaf border was quilted in the dark rust areas. The patchwork was "ditched."

Join the five 2 1/2" wide strips of Fabric X for straight-grain binding.

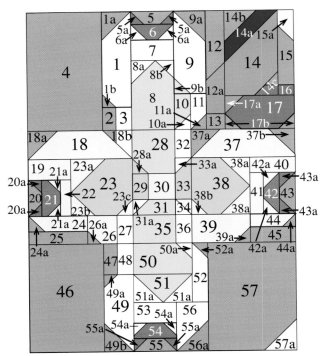

Block A. Make 1. When completed, block
should measure 13" x 17"

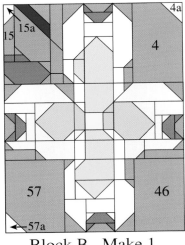

Block B. Make 1.

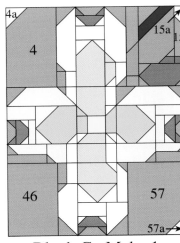

Block C. Make 1.

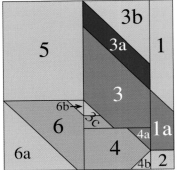

Block L. Make 3. When
completed, block should
measure 6 7/8" x 7 1/8"

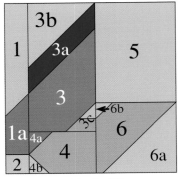

Block M. Make 3. When
completed, block should
measure 6 7/8" x 7 1/8"

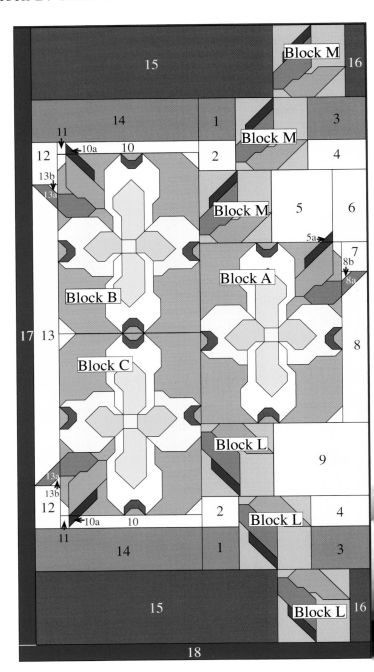

Wall Quilt finishes to: 36 1/2" x 53"
Techniques used: diagonal corners, diagonal ends, strip sets used
as diagonal corners, diagonal corners used as diagonal corners.

Materials

☐	Fabric I (white with tan flower print) 1 yard	Need 32 7/8"
■	Fabric II (dark blue floral print) 1/2 yard	Need 12 1/2"
▦	Fabric III (light blue print) Scrap	Need 4" x 9"
■	Fabric IV (dark green print) 1/4 yard	Need 4 3/4"
▦	Fabric V (medium green print) 3/8 yard	Need 9 3/4"
▦	Fabric VI (light green print) 1/4 yard	Need 4"
▦	Fabric VII (dark salmon print) 1/4 yard	Need 3 1/4"
▦	Fabric VIII (medium salmon print) 1/4 yard	Need 3 1/4"
▦	Fabric IX (medium peach print) 1/8 yard	Need 2 3/4"
☐	Fabric X (light peach print) 1/4 yard	Need 4 1/4"
▦	Fabric XI (rust print) 1/8 yard	Need 1 3/8"
■	Fabric XII (solid dark brown) Scrap	Need 2 3/4" x 4 3/4"
☐	Fabric XIII (solid light tan) Scrap	Need 2 1/2" x 4 3/4"
▦	Fabric XIV (medium honey tan print) 3/8 yard	Need 9 3/8"
■	Fabric XV (dark brown print) 1 yard	Need 29"
☐	Fabric XVI (light yellow print) Scrap	Need 3" square
	Backing	1 5/8 yards

Cutting

☐   **From Fabric I, cut: (white with tan flower print)**
- One 12" x 42 1/8" strip. From this, cut:
  * One - 5 5/8" x 12" (63)
  * One - 8 5/8" x 11 7/8" (6)
  * One - 5 1/4" x 11 7/8" (9)
  * One - 2 3/4" x 11 1/4" (A59)
  * One - 1 3/4" x 10 7/8" (55)
  * One - 3 7/8" x 10 1/8" (36)
  * One - 4" x 6 3/8" (A40)
  * One - 2 3/4" x 5 7/8" (59)
  * One - 4 5/8" x 5 3/4" (A58)
  * One - 2 7/8" x 5 1/2" (26)
- From scrap, cut:
  * One - 3 5/8" x 4 1/8" (48)
  * One - 2 1/8" x 5 1/8" (A15)
  * One - 2 5/8" x 4 1/2" (62)
  * One - 2 7/8" x 4 1/4" (30)

PLEASE NOTE:
There are several units in this design where diagonal corners are a lighter color on top of a dark background. Do not trim the center seam on the diagonal corners as the darker color will show through.

Bottles

- One 5 7/8" wide strip. From this, cut:
  * One - 5 7/8" square (56)
  * Two - 5 1/4" squares (10a)
  * One - 1 3/8" x 4 7/8" (A11)
  * One - 1 1/2" x 4 1/2" (2)
  * One - 1 7/8" x 4 1/4" (A16)
  * One - 1 3/4" x 4 1/8" (64a)
  * One - 1 1/4" x 4 1/8" (40)
  * One - 4" x 7 1/4" (A1)
  * One - 3 3/4" x 7 7/8" (1)
- From scrap, cut:
  * Ten - 1 1/4" squares (3a, 4a, 50c, A10a, A14b, A39a, A49a, A54a)
- One 4 3/8" wide strip. From this, cut:
  * One - 4 3/8" x 28 1/4" (65)
  * One - 1 7/8" x 13 1/4" (52)
- From remaining 2 1/2" x 13 1/4", cut:
  * One - 2 1/4" x 2 1/2" (34)
  * One - 1 1/4" x 2 1/2" (A38)
  * One - 1 1/8" x 2 1/2" (A52)
  * One - 2 3/8" x 3 5/8" (50b)
  * One - 2 3/8" square (32a)
- One 3 7/8" wide strip. From this, cut:
  * One - 3 7/8" x 21 1/2" (33)
  * One - 2 3/8" x 18" (38)
- From scrap, cut:
  * Three - 1 1/2" squares (32c, 35a, 39a)
  * One - 1 1/4" x 1 3/8" (A12)
  * One - 1 1/4" x 2 1/8" (A56)
  * One - 1 1/8" x 2 1/4" (A21)
  * One - 1 1/8" x 2" (A42)
  * Two - 1 1/8" x 1 7/8" (A19b, A57)
  * Two - 1 1/8" x 1 5/8" (A7, A13c)
  * Two - 1 1/8" squares (A6a, A44a)
- One 3 3/4" wide strip. From this, cut:
  * One - 3 3/4" x 21 1/8" (5)
  * One - 3 1/2" square (A18a)
  * One - 3 1/8" square (11a)
  * One - 2 7/8" x 3 1/8" (16)
  * One - 3" x 7" (51)
  * Two - 2" x 3" (A2)
- One 3" wide strip. From this, cut:
  * One - 3" square (A13b)
  * One - 2 1/8" x 2 3/8" (A3)
  * One - 2" square (A53a)
  * Four - 1 7/8" squares (61a, A19a, A33a, A44b)
  * One - 1 3/4" x 15 7/8" (37)
  * One - 1 3/4" square (A33b, 54a)
  * One - 1 5/8" square (32d)
  * One - 1 1/2" x 3 7/8" (49a)

From Fabric II, cut: (dark blue floral print)
- One 12 1/2" wide strip. From this, cut:
  * One - 12 1/2" x 14 1/2" (10)
  * One - 4 7/8" x 5 1/8" (11)
  * One - 2" x 4 7/8" (15) Stack under above cut
  * One - 3" x 4 5/8" (8) Stack under above cut
  * One - 1 1/4" x 3 7/8" (12) Stack under above cut
  * One - 2 7/8" x 3 1/8" (18)
  * One - 2 1/2" x 4 1/4" (29) Stack under above cut
  * One - 1 1/2" x 3 5/8" (14) Stack under above cut
  * One - 2 1/2" x 3 1/8" (22)
  * One - 2 1/2" x 2 7/8" (23) Stack under above cut
  * One - 2 1/8" x 2 1/2" (35)
  * Two - 2" squares (13c, 17c) Stack under above cut
  * One - 1 7/8" square (16a)
  * One - 1 5/8" square (19a)
  * Two - 1 1/2" squares (13a, 17a) Stack under above cut
  * Two - 1 3/8" squares (13b, 17b) Stack under above cut
  * Two - 1" squares (24a) Stack under above cut

  * One - 1 1/4" x 4 1/2" (4)
  * Two - 1 1/4" squares (3b)

From Fabric III, cut: (light blue print)
- One - 3" x 7 3/4" (7)

From Fabric IV, cut: (dark green print)
- One 4 3/4" wide strip. From this, cut:
  * One - 4 3/4" square (53a)
  * One - 2 3/8" x 4 1/4" (50a)
  * One - 3" x 4" (A13a)
  * One - 2 3/8" x 3 3/8" (47)
  * One - 2 1/4" x 3 1/4" (43)
  * One - 1 1/2" x 3 1/8" (49)
  * One - 1 1/2" x 3" (39)
  * One - 2 3/4" x 10 7/8" (54)
  * One - 2 3/4" x 2 7/8" (58)
  * One - 2 5/8" x 2 7/8" (61)
  * Two - 1 7/8" squares (53b, 60a)
  * One - 1 1/4" square (46a)

From Fabric V, cut: (medium green print)
- One 9 3/4" wide strip. From this, cut:
  * One - 9 3/4" x 10 7/8" (53)
  * One - 2 3/8" x 7 5/8" (50)
  * One - 2 5/8" x 5 5/8" (60)
  * One - 2 3/4" x 5 1/2" (57)
  * One - 3" x 4 5/8" (A13)
  * One - 3 3/4" square (31)
  * One - 3 1/4" x 3 3/4" (19)
  * One - 2 3/8" x 3 3/4" (21)
  * One - 2 1/4" x 3 3/8" (42)
  * One - 2 1/2" x 3 1/4" (45)
  * One - 2" square (20b)
  * One - 1 3/8" x 3" (A11a)
  * One - 1 5/8" square (10a)
  * Four - 1 3/8" squares (14a, 20a, 44a)

From Fabric VI, cut: (light green print)
- One 4" wide strip. From this, cut:
  * One - 2 7/8" x 4" (17)
  * One - 2 7/8" x 3 7/8" (13)
  * One - 2 7/8" x 3 3/4" (20)
  * One - 2 5/8" x 3 1/2" (A18)
  * One - 1 3/8" x 3 1/4" (44)
  * One - 2 1/8" x 3" (A14)
  * One - 1 1/4" x 2 3/8" (46)
  * One - 1 1/4" x 2 1/4" (41)
  * One - 1 3/8" x 1 7/8" (A17)
  * One - 1" x 1 5/8" (A13c)
  * Two - 1 3/8" squares (47a, A15a)
  * Six - 1 1/4" squares (15a, 21a, 23a, 40a, 43a, 48a)

From Fabric VII, cut: (dark salmon print)
- One 3 1/4" wide strip. From this, cut:
  * One - 3 1/4" square (A24)
  * One - 3 1/8" x 3 1/4" (A34)
  * One - 1 1/4" x 2 1/2" (A31)
  * One - 1 1/4" x 1 3/4" (A28)
  * One - 1 1/4" square (A27a)

From Fabric VIII, cut: (medium salmon print)
- One 3 1/4" wide strip. From this, cut:
  * One - 3 1/4" x 3 7/8" (A9)
  * One - 3 1/4" x 3 3/8" (A48)
  * Two - 1 7/8" x 2 1/2" (A25, A45)
  * Two - 1 1/4" x 2 1/2" (A27, A30)

From Fabric IX, cut: medium peach print)
- One 2 3/4" wide strip. From this, cut:

* One - 1 1/4" x 2 3/4" (A35)
* One - 1 1/2" x 2 5/8" (A20)
* One - 1 1/4" x 2 1/2" (A36)
* One - 1 1/8" x 2 1/4" (A23)
* One - 1 1/8" x 2 1/8" (A55)
* One - 2 1/8" square (A24a)
* One - 2" square (A34a)
* Two - 1 7/8" x 5 3/8" (A19, A33)
* One - 1 7/8" x 2 3/8" (A54)
* One - 1 1/4" x 1 7/8" (A47)
* One - 1 3/4" square (A34b)
* One - 1 5/8" square (A24b)
* One - 1 1/4" x 4" (A39)
* Three - 1 1/4" squares (A32, A34c, A37a)
* Five - 1 1/8" squares (A22a, A37b, A40a, A57a)

From Fabric IX, cut: medium peach print)
• One 2 3/4" wide strip. From this, cut:
* One - 1 1/4" x 2 3/4" (A35)
* One - 1 1/2" x 2 5/8" (A20)
* One - 1 1/4" x 2 1/2" (A36)
* One - 1 1/8" x 2 1/4" (A23)
* One - 1 1/8" x 2 1/8" (A55)
* One - 2 1/8" square (A24a)
* One - 2" square (A34a)
* Two - 1 7/8" x 5 3/8" (A19, A33)
* One - 1 7/8" x 2 3/8" (A54)
* One - 1 1/4" x 1 7/8" (A47)
* One - 1 3/4" square (A34b)
* One - 1 5/8" square (A24b)
* One - 1 1/4" x 4" (A39)
* Three - 1 1/4" squares (A32, A34c, A37a)
* One - 1 1/8" x 1 7/8" (A41)
* Five - 1 1/8" squares (A22a, A37b, A40a, A57a)

From Fabric X, cut: (light peach print)
• One 4 1/4" wide strip. From this, cut:
* One - 1 7/8" x 4 1/4" (A44)
* One - 1 1/4" x 3 7/8" (A10)
* Two - 1 1/4" x 3 3/8" (A43, A49)
* Three - 2" x 2 7/8" (A2a, A53)
* One - 1 7/8" x 2 3/4" (A6)
* One - 1 1/2" x 2 1/2" (A50)
* One - 1 1/2" x 2 3/8" (A5)
* One - 2 1/8" square (A9b)
* Two - 1 7/8" squares (A48b)
* Three - 1 1/4" x 1 7/8" (A19b, A26, A46)
* One - 1 5/8" square (A9a)
* One - 1 1/4" x 1 5/8" (A8)
* Six - 1 1/4" squares (A9c, A24c, A30a, A31a, A32, A48a)
* Four - 1 1/8" squares (A4a, A51a)

From Fabric XI, cut: (rust print)
• One 13/8" wide strip. From this, cut:
* One - 1 3/8" x 2 1/4" (A22)
* Two - 1 1/4" x 2 1/2" (A37, A51)
* One - 1 1/4" x 2 3/8" (A4)
* Two - 1 1/4" squares (A38a)
* Six - 1 1/8" squares (A3a, A21a, A52a)

From Fabric XII, cut: (solid dark brown)
• One - 1 3/4" x 3 3/4" (24)

From Fabric XIII, cut: (solid light tan)
• One - 1 1/4" x 3 3/4" (25)
• Two - 1 1/4" squares (24b)

From Fabric XIV, cut: (medium honey tan print)
• One 2 1/2" wide strip. From this, cut:

120

* One - 2 1/2" square (32b)
* One - 2" x 4 1/2" (3)
• Cut remainder of strip into two 1 1/4" widths. From these, cut:
* Two - 1 1/4" x 34" (67) Stack this cut.
• One 1 7/8" wide strip. From this, cut:
* One - 1 7/8" square (30a)
* One - 1 7/8" x 2 7/8" (28)
* One - 1 3/4" x 5 3/8" (64)
* One - 1 3/4" square (56a)
• Four 1 1/4" wide strips. From these, cut:
* Four - 1 1/4" x 24 3/4" (66) Piece together
to = two 49" lengths.
* One - 1 1/4" square (25b)

From Fabric XV, cut: (dark brown print)
• One 12 1/2" wide strip. From this, cut:
* One - 7 3/4" x 12 1/2" (32)
* One - 2 3/8' x 2 7/8" (27)
* Four - 2" x 25 1/2" (68) Stack this cut. Piece two
together to = two 50 1/2" lengths.
• Five 2 1/2" wide strips for straight-grain binding.
• Two 2" wide strips. From these, cut:
* Two - 2" x 37" (69)
* Two - 1 7/8" squares (26a, 28a)
* One - 1 1/4" square (25a)

From Fabric XVI cut: (light yellow print)
• One 1 3/4" square (A29)

Block A Assembly

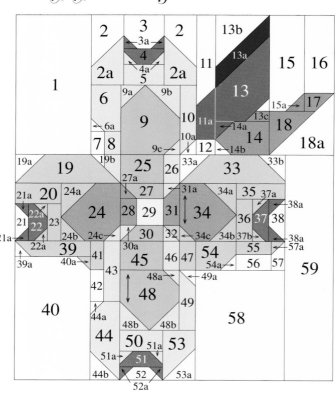

Block A. Make 1. When completed, block should
measure 15 1/4" x 18"

1. Use diagonal corner technique
to make one each of units 3, 4, 6,
9, 10, 13, 14, 15, 19, 21, 22, 24,
27, 30, 31, 33, 34, 37, 38, 39, 44,
48, 51, 52, 53, 54, and 57.
2. Use diagonal end technique to
make two of Unit 2, and one each

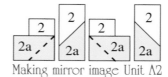

Making mirror image Unit A2

of units 11 and 13.

3. To assemble the block, begin by joining units 3, 4, and 5 in a row; then join mirror image Unit 2 to opposite sides of the combined 3/4/5 units. Join units 7 and 8; then add Unit 6 to top of these combined units. Join units 9 and 10; then add them to right side of the 6/7/8 combined units. Join combined units 2-5 to top of combined units 6-10; then join Unit 1 to left side. Refer to illustration at right for making Unit 11. Join this completed unit to Unit 12. Refer to diagram below for making Unit 13. Follow the instructions for small strip set and the illustrations. Join diagonal end 13a first; then join diagonal corner 13b. As 13b is a light color on a dark background, we do not reccomend trimming the center seam. Press it in place. Place the 13c diago-

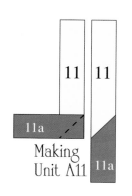

Making Unit A11

for making Unit 19b. Join the two diagonal corners as illustrated.

Unit 32, shown at right is a triangle square. Follow the instructions and illustrations to complete the unit. To assemble the center section, begin by joining units 21, 22, and 23; then add Unit 20 to top of these combined units. Join Unit 24 to right side of other combined units; then add Unit 19 to the top as shown. Join units 28 and 29; then add Unit 27 to the top, and Unit 30 to the bottom. Join units 31 and 32. Add them to the right side of the center units. Join units 25 and 26; then add them to the top of combined units 27-32. Join both combined unit sections together as shown. Join units 36, 37, and 38 in a row; then add Unit 35 to top of these combined units. Join Unit 34 to left side; then add Unit 33 to top. Join these combined units to the right side of the other center units to complete the center section.

Making Unit A32

Place 1 1/4" squares of fabrics IX and X right sides together and raw edges matching. Stitch diagonal as shown. Trim and press.

5. For bottom section of flower, join units 41 and 42; then add Unit 43 to right side of these combined units. Join Unit 44 to bottom as shown. Join units 39 and 40. Add these combined units to left side of other combined units. Join units 45, 46, and 47 in a row. Join units 48 and 49. Join the two combined unit sections together. Join units 50, 51 and 52 together; then add Unit 53 to right side. Join these combined units to the bottom of combined units 45-49 as shown. Join the two combined unit sections together. Join units 55 and 56; then add Unit 57 to right side of these combined units and Unit 54 to left side. Add Unit 58 to bottom of the 54-57 units. Join this completed section to right side of other combined units to complete the bottom of the flower.

6. Join the center section of the flower to the bottom section of the flower, matching seams. Join Unit 59 to right side of the combined sections; then add the top section, carefully matching seams to complete the flower block. Make 1.

Join 1 1/8" x 1 5/8" strip of Fabric I with 1" x 1 5/8" strip of Fabric VI for diagonal corner A13c.

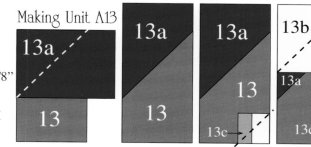

Making Unit A13

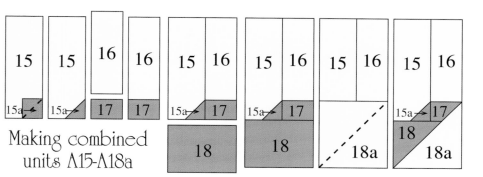

Making combined units A15-A18a

nal corner as shown. Stitch the diagonal and press. Join completed Unit 13 and Unit 14 as shown; then add them to right side of combined units 11/12. Refer to diagram above to make combined units 15-18a. Follow the illustrations and complete the combined units. Join them to right side of ofther combined leaf units. Join the combined leaf units to the right side of the flower combined units to complete the top section of the flower.

4. For the flower center section, make the two units illustrated first. Refer to diagram below of Unit 19, and read the instructions

Making The Bottle Units

1. Refer to the diagram of the wall quilt on page 122. Use diagonal corner technique to make one each of units 3, 4, 10, 11, 13, 15, 16, 17, 19, 20, 21, 23, 24, 25, 26, 28, 30, 32, 35, 39, 40, 43, 44, 46, 47, 48, 53, 54, 57, 60, and 61.

Making Unit A19

19b

19a 19 19b

19a 19 19b

Join 1 1/8" x 1 7/8" strip of Fabric I with 1 1/4" x 1 7/8" strip of Fabric X for diagonal corner A19b

Making combined units 29-31

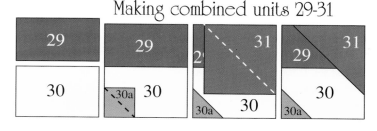

2. Use diagonal end technique to make one each of units 49, 50, and 64. Refer to diagram below to make combined units 29-31.

121

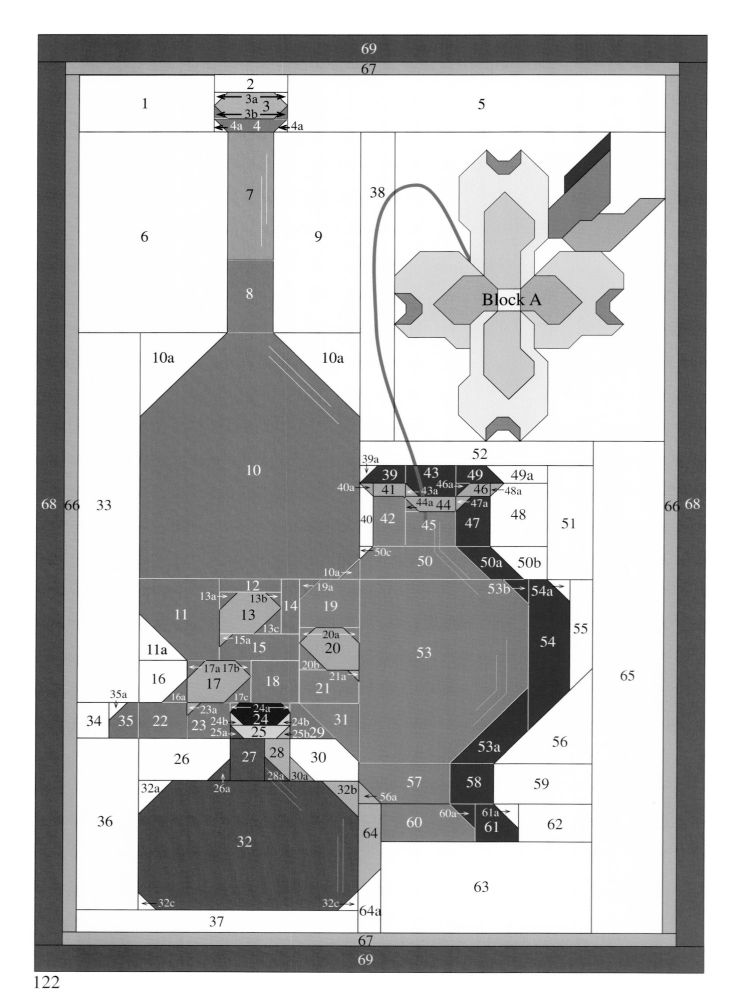

Block A

Join units 29 and 30. Join diagonal corner 30a; then join diagonal corner 31 to complete the combined units.

Making Unit 49

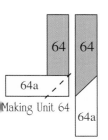

Making Unit 64

Refer to diagram above for making diagonal end, Unit 49. Diagonal end, Unit 64 is illustrated on left. Unit 50 is a continuous diagonal end with a diagonal corner. Join the diagonal ends; then add the diagonal corner. The diagram below shows which way to place and stitch your fabric strips.

3. Refer to the illustration below for making combined units 53-56. Begin by joining diagonal corners 53a and 53b. Join diagonal corner 54a to Unit 54. Join units

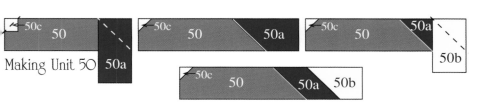

Making Unit 50

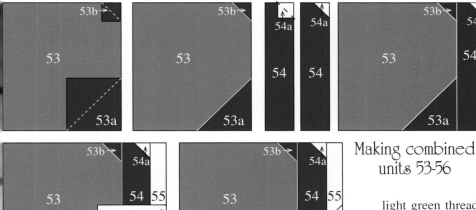

Making combined units 53-56

53, 54, and 55 in a row as shown; then join diagonal corner 56 to bottom of the combined units. As Unit 56 is a light color on dark colors, we suggest that you do not trim the center seam.

Bottle and Quilt Assembly

1. To piece the bottles and the quilt, the top row will be made first. Join units 2, 3, and 4; then add Unit 1 to left side of combined units, and Unit 5 to right side. Set this section aside.

2. Join units 7 and 8; then add Unit 6 to left side of the combined units, and Unit 9 to the right side. Join units 12 and 13; then add Unit 14 to right side of the combined units. Join Unit 15 to the bottom as shown. Join Unit 11 to the left side of these combined units. Join units 16, 17, and 18 in a horizontal row. Add this row to bottom of combined units 11-15. Join unis 19, 20, and 21 in a vertical row and add this row to right side of other combined units. Join this section to the bottom of Unit 10; then add Unit 33 to left side of the bottle combined units. Join these units to bottom of combined units 6-9.

3. Join units 34 and 35; then add Unit 36 to bottom of the 34/35 combined units. Join units 22 and 23; then add Unit 26 to botom of combined 22/23 units. Join units 24 and 25. Join units 27 and 28; then add the previously combined units 29-31 to right side of the 24-28 units. Join combined units 22-26 to left side of the other combined units as shown; then add Unit 32 to the bottom. Join combined units 34-36 to left side of brown bottle units; then add Unit 37 to the bottom. Join the brown bottle section to the bottom of the blue bottle section, matching seams.

4. Join Unit 38 to left side of Block A and set aside. To make the green bottle, begin by joining units 41 and 42; then add Unit 40 to left side of these combined units. Join Unit 39 to the top. Join units 43, 44 and 45 in a vertical row. Join this row to right side of othe combined green bottle units. Join units 46 and 47; then add Unit 48 to right side of combined 46/47 units. Join Unit 49 to the top of these combined units, matching the bottle top seam. Join completed Unit 50 to the bottom as shown. Join Unit 51 to right side of combined units; then add Unit 52 to the top. Join completed combined units 53-56 to bottom of other green bottle combined units. Join units 57, 58, and 59 in a horizontal row and add them to the bottom of other combined units. Join units 60, 61, and 62 in a horizontal row; then add Unit 63 to bottom of this row. Join Unit 64 to left side as shown. Join these combined units to green bottle bottom; then add Unit 65 to right side. Join the flower section to the top.

5. Join the green bottle/flower section to the right side of the blue/brown bottle section, matching seams as shown. Join the top row (units 1-5) to top of quilt, again matching seams.

6. Join border Unit 66 to opposite sides of quilt; then add border Unit 67 to top and bottom. Join border Unit 68 to opposite sides of quilt; then join border Unit 69 to top and bottom.

Quilting & Finishing

Use a medium wide satin stitch with light green thread for the stems coming out of the brown bottle. We used coordinating thread to satin stitch highlights in the bottles, and a decorative stitch for the flower stem.

Mary did a swirl stipple stitch in the ivory background and did some echo quilting in the bottles. She quilted veins in the flowers.

Use the five 2 1/2" wide strips from Fabric XV for straight-grain binding. Refer to page 12 for making the binding, and bind your quilt.

Stockings Finish to: 7" x 19 1/2" long. Techniques used: Diagonal corners, diagonal ends, strip sets used as diagonal corners and triangle-squares as diagonal corners.

Materials For Tree Stocking

Fabric I (dresden blue solid)
Need 11"   3/8 yard
Fabric II (white on white print)
Need 3 5/8"   1/4 yard
Fabric III (white on ivory print)
Need 2 3/4"   1/8 yard
Fabric IV (dark green print)
Need 1 3/8"   1/8 yard
Fabric V (medium green print)
Need 1 3/8"   1/8 yard
Fabric VI (light green print)
Need 2 1/2"   1/8 yard
Fabric VII (dark brown print)
Lg. Scrap
Fabric VIII (medium brown print)
Need 13 1/4"   1/2 yard
Fabric IX solid black)
Need 1"   1/8 yard
1/4" wide green satin ribbon for loop & bow
1/2 yard

Materials For Cabin Stocking

Fabric I (dresden blue solid)
Need 11"   3/8 yard
Fabric II (white on white print)
Need 4 1/2"   1/4 yard
Fabric III (white on ivory print)
Need 2 3/4"   1/8 yard
Fabric IV medium green print)
Scrap
Fabric V (dark brown print)
Need 2 1/4"   1/8 yard
Fabric VI (medium brown print)
Need 13 1/4"   1/2 yard
Fabric VII (rust print)
Need 1 3/8"   1/8 yard
Fabric VIII (bright red print)
Need 2 7/8"   1/8 yard
Fabric IX (solid black)
Need 1"   1/8 yard
Fabric X (gold print)
Scrap
1/4" wide green satin ribbon for loop
and bow 1/2 yard

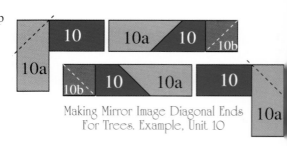

Making Mirror Image Diagonal Ends
For Trees. Example, Unit 10

Cutting For Tree Stocking

From Fabric I, cut: (dresden blue solid)
- One 11" wide strip. From this, cut:
  * One - 11" x 20 1/4" (to cut stocking back)
  * One - 8" X 11" (to cut stocking foot)
  * One - 1 1/4" x 7 1/2" (13)
  * Two - 2 1/2" squares (11) Stack this cut.
  * Two - 2" x 2 1/2" (12) Stack this cut.
  * Two - 1 3/8" x 2 3/4" (2, 3) Stack this cut.
  * Two - 1 3/8" x 2 1/2" (10a) Stack this cut.
  * Two - 1 3/8" x 2 1/8" (9a) Stack this cut.
  * Two - 1 3/8" x 1 3/4" (8a) Stack this cut.
  * Two - 1 3/8" squares (7a) Stack this cut.
  * Two - 1" x 1 3/8" (6) Stack this cut.

From Fabric II, cut: (white on white print)
- One 3 5/8" wide strip. From this, cut:
  * Four - 3 5/8" squares (4a, 4b)
  * Four - 1 3/8" x 3 5/8" (5)
  * Four - 1 3/8" squares (7a)

From Fabric III, cut: (white on ivory print)
- One 2 3/4" wide strip. From this, cut:
  * Two - 2 3/4" x 5 3/4" (4)
  * One - 1 3/8" x 7 1/2" (14)

From Fabric IV, cut: (dark green print)
- One 1 3/8" wide strip. From this, cut:
  * Two - 1 3/8" x 3 1/8" (7)
  * Four - 1 3/8" squares (6a, 8b)

From Fabric V, cut: (medium green print)
- One 1 3/8" wide strip. From this, cut:
  * One - 1 3/4" x 7 1/2" (16)
  * Two - 1 3/8" x 3 5/8" (8)
  * Two - 1 3/8" x 2 7/8" (10)
  * Four - 1 3/8" squares (9b, 11b)

From Fabric VI, cut: (light green print)
- One 2 1/2" wide strip. From this, cut:
  * Two - 2 1/2" squares (11a)
  * Two - 1 3/8" x 3 1/4" (9)
  * Two - 1 3/8" squares (10b)

From Fabric VII, cut: (dark brown print)
- Two 1 1/4" x 1 3/8" (1, 6)

From Fabric VIII, cut: (medium brown print)
- One 11" wide strip. From this, cut:
  * Two - 11" x 20 1/4" (to cut stocking lining)
- One 2 1/4" wide strip. From this, cut:
  * Eight - 2 1/4" squares for prairie points

From Fabric IX, cut: (solid black)
- One 1" wide strip. From this, cut:
  * Two - 1" x 7 1/2" (15, 17)

Cutting For Cabin Stocking

From Fabric I, cut: (dresden blue solid)
- One 11" wide strip. From this, cut:
  * One - 11" x 20 1/4" (to cut stocking back)
  * One - 8" X 11" (to cut stocking foot)
  * Two -1 5/8" x 7 1/4" (11)
  * One - 2 3/8" x 5 1/4" (10)
  * One - 2 7/8" square (8b)
  * One - 1 3/4" x 2 7/8" (9b) Stack. Cut under 2 7/8" sq.
  * Three - 1 1/8" x 2 7/8" (7, 9b) Stack this cut.

From Fabric II, cut: (white on white print)
- One 4 1/2" wide strip. From this, cut:
  * Two - 4 1/2" squares (15a, 15b)

From Fabric III, cut: (white on ivory print)
- One 2 3/4" wide strip. From this, cut:
  * One - 2 3/4" x 7 1/2" (15)
  * One - 1 3/8" x 7 1/2" (12)

From Fabric IV, cut: (medium green print)
- One 1 3/4" x 7 1/2" (14)

From Fabric V, cut: (dark brown print)
- One 2 1/4" wide strip. From this, cut:
  * Two - 2 1/4" squares (8a, 9a)
  * One - 1" x 2 7/8" (9b)

From Fabric VI, cut: (medium brown print)
- One 11" wide strip. From this, cut:
  * Two - 11" x 20 1/4" for stocking lining.
- One 2 1/4" wide strip. From this, cut:
  * Eight - 2 1/4" squares for prairie points

From Fabric VII, cut: (rust print)
- One 1 3/8" wide strip. From this, cut:
  * One - 1 3/8" x 4" (6)
  * One - 1 1/4" x 2 5/8" (3)
  * One - 1 1/8" x 2" (5)
  * Two - 1 1/8" x 1 1/4" (2)

From Fabric VIII, cut: (bright red print)
- One 2 7/8" wide strip. From this, cut:
  * Two - 2 7/8" x 3" (8, 9)
  * One - 1 1/4" x 2" (4)
  * Two - 1 1/8" squares (7a)

From Fabric IX, cut: (solid black)
- One 1" wide strip. From this, cut:
  * Two - 1" x 7 1/2" (13, 16)

From Fabric X, cut: (gold print)
- One - 1 1/4" x 1 3/8" (1)

Tree Stocking Units

1. Use diagonal corner technique to make one of Unit 6, two each of units 7, 8, 9, 10, and 11.

2. Diagonal ends are made in conjunction with diagonal corners. Diagonal ends all have diagonal corners joined to them when they are completed.. Make two of mirror image units 7, 8, 9, and 10. Refer to illustration at left on page 124 for making the diagonal ends for all of the tree layers.

3. Unit 6, shown at right is a Flying Geese block. The small strip

Making Unit 6

set is made by joining 1" x 1 3/8" strips of Fabric I to opposite sides of 1 1/4" x 1 3/8" strip of Fabric VII. Join diagonal corner 6a as shown. Trim seam and press; then add another diagonal corner 6a. Trim seam and press.

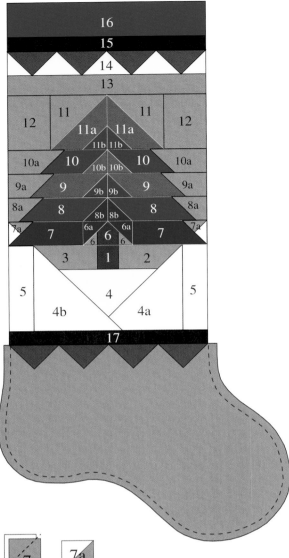

Making Mirror Image Unit 7

Folding Prairie Points

and add it to the top of the 7/6/7 row. Join mirror image Unit 9 's together and add to other combined tree units. Join mirror image Unit 10's, again joining to top of other tree combined units. Join mirror image Unit 11's together; then join Unit 12 to opposite sides of the joined Unit 11's. Join Unit 13 to top; then join the 11-13 combined units to the top of the tree. Join previously joined units 1-5 to tree bottom, matching the trunk seam to complete the tree block.

3. Refer to illustration below showing how to fold the 2 1/4" squares for Prairie Points. The long bias edge of each prairie point will be sewn into the seams. Fold all of the prairie points from Fabric VIII.

A tip that works for placing the prairie points so that they don't shift is to cut a small strip of Steam-A-Seam 2 (approx. 1/4" wide) and press one side down along the raw edge of Unit 14 and along stocking foot top. Remove the paper from the other side and begin to place your prairie points. They should overlap 1/4". Be careful when handling them so that they do not stretch because of the bias edge. When all of the prairie points are in position, lay a press cloth over them, and with your iron on a hot, steam setting, press them in place. This will hold them securely until they are sewn into the seam.

Stocking Assembly

1. Join Unit 17 to bottom of tree block. Join units 16, 15, and 14, making sure to catch prairie points into the seam. Join this row to stocking top. As both stockings are the same from this point on, follow these instructions for both stockings.

2. Cut one foot from pattern given on page 128. Join the foot to the stocking top. Press seam towards stocking bottom. For stocking back, press stocking front, and using it as a pattern, lay it right sides facing on fabric for stocking back. Cut out back of stocking.

3. For lining, fold fabric right sides together and once again use stocking front as pattern. Cut two stocking linings.

4. Using 1/4" seam, place stocking front and back right sides together and stitch around stocking, leaving top open. Stitch around lining, leaving about a 3" opening on one long side. Reinforce seams at opening. Clip all seams around curves to stitching.

5. Turn stocking wrong side out. Turn lining right side out. Place stocking lining inside of stocking. Match back and front seams at stocking top. Pin generously around stocking top. Again using 1/4" seam, stitch around stocking top.

6. Pull lining out. Bring stocking through lining opening; then stitch the opening closed by machine. Place lining inside of stocking, finger pressing along top edge. Smooth lining out inside of stocking so that toes match. Press.

7. Make a loop from the ribbon, and attach it to top left side of stocking by hand or machine. Tie remaining ribbon in a bow with long streamers and tack it in place.

4. To assemble Unit 7, Unit 7a triangle-square must be joined first. Place 1 3/8" squares of fabrics I and II right sides together and stitch a diagonal seam as shown. Trim seam and press. Make two. One for the right side of Unit 7 and one for the mirror image left side of Unit 7.

5. Unit 11 is a triangle-square with a diagonal corner. To assemble Unit 11, place 2 1/2" squares of fabrics I and VI (Unit 11a) right sides together. Stitch diagonal down the center. Trim and press. Add diagonal corner 11b. Trim and press.

Tree Assembly

1. To assemble the tree block, begin by joining units 1, 2 and 3; then add Unit 4 to bottom of these combined units. Join Unit 4a diagonal corner. Trim seam and press. Join diagonal corner 4b as shown. Trim and press. Join Unit 5 to opposite sides of the combined units as shown.

2. For the tree, begin by joining mirror image units 7, 6, and 7 in a row. Join mirror image Unit 8 together as shown

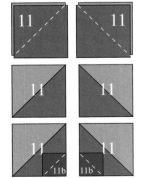

Making Mirror Image Unit 11

shown. Stitch diagonal, trim seam and press. This forms the chimney.

Cabin Assembly

1. To assemble the cabin block, begin by joining units 2, 1, and 2 in a row. Join Unit 3 to bottom of these combined units. Join units 4 and 5; then add these combined units to the left side of combined units 1-3. Join Unit 6 to top of combined units; then add Unit 7 to opposite sides of cabin. Join units 8 and 9 as shown in stocking diagram at left. Join these combined units to top of cabin, matching Unit 7 seams. Join Unit 10 to top of combined units; then add Unit 11 to opposite sides. Join Unit 15 to bottom as shown. Join diagonal corner 15a. Trim seam and press. Join diagonal corner 15b. Trim seam and press to complete the cabin block.

Stocking Assembly

1. Join Unit 16 to bottom of cabin block. Refer to Step 3 under Tree Assembly on page 126 for instructions on making and placing the prairie points. Join units 14, 13, and 12 making sure to catch prairie points into the seam. Join this row to stocking top.
2. Refer to Step 2 under Stocking Assembly on page 126 to complete the stocking.

Making Unit 8

Cabin Stocking Units

1. Use diagonal corner technique to make two of mirror image, Unit 7, and one each of units 8 and 9.
2. Refer to diagram on left for making Unit 8. Join Unit 8a diagonal corner. Trim seam and press. The diagram at left shows the 3" side of the unit for correct placement of the diagonal corners. Join diagonal corner 8b as shown. Trim seam and press.
3. For Unit 9, shown below, begin by making 9b. Join 1 1/8" x 2 7/8" strip of Fabric I with 1" x 2 7/8" strip of Fabric V. Press seams towards dark fabric. Join 1 3/4" x 2 7/8" piece of Fabric I on right side of the other two combined pieces. Referring to diagram below, join diagonal corner 9a to Unit 9 as shown. Trim seam and press. Use the strip set just completed for diagonal corner 9b. Place it on top of Unit 9 as

Making Unit 9